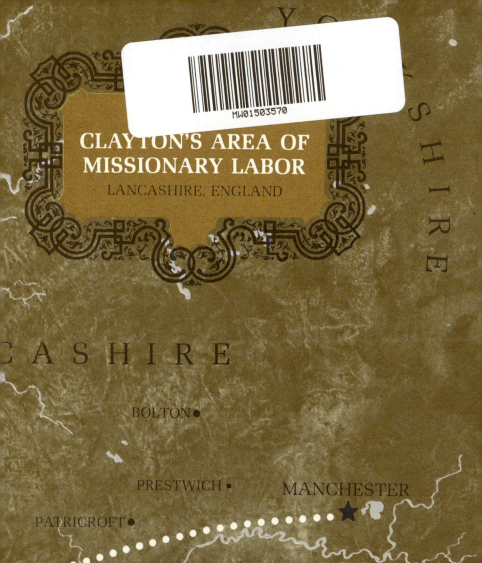

CLAYTON'S AREA OF MISSIONARY LABOR
LANCASHIRE, ENGLAND

YO·····SHIRE

CASHIRE

BOLTON •

PRESTWICH •

MANCHESTER
★

PATRICROFT •

CHESHIRE

• STOCKPORT

MANCHESTER MORMONS

The Journal of William Clayton

1840 to 1842

Courtesy L.D.S. Church Archives

William Clayton, 1814-1879

MANCHESTER MORMONS

The Journal of William Clayton
1840 to 1842

EDITED BY
JAMES B. ALLEN
AND
THOMAS G. ALEXANDER

VOLUME I IN THE CLASSIC MORMON DIARY SERIES

Peregrine Smith, Inc.
SANTA BARBARA AND SALT LAKE CITY
1974

The Classic Mormon Diary series includes previously unpublished works
from one of the richest traditions of diary-keeping in American history.
The titles have been selected for the unique qualities of the authors
or special facets of Mormon history that they illuminate.
Each work is edited by one or more scholars, who supply the annotations
and identifications necessary for a full appreciation of the work.
The 1840-1842 diary of William Clayton, edited by James B. Allen and
Thomas G. Alexander, has importance out of proportion to its size.
With annotations and a substantial introduction, it now stands as an
indispensable source for the early introduction of Mormonism
into Great Britain.
The volumes in the series are edited according to guidelines that
combine readability with textual reliability. None of the
minor editorial changes alters the meaning of the original text.

DAVIS BITTON, General Editor
Classic Mormon Diaries

Library of Congress CIP Data

Clayton, William, 1814-1879.
Manchester Mormons; the journal of William Clayton, 1840 to 1842.

(Classic Mormon diary series, v. 1)
1. Mormons and Mormonism in Manchester, Eng. 2. Manchester, Eng.—
Religion. 3. Clayton, William, 1814-1879. I. Title.
BX8617.G7C55   1974   289.3'427'2   73-89749
ISBN O-87905-024-1

To Our Parents

Harold T. and Edna B. Allen
and
Glen M. and Violet B. Alexander

Acknowledgements

The editors of this volume express gratitude to the following
for their valuable help in preparing it: Mr. and Mrs. Comstock Clayton,
for donating the William Clayton Journal to the Brigham
Young University Library, and for their interest in
seeing it published; Donald K. Nelson, Director of the BYU Library,
for encouraging the publication; Chad Flake, Special Collections
Librarian, for making the journal and other manuscripts
available; The Research Division of Brigham Young University,
the Charles Redd Center for Western Studies, and the
Historical Department of the Church of Jesus Christ of Latter-day
Saints for providing time and research facilities to the editors; John
Bluth, Herbert LePore, and Keith Smith, graduate students at
BYU, for assistance in the early stages of editing and
research; Janet Hauck, Marcia Sayer, and Earline Whetten
for their painstaking editing and typing,
and Jessie Embry for assisting with the index.

PROVO, UTAH, 1974
JBA AND TGA

MANCHESTER MORMONS

The Journal of William Clayton

1840 to 1842

TABLE OF CONTENTS

CLUSTER OF DECORATIVE BORDER ORNAMENTS

INTRODUCTION

CLUSTER OF DECORATIVE BORDER ORNAMENTS

On January 1, 1840, William Clayton, a twenty-five year old Elder presiding over the branch of the Church of Jesus Christ of Latter-day Saints in Manchester, England, began what is one of the earliest daily journals now extant of a native-born English Mormon official. Highly conscientious and concerned with the intimate problems of the members of his congregation, Clayton purchased a small notebook in which he registered his intent, "Dei Gratia," to record impartially "all particular incidents and events which transpire," and prayed for ability to discern the truth in all cases. In a search for this ideal, Clayton detailed his daily activities from the beginning of the year until his migration to America in September. He then continued the journal intermittently until the end of 1841.

The manufacturer called the volume "Harwoods Patent Memorandum With Metalic Pencil" and declared that the writing would be permanent. Though that claim may have helped in its promotion, one-hundred thirty odd years have left it unfulfilled, for portions of the journal have become smudged with use or faded with age. Today the diary, housed in Brigham Young University Library, is readable only with difficulty, but it provides significant insight into the nature of the early Mormon community in Victorian England.

When apostles Brigham Young and Willard Richards arrived in England in 1840, they soon became acquainted with the laboring classes, who made up a large portion of the early Mormon converts. Both William Clayton and the apostles were highly sensitive to the needs of these factory workers and artisans. The apostles particularly sensed the need to write history not only from the perspective of great leaders but also with the views, aspirations, and needs of the common folk in mind. Indeed, the Mormon leaders accused traditional historians of too much elitism and decried what they considered to be a tendency to ignore the masses. Writing from Manchester to the First Presidency of the Church on September 5, 1840, they complained that

the man who has only read the histories of the people of England, which we had seen before we left America, is liable to meet with some disappointments, at best, when he comes to make his introduction amongst them. This may in part be owing to the historian . . . for it is generally the case that what we find in history relates more particularly to the higher classes in the nations, for England, unlike America, is divided into classes; many indeed, but they may all be comprised in three, so far as we need designate at this time: (viz) Lords, Tradesmen, and Mechanics or laborers, or, in other words, the highest, Middle, and lowest classes, each of which have their particular customs, and manners. But the histories . . . we refer to have more generally treated of those of the higher order, or, at least, we find on acquaintance that those histories are now more applicable to the higher middle classes than any others.[1]

In spite of the belief that the U.S. enjoyed a classless society, these men realized that history, then as now, was too

2

often written to interpret the course of great movements, important ideas, and outstanding leaders. All too often the feelings of the common man, his thoughts and day-to-day existence are not sufficiently appreciated. Even though the masses may not have participated in making great decisions, it was they who endured the consequences, fought the wars, and, in the case of Mormon history, carried the daily burden of applying the principles and regulations given by their leaders. Only the history of these people can provide the personal dimension necessary to understand how the society of any age really functioned. Frederick Law Olmstead once bluntly declared that men

of literary taste . . . are always apt to overlook the working-classes, and to confine the records they make of their own times, in a great degree, to the habits and fortunes of their own associates, or to those of people of superior rank to themselves, of whose sayings and doings their vanity, as well as their curiosity, leads them to most carefully inform themselves. The dumb masses have often been so lost in this shadow of egotism, that, in later days, it has been impossible to discern the very real influence their character and condition has had on the fortunes and fate of nations.[2]

And social historian Jesse Lemisch recently challenged others to add depth to their writing by studying the "inarticulate" masses whose experiences seldom find their way into major histories.[3]

The missionary journal of William Clayton provides an opportunity to do just that with the Mormon Church in Manchester, a major industrial city in England. Although Clayton was no "common" man in his abilities, his sensibilities provide an insight into the life of the ordinary folk of the branch. Their personal problems, weaknesses, and concerns were all part of his life and were recorded in his diary. Most of the well-known Mormon diaries of the period were written by American apostles, such as Brigham Young, Wilford Woodruff, Willard Richards, and Parley P. Pratt, who, in spite of

3

their concern for the laboring classes, seldom wrote of the day-to-day activities of ordinary members of the Church. This is understandable, since the apostles were engaged in proselyting work, in supervising the general affairs of the mission, and in establishing a publishing program for the Church in England. They had little time to become involved with the routine of local administration. Even when they were in Manchester they seldom mentioned local members in their diaries, not even William Clayton. But it is largely from their records that the history of the Church in England has heretofore been written. This volume attempts to bridge a gap in our knowledge of Mormon history by looking at the Church from the perspective of the native members rather than the itinerant American missionaries.

The Beginning of Mormon Activities in England

Forasmuch as many have taken in hand to set forth in order a declaration of those things which are most assuredly believed among us, and which must shortly come to pass: It seemeth good unto me, and also unto the Holy Spirit, to write unto you, that you may know of a certainty your standing and relation to God; and also of the times and seasons of the fulfillment of the words of his servants the Prophets.[4]

These apocalyptic words of Orson Hyde represent the spirit in which a group of young Mormon elders set out from New York City for England on July 1, 1837.[5] Organized seven years earlier, Mormonism was still an American religion which intended to send its message throughout the world. The missionaries taught that the ancient Gospel of Christ which had been taken from the earth because of apostacy had been restored through Joseph Smith, with the basic principles and authority of old. The Millennium was rapidly approaching, and as part of the cleansing process preparatory to the Second Coming of Christ great catastrophes would befall the nations of the earth. The elders were impressed

4

with the imminence of these cataclysmic events and felt the utmost confidence in predicting that they would occur within their lifetimes.

The young men who boldly set out to proclaim this awesome message in England included two apostles, Heber C. Kimball and Orson Hyde. There were also several recent converts to the Church: Willard Richards, a native of Massachusetts; Joseph Fielding, an English native who had emigrated to Canada; and three missionaries who had been working in Canada, John Goodson, Isaac Russell, and John Snyder.

It was Orson Hyde, shortly to become one of the most prolific and outspoken writers of the early Church, who wrote a major essay, *Timely Warnings*, which the missionaries distributed in New York City. After they arrived in England the Apostles had it reprinted first as a pamphlet then as a broadside entitled *A Timely Warning to the People of England* and used it as a basic missionary tool.[6] Hyde emphasized the apostacy from the ancient Church, proclaimed the imminence of the Second Coming, and stressed that apostles, prophets, and the gifts of the spirit were evidence of the restoration of the Kingdom of God.

Hyde's words reveal the total confidence of the elders in their message of restoration, impending cataclysm, and millennialism. Like a voice from Sinai he proclaimed that

God will soon begin to manifest his sore displeasure to this generation, and to your own country by distressing famine; for the season will hence forth be more irregular and uncertain in causing the earth to yield her bounty for the sustenance of her inhabitants. The trade and commerce of nations which have hitherto been a source of great wealth and pride, already begin to feel the withering touch of the Almighty, and must fade and sink to rise no more. Your nation is now, probably, at peace; and so are most nations. The sun of prosperity has shone upon them for some length of time, with scarcely a cloud to obstruct its rays. But the golden luminary of peace is now fast reclining behind the western waters; and then comes a night darkened by war-clouds, arising from almost every quarter and fiiling the political horizon with terror and dismay. The hearts of kings, rulers, and nobles, will then faint because they know not the time of their visitation; and will know not what measures to adopt to avert the calamities of war.

O ye shepherds! ye teachers! ye rulers in Israel! hear the word of the Lord concerning you—the Lord who shall suddenly come to his temple--the Lord who shall come down upon the world with a curse to judgment, and upon all the ungodly among you. Wo! Wo!! unto them, saith the Lord, who preach for hire and *pervert* the ways of *truth*. . . . Wo! be unto all the wicked ones of the earth; for the fire of God's jealousy will consume them, root and branch, except they speedily repent.

Earthquakes, strange things and fearful sights, together with the waves of the sea heaving themselves beyond their bounds, will cause men's hearts to fail them. . . .

The apostacy of the church is the prime cause of the earth being visited by the judgments of God. . . .

. . . .

I am unwilling to dismiss this subject without telling you what the Lord has done for his creatures in these latter times, and, also what he requires of you, that my garments may be clean of your blood in a coming day. The Lord has been pleased to send his holy angel from heaven to announce the joyful tidings to witnesses now living, that the time has come for him to set his hand the second and last time to gather the remnants of Israel; and with them the fulness of the Gentiles—to establish permanent peace on Earth for One Thousand Years. . . .

As John was sent before the face of the Lord to prepare the way for his first coming, even so has the Lord now sent forth his servants for the last time, to labour in his vineyard at the eleventh hour, to prepare the way for his second coming. . . .[7]

Convinced that they were, indeed, living in the eleventh hour, the missionaries set out on their venture. Arriving at Liverpool on July 20, 1837, Kimball, Hyde and Richards were penniless but nevertheless convinced that by putting their trust in God they would succeed. Opposition, especially from other ministers, dogged them nearly everywhere. Even the Reverend James Fielding of Preston, a brother of Joseph Fielding, turned against them. He found their message too persuasive, for after first welcoming the Elders to preach in his chapel he lost several members of his congregation to the Mormons. It was only natural that the Reverend Mr. Fielding and other ministers should resent what appeared to be sheep stealing and should oppose the Mormons. Fielding probably represented the feeling of many when he wrote his brother:

> With regard to your robbing me of my flock I abide by what I said before—we must proceed upon an acknowledged principle or data. Now I do not believe at all that you were sent of God to rend my little church to pieces. Were I to speak as "plain" as you do I should boldly declare that it was not God but Satan as an angel of light sent you here.[8]

The opposition became so intense in Preston that Elders Hyde and Richards finally, upon the advice of a lawyer, applied for licenses as preachers. This required them to swear an oath of allegiance to the queen, and to take an oath of abjuration provided for unnaturalized foreigners. Though an oath to a foreign monarch may have made the young Americans somewhat uncomfortable, they apparently considered it necessary to fulfill their mission, and they used their licenses to good advantage. After they found that only a few Preston ministers were licensed, Kimball bluntly told any who bothered him that if they continued their abuse, he would report them to the authorities. This tended to quiet the opposition.[9]

In spite of their problems, by April, 1838, the work of the missionaries had yielded over 400 converts in Preston and more than 1500 members scattered throughout the country. Goodson and Snyder had previously returned to America, and on April 20, Kimball, Hyde, and Russell also sailed for home. They left behind Joseph Fielding and Willard Richards as president and first counselor of the mission and chose William Clayton, a convert from Penwortham, as second counselor.

Clayton, the eldest of fourteen children, was a talented and unusually persevering young man. Having been tutored by his father, a teacher, Clayton eventually became a bookkeeper in a large factory in Penwortham. In his leisure hours, he played the violin and was a member of a band in Penwortham. He was orderly and methodical in nature, even

7

refusing to carry a watch that did not keep accurate time. Clayton, who seems to have been a man of decisive action, was baptized in the River Ribble, which separated Penwortham from Preston, at 11 p.m. on October 21, 1837. Though he had been married just a year to Ruth Moon at the time of his conversion, he became enthused with the work of the Church and felt so responsible in his calling as a member of the mission presidency that on October 19, 1838, he left his job in Penwortham and gave himself wholly to the ministry. Shortly after this momentous decision he left his wife and two daughters with her mother in Penwortham and became the first missionary to preach Mormonism in Manchester. New Years Day, 1840, found him living in a Manchester boarding house operated by Church members and depending entirely for his livelihood on donations from those among whom he labored.

Clayton and his two colleagues who were left to preside over the Church in England served from April, 1838, until July, 1840. In that time, Clayton succeeded in building a membership in Manchester of about 240, which rivaled the number in Preston. Although Clayton spent most of his time in Manchester, Joseph Fielding and Willard Richards apparently traveled widely. All three endured financial hardships and Richards suffered a period of illness. The mission leaders were plagued not only by opposition from outside the Church, but also by serious personal problems and petty bickering within the Church. For example, when Richards married Jennetta Richards, the daughter of an upper middle class minister, members of the Church criticized her for wearing clothing that seemed too fine for someone devoted to full time Church service. In her defense it was pointed out that, being in ill health, she wore a muff to protect herself in cold weather. To poverty-stricken Saints, however, even this seemed too much, and for the sake of harmony she wore the poorest clothes she had. This did not soften the bitterness, and members criticized her husband further for allegedly not leaving her often enough to preach the gospel.[10]

Such difficulties were compounded by myriad personal problems among the members of the Church, and letters from the three mission leaders reveal that they spent a great deal of time with the moral, spiritual and economic welfare of the new converts. In addition, they had to deal with at least one problem created in America. Isaac Russell, who had established a branch at Alston, wrote a secret letter to his converts claiming to have received a special prophetic calling through which he and others were to go into the wilderness "to be fed and directed by the hand of the Lord until we are purified and prepared to minister to the Lamanites. And with us the Lord will send those three, who are spoken of in the book of Mormon, who were with Jesus after his resurrection and have tarried." Russell informed his followers that members of the Church in America did not accept his mission but that "God is sending us before to prepare a place for you and for the remnant who will survive the judgments which are now coming on the Church of Latter-day Saints, to purify them, for we are sent to prepare a Zion . . . a city of Peace, a place of Refuge." After Richards saw a copy of the letter, it was only with great difficulty that he convinced the Alston saints that Russell had misled them.[11]

Such blandishments, as well as the pettiness of some Church members, are only typical of the problems constantly faced by the beleaguered, but intensely dedicated, English triumverate. On July 25, 1839, Heber C. Kimball wrote that they were to "Feed the hungry, clothe the naked, and visit the widow and the fatherless, and turn not the stranger away empty, feed thine enemy, do good to them that revile you and say all manner of evil, if it be false great is your reward in heaven."[12] Their letters and journals reveal that it was, indeed, with such faith and charity that they conducted their mission. On March 27, 1839, Joseph Fielding wrote a tender letter to his wife, Hannah, which reveals both his frustrations and his determined spirit:

My Dear Hanna

All is well, All is well. I felt when I left you last, with Tears in your Eyes very different from what I felt when I left you agrieved. There was nothing wanting but a kiss, and that will be made right; my Prayer was and is still that you might not be sorrowful or discouraged at my leaving you so oft. You know and approve of the Work in which I am engaged and that if you bear the Cross with me, you shall also wear the Crown with me.

. . . .

The moral condition of the world looks worse and worse, and I rejoice the Lord of the Harvest has sent me into his vineyard. Pray for me, my love, that I may be faithful and successful, and so shall you do your Part in the great and important work, and we will at last rejoice together in the Kingdom of God. Never was anything more needed since the World stood than the Gospel is now. . . . Seek for more of his Spirit. This is the greatest of all blessings. Nothing can be A Blessing without it. Pray and strive for it, my Love, and you shall have it and remember that *Joseph is ever the same whether present or absent, in Life as in Death.* Do all you possibly can to make and preserve Peace in the Church, in Word and in Deed, at home and abroad. Give my Love to all who inquire after me especially at home. *Never encourage a party Spirit.* Strive rather to promote unity. Blessed are the Peace Makers for they shall be called the Children of God. Blessed are the pure in heart for they shall see God. O that we might stand in his Presence together, then the parting Tear shall be unknown forever.[13]

By 1840 there were few more than 1500 members of the Church in England, only a slight increase over the membership when Kimball and Hyde left in 1838.[14] It seems probable, in fact, that almost as many left the Church as joined between 1838 and 1840. With all the problems of that two year period, however, it is almost a wonder that the dedicated core of members and leaders held the Church together at all. Nevertheless, after Kimball returned, he wrote to the Saints in the United States that

10

The work of the Lord is progressing here, and has been ever since Elders Orson Hyde and H. C. Kimball left this country. According to the account that the Elders give of their labors, there have been about eight or nine hundred persons baptized since they left.[15] The Gospel is spreading, the devils are roaring. As nigh as I can learn, the priests are howling, the tares are binding up, the wheat is gathering, nations are trembling, and kingdoms totering; "men's hearts failing them for fear, and for looking for those things that are coming on the earth." The poor among men are rejoicing in the Lord, and the meek do increase their joy. The hearts of the wicked do wax worse and worse, deceiving and being deceived.[16]

By 1840, then, the Church had established a small, unstable community in England. In that year the Twelve Apostles arrived on a special mission and within a year had baptized seven to eight thousand souls.[17] Thereafter membership grew at such a rapid rate that England became the source of a much-heralded movement to America. By 1870, some 38,000 British Saints had migrated to America. That emigration began, in fact, in 1840, and Clayton himself was a member of the second group to leave. But these English Saints did not live in a vacuum, and in order to understand their condition it is necessary to examine the British society from which they came.

England in 1840

In 1837 Queen Victoria ascended the throne, and during the early years of her reign England suffered bitter social cleavage and dislocation. England had become an industrial nation, and about half its people lived in urban manufacturing or mining communities. The possibility for making a livelihood in agriculture had declined, forcing many to seek employment in the cities. At the same time, industrialization seemed to leave many workers rootless and subject to attraction by labor organizations and various radical groups. The dislocation is illustrated by the fact that in 1841-42 unemployment in Bolton averaged over 50 percent for all trades;

similar conditions prevailed in Liverpool, and from 1835 to 1842 purchases in Manchester declined by 40 percent.[18]

A cleavage developed between agriculture and industrial laborers. Farmers demanded and got a series of corn laws, which restricted the importation of grain, thus raising prices within England. Workers, on the other hand, blamed these laws for the high cost of living and demanded their repeal. At the same time many working class people who felt oppressed by landlords, factory owners, and the government were attracted to the Chartist movement. In an effort to make the government more responsive to the masses, Chartists demanded such radical measures as universal male suffrage, equal electoral districts, annual parliaments, and the elimination of property qualifications for membership in Parliament. The movement withered away after 1848, but together with the anti-corn-law agitation it symbolized the economic distress and social discontent that characterized the industrial communities of England in the 1840s.

The problems of the mid-19th century resulted not only in migration from the countryside to the city but also in mass emigration to Canada and the United States. In this sense the Mormon migration was part of a well defined pattern. In 1813 some 2,000 people left England; by 1830 the number jumped to over 55,000; and in the late 1840s and early 1850s over 250,000 subjects left Great Britain annually in search of more promising economic conditions. It may well be that the promise of a better life in America, which Mormon missionaries did not hesitate to preach, attracted Mormon emigrants as well as other British subjects. Emigration became a well-organized industry with appurtenances such as agents, propaganda offices, and shipping rebates. It is little wonder that the Mormons found it easy to organize their own emigration companies, for such things were commonplace during

12

the period.[19] British emigration was often considered, in fact, a sort of "safety valve" for the mother country, which tended to siphon off the worst effects of economic discontent by holding out hope for another economic frontier, and it was not uncommon for migrants to sing such verses as:

Brave men are we, and be it understood
We left our country for our country's good,
And none may doubt our emigration
Was of great value to the British nation.[20]

It was in the urban, industrial centers of England that the Mormon Church grew most rapidly in the late 1830s and early 1840s. In this sense, the Mormon people in England were a somewhat different breed than those in America. While some had lived in New England factory towns, the social background of the American Mormons was, in large measure, rural or smalltown. Joseph Smith and Brigham Young, for instance, both came from rural, agricultural areas.[21] The cooperative experiment known as the Law of Consecration and Stewardship, which was attempted both in Ohio and Missouri, was based largely on agricultural enterprise and handicraft. Before the flowering of Nauvoo, no Mormon-built community had a population exceeding 4,000.

In England, which was far ahead of America in the industrial revolution, most Mormons in 1840 were located in major industrial centers. These large cities were inhabited mostly by operatives and displayed all the social and economic distress that attended the rapid industrialization of the country. In April, 1840, for example, there were some 33 Mormon congregations represented at the general conference held in Manchester. At least 15 of these congregations were clearly located in industrial communities, and some 61.5 percent of the total membership represented came from these industrial areas.[22]

13

Mormon emigration reflected the same orientation. During the 1850s some 42 percent of all the emigrants came from cities of over 50,000 population, 32.5 percent from those with populations between 10,000 and 50,000, and 15.6 percent from towns between 2,500 and 10,000. Only 10 percent of the emigrating Mormons came from rural areas even though the population of Great Britain itself was still about half rural.[23] The occupations of British Mormons, furthermore, generally reflected this urban origin. Some 21.2 percent were "general laborers" (some of whom may have been farm laborers), while other occupations, in order, included miners (14.8 percent), metal and engineering workers (10 percent), textile workers (9.2 percent), carpenters (6.7 percent), boot and shoe workers (5.9 percent), farmers (4.9 percent), brick and stone workers (3.8 percent), shopkeepers (3.4 percent), clothing workers (2.9 percent), farm workers (2.3 percent), and a smattering of clerks, domestic servants, professionals and miscellaneous.[24]

The Mormon Church in Great Britain was an urban church, and the various social and economic problems and attitudes of its members must be related to their urban orientation. It is instructive, furthermore, that the rise of the Church's first major urban center at Nauvoo coincided with the emigration of the British urban converts to the United States, and that members of the Council of the Twelve who had interacted in the British urban setting increasingly displaced agrarians like Sidney Rigdon in the Church's leadership. Clayton himself, after his emigration, became a secretary to Joseph Smith.

Manchester

The largest city in Britain to host a Mormon congregation in 1840 was Manchester, which had a branch of some

14

240 members. Manchester was the chief city in highly industrialized Lancashire, which alone possessed some three-fifths of the British spinning and cotton weaving factories. Over 100 of these were located in Manchester. Other industries in Manchester and surrounding towns included flax, wool, and other textile enterprises, chemical works, dying, brewing, colliers, sawmills, iron works, hat making, and machine making. Manchester had a population of some 170,000 people, and nearly 70 percent of the workers were employed as factory operatives.[25]

General descriptions of Manchester and its people in the early Victorian era go far to explain the conditions, problems and attitudes of the Mormons with whom William Clayton had to deal. Clayton's diary leaves the impression that they were mostly of the working class; many lived in boarding houses, some were transient and some were illiterate. In 1836, it was said that some 7.3 percent of Manchester's population consisted of migrant families, living in boarding houses as they wandered through the countryside seeking work.[26]

Manchester was located in southeastern Lancashire on the east bank of the River Irwell, north of its confluence with the River Medlock, and its chief suburb, Salford, was on the Irwell's west bank. Girdling the town were the various factories and machine shops, which lined a series of canals. These arteries and the city's railroads brought boatloads of coal and cotton to the industrial plants. Undoubtedly the smoke and other pollutants created the same unsightly and unhealthy atmosphere that concerns modern ecologists. There were no great boulevards, the streets were usually small and narrow, and the houses which lined them were generally of a uniformly drab architectural pattern.

The rapid industrialization wrecked havoc with Manchester's health and sanitation facilities. After an 1832 cholera

15

epidemic, a newly organized board of health inspected the city's dwellings and streets and discovered that of 687 streets 284 were unpaved, 53 were poorly paved, and 112 were poorly ventilated. Heaps of refuse, stagnant pools, and other filth dotted 352 streets. Of the 6,951 houses visited, 2,565 were so infected as to require immediate whitewashing, 960 were in need of repair, 1,435 were damp, 452 were inadequately ventilated, and 2,221 needed privies. The so-called "damp" houses were undoubtedly those located in a low, swampy, frequently flooded area between a high bank over which the Oxford road passed and a bend of the river Medlock. This unhealthy spot was so low that the chimneys of the houses, some of which were three stories high, barely crested above the road. Some 200 houses were clustered there, often with three or four Irish families packed into each. The whole area was surrounded by large factories whose chimneys were said to "vomit forth dense clouds of smoke, and which hang heavily over the insalubrious region." By 1840, one writer observed that things had become even worse in so-called "Little Ireland," with several piggeries having been added and the still unpaved streets filled with rubbish.[27]

Leon Faucher, a Frenchman who was highly critical of industrial society, wrote of the worst side of England's most prominent industrial community in 1844. Misery and corruption, he believed, grew directly from the industrial society, which created large numbers of unemployed migrants who ended up with pitifully low wages when they could find employment at all. In 1840 some 1,200 paupers inhabited the Manchester workhouse, two other workhouses served the suburbs, about one-sixth of the population received medical aid in public infirmaries, and half the children were born in charitable institutions. It appeared also that while crime increased in England as a whole by 50 percent be-

16

tween 1836 and 1842, it increased in the manufacturing districts by 100 percent. Women and children committed a large portion of the crime, although in Manchester they were responsible for "only" 43 percent. Faucher seemed especially intrigued with prostitution and reported that in 1840 the police had listed 285 brothels and 629 prostitutes, although an unnamed Protestant missionary had asserted that there were more like 1,500. Faucher took some comfort, however, in the belief that such activities gave less trouble in Manchester than elsewhere, for he wrote, the "more decent prostitutes" flocked there in order to appeal to the wealthy classes who rendezvoused in Manchester, and that prostitution for money had little attraction for the inferior classes, where chastity was the exception rather than the rule.[28]

Nevertheless, the picture was not entirely bleak. A local, probably promotional, study of Manchester in 1839 found some signs of progress in dealing with what were admittedly serious social problem. At least there *were* charitable institutions, including a royal infirmary, royal lunatic asylum, royal dispensary, several hospitals, a humane society, a workhouse, a night asylum for the destitute poor, and a number of others. Case loads were extremely high. From February, 1838, to February, 1839, for instance, the night asylum for the destitute poor handled some 11,006 adult males, 3,877 females, and 2,523 children, almost ten percent of the city's population. The city enjoyed the services of various educational institutions, including several schools for poor children, as well as a college, a school of medicine and surgery, literary and scientific institutions, and libraries. In addition, at least 29 factories provided education for child employees. This report tended to confirm the belief that there was considerable poverty, but it also suggested that there was at least some social responsibility on the part of public officials and factory owners and that efforts were being made to alleviate at least the worst ills created by a congested industrial complex.[29]

A majority of Manchester's adults expressed some religious preference. Some 50,429 adults professed adherence to some denomination. Over half of these claimed membership to the Church of England, over 12,000 to various other Protestant denominations, and over 7,000 to the Roman Catholic Church. There were 51 Jews and about 4,400 who either had no preference or declined to state it.[30] These statistics seem to be official. Faucher's impressions were, however, that the "latest imported [religious sect] is generally the most acceptable."[31] He thought that there were more Methodists, Quakers, and Independents than adherents to the established Church. There were, he said, some 137 places of worship in Manchester and Salford, only 39 of which belonged to the Church of England, plus many preaching-rooms and assemblies of sectarians who were not influential or wealthy enough to erect chapels of their own. The Mormon congregation in Manchester belonged to this category.

In addition to the regular churches in Manchester, there were a number of benevolent and reform societies which seemed to appeal to the working classes. The town mission, established among the poor in a densely populated area, promoted scripture reading, religious meetings, and education. Especially popular among some groups was the Manchester and Salford Temperance Society. The first public meeting on temperance in Manchester was held in 1830, after which the society was formed and public meetings began on a regular basis in 1835. Members of the society rejected any pledge of moderation in favor of a firm pledge to abstain totally from intoxicating beverages. By 1839 the society had 12 branch associations in Manchester and Salford, and approximately 8,000 members, including 500 reformed alcoholics.

18

Its members came largely from the working classes, although some more wealthy and benevolent individuals gave limited financial support.[32]

The city of Manchester was also a center for at least two political reform movements that illustrated the impact of industrialization and the conflict between the urban centers and the agricultural communities of England. The Chartists, who advocated political reform to make government more responsive to the people, had a substantial following in Manchester. In addition, politicians in Manchester led the movement for incorporation as a borough. Richard Cobden, a Manchester textile manufacturer and statesman, became the leader in this fight when, after being summoned to serve as a juror in the manorial court, he saw how inadequately such rule suited an industrial city. The movement succeeded in bringing about Manchester's incorporation in 1838. Cobden was also a leader in the so-called "Manchester School" of laissez faire political and economical liberalism which made this manufacturing town the center of the Anti-Corn-Law League.[33] The industrial workers saw the corn laws as a means of raising food prices, though the farmers saw them as a way to preserve prices. The corn laws were repealed in 1846, but the bitterness caused by this and other social and economic issues seemed to some people to threaten class war and revolution in the 1840s.

In the period of time covered by William Clayton's missionary journal, then, Manchester was the center of considerable ferment. Reformers both at home and abroad engaged in examining the social and economic structure of the community. Progressive political elements called for governmental reforms, and they seemed to have the backing of the general populace. Manchester was characterized by poverty, crime, and "rioting propensities." City life had its defenders, however. In 1839 the Reverend R. Parkinson of Manchester's Collegiate Church deplored the idea that "there is something in the character of manufactures which is unnatural and opposed to the will of God." He defended the urban industrial society as being just as moral as rural agrarian society.[34] Though he seemed to have had little more than his own feelings as evidence, he evinced the usual tendency of the establishment to defend Manchester and its life. Interestingly, the Mormon apostle Wilford Woodruff was not unimpressed by the city, for he described Manchester as being "the metropolis of the manufacturing Districts in England" and "a beautiful borough." Parley P. Pratt described Oldham Road, where the office of the *Millennial Star* was located, as one of Manchester's larger thoroughfares and he found his house and office good though inexpensive.[35]

The Urban Saints: A Social Profile

William Clayton's missionary journal is primarily valuable not for any insight into reform movements but for its intimate social picture of the Manchester Saints. Clayton's diary allows us to answer a number of questions about the community of English Mormons: Who were they? What social and economic class, or classes, did they represent, and how did they work together within the Church? How did the Church administration function and how did it affect the lives of its members? What were their attitudes toward the religious teachings of the Church, and how well did their lives reflect these teachings?

Clayton revealed the day-to-day activities, problems, disappointments and accomplishments of a group of new converts in an industrial town. Their religious attitudes, social problems and economic concerns are important, for they tell us what kind of people the English Mormons really were and how they differed from modern Mormons. When we attempt to view them as real people, warts and all, we do not discover an idyllic picture of a faithful community of highly spiritual, loving, and fully cooperative Saints. Rather, we see real people struggling with everyday problems and displaying the weaknesses of all human beings. At the same time, their lives were characterized by genuine religious devotion and cooperation. It may well be, in fact, that their concern for spiritual experience and their struggles in everyday life go further in illuminating the aspirations of the common Manchester factory operative than do detailed studies of the Anti-Corn-Law agitation or the Chartists.

The members of the Mormon Church in Manchester probably represented a cross-section of the young lower-class citizenry of the town. Many had belonged to the Church of England and others to the more prominent dissenting churches such as the Methodists or the United Brethren. William Clayton had been an Anglican, although he had not been particularly active. It is not strange that people from the working classes of Manchester should be attracted to Mormonism. By the late 1830s the preaching of fundamentalist, revivalist religion was becoming commonplace in England. American evangelists regularly crossed the Atlantic and seem to have had a greater appeal in England than in America. The search for social justice through utopian socialistic movements, such as that of the Owenites, together with religious fundamentalism, tended to create interest in faiths which emphasized personal religion and salvation and promised hope for a better life here and hereafter. The Mormon emphasis on prophecy, millennialism, progress, apostolic authority, religious ordinances, and universal salvation appealed to the working classes.[36] Those horrified by the corruption and poverty on every hand undoubtedly found a satisfying sense of identity and community in associating with religious sects like Mormonism that tried to remain in the world but not of the world.

According to the records of the Manchester branch, perhaps 80 percent of the members were not married, and there were more women than men.[37] Most of them were young, generally in their 20s or early 30s. Nearly all were baptized in 1839 or 1840, and none was baptized earlier than November, 1838. Most, therefore, were inexperienced in the faith, and there was considerable instability in the membership. Either the sense of community in the Church was weak or many of these working-class converts wandered from one group to another in search of temporal and eternal salvation. At any rate, branch records seem to indicate that 50 percent of those members in 1840 who did not emigrate were eventually excommunicated from the Church.

Church records give little specific information as to the occupations of the Mormon converts. The Clayton diary suggests that they were generally of the working class. Many lived in boarding houses, and some had serious financial problems as well as anxiety relating to jobs or living places.

Some of the attraction of the Church may have come from the sympathy the American apostles showed for the problems of the working classes. They showed great interest in some of their reform movements and liberal political and social attitudes. Heber C. Kimball said that when he arrived in Liverpool "wealth and luxury abounded, side by side with penury and want. I there met the rich attired in the most costly dresses, and the next minute was saluted with the cries of the poor with scarce covering sufficient to screen them from the weather. Such a wide distinction I never saw before."[38] Wilford Woodruff was also alarmed by the high unemployment and wretched social and economic conditions in Manchester. On January 20, 1840, he wrote that:

> The distress of nations is at the door in fulfillment of the word of God. While confusion is through America, great trouble is manifest in England. Beginning in all nations there is trouble. This morning in the town of Manchester about 8000 souls is flung out of employ at the factories because of the pressure of times and the lowering of the wages and they are standing in every corner of the streets in groups counciling what to do, and their are at the present time (I have been informed) thousands of souls almost in a state of uter starvation.[39]

Brigham Young and Willard Richards wrote Joseph Smith from Manchester in September, 1840, of the plight of both farm tenants and city dwellers who suffered from contemporary economic readjustments.

> A few years since, and almost every family had their garden . . ., their cow on the common and their pig in the Stye, which added greatly to the comforts of the household; but now we seldom find either garden, cow or pig.
> As we pass around among the country cottages to see the stone walls which are thrown down, but more commonly the hedges in a decaying and mutilated state, it is very naturally for us to enquire what have you here? and what the cause of this destruction? and we generally get but one answer: "A few years ago I had a flourishing garden on the spot you now see and it was surrounded¹ with this hedge which was planted by my own hand; I had a cow of my own which fed on yonder common. I labored on my masters farm, and had plenty of time, morning, and evening, to till my garden, in which I raised sauce Enough for my family, and every year I had a good pig, plenty to eat, and we were happy. But our Lords and masters have become more avoricious, and they are trying to get all they can for themselves, and will hardly let the poor live. You see my landlord has made my garden into a meadow and feeds his own cattle upon it; the Lord of the manner fenced in the common, so that I had no place to keep my cow and I was obliged to sell her; I killed my pig to prevent its starving. The small farms are united and made into large ones, so we could get nothing to do on the land. I have been obliged to go into the factory with my wife and children, to get a morsel of bread." Or, "I have taken to hand loom weaving, to keep my wife and little one from starvation."
>
> .   .   .   .
>
> Manufacturing is the business of England. The cotton mills are the most numerous. The weavers will get from 6 to 10 shillings per week, the spinners something more. The hand loom weavers have to work hard to get 6 shillings per week. Now after paying 2 or 3 shillings rent per week, 1/1 shilling for coal, beside taxes of *every kind*, we might say, for smoke must not go up chimney in England without

a tax, light must not come in at the window without paying duties, many must pay from 1 penny to 5 pence per week for water, and if we should attempt to tell all we should want a government list, after paying all taxes what think you will a family have left for bread stuff? Add this to the tax on corn, which is a great share of the expense of this article, and what is left but starvation, leaving out of account all seasonings, such as Peppers, Spices, &c. which by taxation is four times the value it is in the United States. So you may well suppose that the poor are not troubled much with these things. The poor are not able to keep dogs, and if they were they would have to pay from 8 shilling to 1 £ per head per annum tax. There are taxes for living and taxes for dying, inasmuch that it is very difficult for the poor to get buried any how, and a man may emigrate to America to find a grave, for less money, than he can get a decent burial for in old England. We scarce recollect an article without a tax except cats, mice and fleas.[40]

If such a negative impression accurately reflected the economic opportunities afforded the common man in England, the Mormon apostles could well have preached emigration to America not only for the sake of the Gospel, but also for the temporal salvation of the distraught masses. Either message or some combination of both would have appealed to the industrial workers of Manchester. For whatever reason, over 62 percent of the Manchester membership in 1840 eventually emigrated.[41]

Church growth in the early 1840s did not come without difficulties in public relations. Theodore Turley, for example, who had emigrated to the United States seventeen years before returning as a missionary in 1840, was arrested on the affidavit of an unfriendly Methodist who swore that Turley had defaulted on a debt before leaving for the United States. Turley was held without trial and released only after his missionary friends threatened to expose certain illegalities in his arrest.[42]

Just as James Fielding believed the missionaries came from Satan, so the elders, true believers in their own right, averred that much of the opposition to their efforts came from the same source. Clayton wrote to Willard Richards in February, 1840, that:

We have some mighty opponents and surely Satan is seeking not only to disturb the peace of the Saints, but to destroy the body and spirit also. If my judgment is correct in these things, we are only just beginning to feel the smart.[43]

On occasion, the opposition tried to discredit the Mormons by publishing unfriendly stories of some of their activities. In October, 1840, according to one of these accounts, Elder James Mahon accepted a challenge to appear before anyone and convince them of his ability to speak in tongues. A meeting was held. When some Hebrew was read to Mahon, he could not understand it. When he spoke what he claimed to be Hebrew none of the teachers of Hebrew in the audience could find a word of the language in what he said.[44] The publication and circulation of such stories undoubtedly did little to speed the growth of the Church.

Clayton's diary reveals a great deal about the life of a Mormon clergyman in Victorian England. When William Clayton gave himself wholly to the ministry, he preached "without purse or scrip" and relied almost totally upon members of the Church for his livelihood. It is unclear what hardships this placed upon his wife and two small children whom he left behind in Penwortham. It is also unclear whether he paid for his lodging. What is clear, however, is that he relied heavily upon gifts from branch members for his meals and clothing. The good people who befriended him were themselves not generally well off, yet their willingness to share illustrates the desire on the part of many to promote the work of the Church. Clayton often recorded in his diary not only where he took his daily meals, but also when and from whom he received such offerings as cake, fruit, drinks, clothing, and money. On January 27, for example, he had breakfast at the Hardman boarding house, dinner at the home of Thomas Miller, and supper with Ellen Battersby, where he also drank a pint of porter.[45] On February 4, he recorded

25

having breakfast at Hardman's and dinner at the Bewsher home. The same day Sarah Perkins gave him a cup of red wine, five people gave him money to give to Willard Richards, Amby Sands gave him some optical dye for his baby daughter, and Sarah Crooks gave him some raisins, some articles for his wife, and an orange. Clayton frequently even noted that he had water at various places, which seems curious to the modern reader. It may be, however, that he made such a notation because culinary water was so scarce in Manchester in the period, or it may have been that he was referring to some sort of special mineral water rather than culinary water.

The myriad problems which confronted Clayton as branch president reveal a number of things about the Mormons in Manchester. Though these people were Latter-day Saints, they were not holy, and running a branch was a challenging exercise in human relations. Church members tended to rely heavily on local leadership in handling their personal problems. Nevertheless, Clayton's attitude toward them suggests that he himself was devoted not only to the faith, but also to the individual well-being of his urban flock.

Two cases which play a prominent part in the diary are illustrative of the diverse problems with which Clayton had to deal. One concerned Arthur Smith and Betsy Holden,[46] whose romance was tragically complicated by the fact that Betsy was already married to John Holden, a soldier who had left England three or four years earlier and had not been heard from since. Local Church leaders objected to their marriage plans on the grounds that there was no evidence that Holden had actually died. Clayton counselled long and hard with the couple and was finally informed by Betsy that they had decided to cut off their relationship until the matter was legally settled. The fact that Arthur was courting a married woman, however, caused considerable stir in the Church, and on

November 22, 1839, he was finally brought before the branch council. Clayton sympathized with Betsy. "We know the natural weakness of woman," he wrote to Willard Richards, and refused to cast any blame on her. He did suggest that she should give satisfaction to the Church, apparently by making some kind of public statement. This the sensitive young woman found herself unable to do, for, she said, it would almost break her heart.

Arthur Smith became embittered at what he considered Church interference in a private matter and refused to partake of the sacrament. In an impassioned exchange with Clayton, he complained that some of the elders had told him that his marriage plans were from Hell. He rejected this idea, of course, and declared that he would wait until God showed him the way. Clayton pleaded with him to accept the counsel of the Lord's servants. Smith remained adamant, however, even after Clayton threatened him with disfellowship. The discussion ended on a more mellow note as Smith expressed his love for the members of the Church, his faith in the gospel, and his belief that if God showed him he was wrong and he repented he would be under no condemnation. Clayton, ever concerned with the spiritual welfare of his flock, wrote to his brethren in the presidency that Smith's conduct did not altogether "agree with the spirit of God," and that if he found the two really intended to marry he would write Betsy's father.

Smith gave the branch leadership further reason for concern. He held the office of deacon in the branch and became concerned for his perogative in office when he found that, in his absence, it was proposed that the branch collect funds to help the indigent Sarah Duckworth. Arthur insisted that the regular collection box should be used for that purpose, and severely criticized the Saints for not following proper procedures. Clayton, who was trying valiantly to be fair in all his judgments, told Smith to take his complaint to the council, but wrote to Willard Richards that Smith "is not one with us." He soon heard via the branch grapevine that Smith had lost confidence in him.

Such problems were not easily solved, for personal feelings ran deep and some members found it difficult to accept instruction by Church leaders in the temporal aspects of their lives. Though Smith was apparently devoted to the Church in principle, he found it hard to give unqualified obedience to Church leaders whom he also knew as merely men. The mission presidency counseled Clayton to take Smith's license, but before this happened both the question of his marriage and that of the collection came before the council. When Clayton patiently explained that the disputed collection had been taken up as an emergency measure, Smith was finally reconciled on the matter and asked the forgiveness of the council, which he received. He also agreed to partake of the sacrament, but a new debate flared up over the matter of his marriage to Betsy. He refused to break off his connection with her and the council voted to take his office from him.

The sequel of this story of love, Church discipline, and human antagonism is somewhat sketchy, but reveals the unpredictableness of human nature. Clayton later discovered that Arthur and Betsy had been secretly married, and the council soon excommunicated them. But after all this, Smith continued to respect Clayton. One day Clayton heard that Smith "wept yesterday because I looked distant & did not say brother." Arthur and Betsy were apparently reconciled to the idea that theirs was not a legal marriage and had it performed again after proper legalities had been taken care of, for church records indicate that they were married in May, 1840, in Liverpool. Their reconciliation with Clayton and the

Church is seen in the fact that when Clayton was preparing to emigrate to America, Smith, a tailor by trade, purchased cloth for Clayton's trousers and cut out his clothes. Arthur and Betsy later emigrated to Utah, where Arthur became a high priest and served nine years as a steward to Brigham Young. The couple had four children and finally settled in Laketown, Utah, where Betsy died in 1874 and Arthur in 1878.

A second case in which Clayton became involved concerned the family of James and Ann Lee, who lived in Leicester before moving to Manchester.[47] In Leicester, where James had been sent by his employer, the Lees found themselves far from other Mormons and the fellowship of the Church. Penniless, Lee and his family moved to Manchester, after which a controversy developed over a debt which he allegedly owed his former employer. The latter even followed them to Manchester to try to collect.

The Lees were happy to be in Manchester, but their problems were not yet over. For one thing, the mission leaders cautiously refused to allow James to function in the priesthood until they checked on his standing. In addition, Mrs. Lee became extremely ill about a month after they arrived in Manchester. Clayton prayed with her and blessed her, which made her feel somewhat better, but later in the day she began experiencing hallucinations—alternately screaming, laughing, and praying. Wilford Woodruff visited her the next day, prayed to rebuke the foul spirits, then joined with the other elders in annointing her head with oil. They then had her drink some oil and washed her forehead with rum. She apparently recovered for Clayton made no further mention of her illness in his diary.

That the branch members had developed a strong sense of community is apparent from the events which followed.

On January 19, two days after Mrs. Lee's healing, Clayton presented Lee to the Church members, who forgave him his transgressions and offered him full fellowship. Several days later, Clayton reported to Willard Richards that the preceding Sabbath day had been one of fasting and prayer in behalf of Brother and Sister Lee, in the hope of their repentance. Apparently, it was a common practice not only for members to confess their sins before the body of the Saints, but also for members to exhibit a genuine brotherhood by assisting one another to overcome their sins.

The Lees seem to have become integrated very well into the branch. Clayton noted on several occasions that Lee was sent to make visits and perform baptisms. Clayton wrote in support of Lee's application for employment, and Lee was apparently offered a position as a clerk in a shop.

In addition to problems such as those of Arthur Smith and the Lee family, Clayton found himself constantly confronted with branch members who seemed to rely on him to help and counsel them. Typical problems included family quarrels and petty jealousies, welfare cases and other financial difficulties, petty arguments between members of the branch over finances and other matters, members seeking advice on economic affairs, and unexemplary public conduct of some members of the Church. Clayton's faithful recording of all these difficulties leaves today's reader with an intimate insight into the human nature of the Church in Manchester.

At the same time, the diary reveals the genuine devotion of William Clayton to the work of the Lord and to the well-being of the members of the Church. He was capable of genuine sympathy, as illustrated by his notation after dealing with Betsy Crooks: "I feel to weep over her." He seemed especially grieved over hard feelings among the Saints, and made every effort to play the role of peacemaker, but his diary is filled with sad notations regarding personal disputes. Little wonder that on May 17 he finally preached a sermon against "evil speaking and hard feelings," and on May 31 he preached from I Peter, chapter 3, which calls for unity in the home and love and harmony among the Saints.

Some Personal Notes on William Clayton

In spite of all his difficulties, Clayton seems to have functioned well in his position. When he decided to commit his life wholly to the Church, he was prepared to do whatever was required of him. He expressed such an attitude in a letter to Willard Richards when he declared:

I feel I am not my own. I am bought with a price, even the blood of Jesus Christ, and as a servant I must soon give up my account. I desire and strive, brethren, to keep my accounts right with the Lord every day that I may meet him with joy. [James] Lea could get away from his master but I feel always in the presence of mine, and my desire is to live nearer still that I may be ready in the hour to give up my accounts.[48]

Apostle Woodruff, apparently impressed with Clayton's ability wrote in his journal that he was "a wise and worthy brother," and wrote to Willard Richards that Clayton was "a man of wisdom and of God."[49]

Clayton was anxious not to antagonize others. Mention has already been made of his efforts to keep peace among the members of the branch, but he was just as concerned with keeping a good image before the public. He was critical, for example, of one missionary who spoke "too much about his works and other sects," and on at least two occasions cautioned him against rashness in preaching against other denominations. Clayton felt that missionaries should "not speak of anything but the first principles," and that they should be good examples before the world. In his own confrontations with preachers and members of other denominations, he seemed more concerned with expounding the basic principles of Mormonism than with criticizing other denominations.

In spite of Clayton's compassion and good nature, he could not avoid some criticism, some of which he reported in his diary. At least one woman in the branch was bitter against him, and another young lady whom he was counseling called him and other church leaders "abominable liars," but later repented the incident. Some Protestant missionaries called him one of the "worst devils that ever came from hell." But there is little indication that Clayton was held in anything but the highest esteem by most branch members, and they obviously relied heavily on his wisdom and judgment.

Nevertheless, even this devoted leader was subject to the temptations of the flesh. One of the most intriguing aspects of Clayton's personal life was his relationship to a young woman in the Manchester branch by the name of Sarah Crooks. Sarah was about two years younger than William, and apparently they were immediately attracted to each other. Clayton's diary is filled with notations concerning Sarah's feelings, problems, and kindness to him. Only the unobservant would fail to see that they had special feelings for each other. The first time she appeared in his diary was January 13 when he mentioned a grievance she had against another branch member and recorded her gift of money. Six days later he detailed a series of dreams which he and other members of the branch had about his wife. At about the same time, Sarah Crooks dreamed that William had a second wife, and some other sisters dreamed that his wife was dead or dying. While one hesitates to read too much psychological analysis into such events, it may not be amiss to suggest that some branch members, including Sarah, were becoming concerned with Clayton's marital status and his separation from

32

his wife. The dire predictions of some of the Manchester women concerning the fate of his wife were not fulfilled, and there is nothing to suggest that Clayton was in any way losing affection for his family. But it becomes clear throughout the diary that the attachment between Clayton and Sarah was more than a passing fancy and that both of them struggled with their feelings for each other.

As time went on their association became more close and Clayton mentioned her more and more frequently in his diary. He often accepted money from her, took her to missionary meetings both in and away from Manchester, and ate meals with her either alone or with her friend, Rebecca Partington. Finally on February 27, this ambivalent relationship came to a head as he confided in his diary that Sarah contemplated marriage, and he did not want her to get married. Then, revealing the war between his human nature and his great desire to live the principles in which he believed, he wrote, "I certainly feel my love towards her to increase but shall strive against it. I feel too much to covet her and afraid less her troubles should cause her to get married. The Lord keep me pure and preserve me from doing wrong." Other young Mormon elders have undoubtedly shared such feelings. Though most seem to have had his ability to adhere to principles in which they believed, few have been as honest in revealing their inner feelings and conflicts.

As time went on, his association with Sarah grew more frequent. As branch president, he helped Sarah and Rebecca find a place to live. When their first residence proved unsatisfactory, they came to live at the Hardman home, where Clayton also stayed. Six days later Clayton left Manchester for a short visit with his family at Penwortham. Before he left, Sarah gave him some money and a personal letter. He arrived at Penwortham that evening and the next day wrote several letters, one to Sarah, another to Alice Hardman. One gets the impression that Clayton was not attempting to hide anything; his wife and family probably knew that he was on friendly terms with some of the young ladies in the Church at Manchester. When he arrived back in Manchester a week later, Sarah and Rebecca gave him his supper and Sarah washed his tired head with rum, a soothing service which she was to perform frequently during the next several weeks.

Throughout the month of April, Clayton saw Sarah nearly every day. His feelings are difficult to ascertain, for at frequent spots in his diary lines have been crossed out. Often these passages are closely associated with his mention of Sarah, and on one occasion her name can be seen in the deleted material. Who did the crossing out and why may always remain a mystery, but if these passages really did concern Sarah they undoubtedly reflected his growing affection for her. On the night of April 1, for example, he arrived at the Hardman boarding house after a seven or eight mile walk, and Sarah, who was waiting for him, washed his tired feet. At the same time she told him of a dream concerning her possible marriage to a young man and what Clayton had told her about eternity. Clayton wrote that she had decided not to be in a hurry. The next five and one-half lines of the diary are crossed out and illegible. The next sentence states that she (Sarah, undoubtedly) gave him a new pair of shoes. On April 7, Clayton observed that some of the Manchester Saints seemed envious of Sarah for some reason, but the following 21 lines are crossed out in his diary.

Sarah and William Clayton apparently remained the best of friends throughout his stay in Manchester. There is no evidence that their friendship went beyond the bounds of propriety, even though one finds such days as May 18, when he had supper with her, drank a pint of porter, had her wash

34

his feet, then sat up with her until two a.m. the next morning. On July 31 he made a rather cryptic entry in his journal. He had been released from the mission presidency and was preparing to leave Manchester. Sarah gave him money for a new pair of boots to help him along the way. "I feel hard to leave the saints at Manchester," he wrote, "yet willing because it is for the best." Those who have read his diary will always wonder whether he was not relieved to be rid of the nagging problem of an impossible romance.

For those with romantic inclinations the outcome of the story of Sarah Crooks is rather disappointing. As Clayton prepared to sail for America in September, the two were still on very good terms. He received a letter from her on September 3, and on September 6 she not only gave him some linen but cut it for shirts. From then on, however, she disappeared from his diary. It would, indeed, have been a romantic ending to the story if, after the Mormons began the practice of plural marriage, William had sent for Sarah. Such an outcome might have been anticipated when in February, 1843, Joseph Smith explained the principle of plural marriage to Clayton, and volunteered to put up the money for him to send for a sister back in England to whom he was very much attached. Sarah emigrated the following month. But, alas for the romantic historian, William Clayton's first plural wife, whom he married in April, 1843, was his first wife's sister. In 1844 he married Alice Hardman, one of the young ladies whose family owned the boarding house where Clayton and Sarah lived in Manchester. Sarah, however, married William Cook, and on June 29, 1844, these two were placed on a list of those who had "aided and abetted" William Law, Robert Foster, and others in the events that led to the death of Joseph Smith.[50] Thus ended William Clayton's missionary romance.

Church Practices and Ideas

One of the values of William Clayton's journal is in the comparisons one may make between the ideas of Church members in years past and those of today. Awareness of both the similarities and the differences is essential to an understanding of the historical development of the Church itself.

Mormon missionaries of 1840 were clearly devoted to the idea that their Church was a restoration of the ancient Church of Christ, that baptism by one holding authority was necessary to salvation, that the second coming of Christ was near, and that the Holy Ghost could and did operate directly in the lives of individuals. In this, the emphasis was not too different from that of today, except that the millennium seemed more imminent then, and the Saints of Manchester, at least, seemed to expect direct personal communication from God more fully than most Saints today. Clayton frequently mentioned dreams that had some special meaning to him, and he often recorded experiences with speaking in tongues. Such things seemed commonplace among the urban Saints of Manchester in 1840 and reflected a simple faith not often found in the secularized society of the mid-20th century.

At the same time, there were practices which reflect basic differences in interpretation between 1840 and today. The interpretation given the "Word of Wisdom" is a case in point. Today, it is clearly established that active Mormons will abstain from the use of tea, coffee, tobacco, and all alcoholic beverages. In William Clayton's day such rigid adherence to the letter of the law was apparently not required. Almost everywhere the Mormon elders went they could preach in a temperance hall, for teetotalers believed the Mormons made men temperate faster than they did. Heber C. Kimball observed that "as soon as any obeyed the Gospel they abandoned their excess in drinking; none of us drank any kind of spirits, porter, small beer, or even wine, neither did we drink tea, coffee, or chocolate."[51] Clayton's diary and other sources, however, reveal that Kimball exaggerated. When the apostles arrived for a conference in Preston in 1840, for example, William Clayton's mother-in-law celebrated by breaking out a bottle of wine which she had kept for forty years. There was, she explained, "something providential" in its preservation, for she had intended to use it several times before. The Church leaders blessed the wine and each drank a glass.[52] It is clear that on occasion Clayton drank everything listed by Heber C. Kimball and that such habits were not frowned upon. Porter, a light beer, was given to him regularly, and on occasions when he was ill he drank stronger beverages. On May 27, while Heber C. Kimball was staying with him, Clayton had a sick spell and drank six pints of brandy, which he said, "gave me ease." The next morning Kimball himself ordered a pint of porter. From all the entries in Clayton's diary, it can only be concluded that obedience to the Word of Wisdom meant abstinence from the use of tobacco, moderation in the use of alcohol, and very little with regard to tea, coffee, or chocolate. Clayton himself often drank tea, cocoa, and coffee with the members. The use of stronger alcoholic beverages for medicinal purposes was also common, and Clayton frequently recorded such things as the use of rum for bathing his head. Such an interpretation of the Word of Wisdom was not different from that among American Mormons, for it took many years after the revelation to Joseph Smith for the present requirements to become solidified into the accepted practice of the Church.

When illness struck, the Manchester Saints were quick to call on the elders of the church to anoint them with oil and pray for their recovery; an ordinance still very much alive in the Church. Clayton's journal reveals, however, some interesting differences in the way this ordinance was performed. Today the afflicted has a drop of oil applied to the crown of his head, and an appropriate blessing is pronounced. In earlier times it was common to anoint the afflicted part of the body directly or to take the oil internally. The urban Saints in Manchester were great believers in the healing power of the Priesthood, and various entries in Clayton's journal record the rewarding of their faith through healing. While Wilford Woodruff was visiting the branch on January 19, he reported laying his hands on twenty afflicted persons who were healed. "The Saints in England have great confidence in God and His Servants," he wrote in his journal, "and there are so many applying for the laying on of hands that we need as much faith as the Apostle Paul had, so that at the touch of our garments or handkerchiefs they might be healed."

Another intriguing custom was the practice of the Manchester Saints to take seriously the biblical injunction to "salute one another with a holy kiss."[53] In February 1840, Clayton advised the members to give up the practice, apparently because it could have gotten out of hand and become offensive to some, but in April it still continued. On the 18th of that month, George A. Smith, the only eligible bachelor among the apostles, visited the Hardman boarding house. Very quickly several young ladies filled the room and one of them, "decidedly a little beauty" and somewhat shy, as he described her, approached him with what to him must have been a startling request. "Brother Smith," she said, "we want a kiss of you," and her eyes, the apostle reported, "flashed like stars on a clear night." Somewhat taken aback, but no doubt flattered, Smith struggled to summon up resolution enough to tell her that kissing was not part of his mission to England. After that, he said, he was regarded as no lady's man by the girls of Manchester. Smith accused the

English elders of teaching that there was no harm in greeting each other with a holy kiss, and said that some of them had set the example, and that "it required a very decided course both in Manchester and other places to prevent evil corruption growing out of this custom, which might have been firmly established had not the Twelve put it down."[54]

Other differences between past and present may be observed in Clayton's diary. They include the use of collection boxes in church services, the requirement that members in transgression confess their sins openly before the Church, the absence of any meetings except those for preaching and council, the conduct of branch affairs including excommunication and disfellowshipping by a council which included men and women of the branch rather than by a select group of priesthood holders, and the total reliance of missionaries upon the local Saints for their livelihood.

The Emigration of William Clayton

On July 6, 1840, Joseph Fielding, Willard Richards and William Clayton were released from their duties as a mission presidency, and the next day Clayton was assigned to do missionary work in Birmingham. He never fulfilled that mission, however, for sometime in August he decided to emigrate with his family to America. One company of British Saints had already gone, under the leadership of John Moon. Clayton and his family were to go with the second group. His account of the transatlantic voyage and the overland trip to Nauvoo is the earliest-known, firsthand account of the journey of a group of Mormon emigrants and is one more reason why the Clayton diary is of great historical value.

It was natural that by 1840 the British Saints should have felt the pull of a desire to gather to the New World. America, after all, was not only the land where their prophet lived, but also the land of Zion where Adam himself had lived, where the Gospel had been restored, where the Saints would gather in the last days, and where Christ would conduct His Millennial reign. Symbolically, America was indeed "home." Anticipation of calamities incident to the Second Coming combined with economic conditions in England could not help but promote a longing for America in the hearts of European Saints. In the 1840s a massive migration began which eventually culminated in the transfer of over 51,000 European Saints to America, more than 38,000 coming from England.[55]

Although the spirit of fleeing to Zion had begun to catch on among the British Saints by early 1840, Church leaders were at first reluctant to give their approval. As early as January, 1840, Clayton wrote to Willard Richards that some Saints were "making ready for America without council and in their present state of religion only feel to say if *they should go* as soon as they anticipate some of them will wish themselves back again."[56] Clayton's wife's cousin, John Moon, was among those who pressed to go. It is not clear in the correspondence whether Clayton himself wanted to emigrate at that time, but in March the mission president, Joseph Fielding, instructed Clayton and the Moon family that he did not feel it was the will of God for any elders or priests to go unless they had an imperative call. It was apparent, however, that the mission leaders expected the gathering to begin momentarily. In a letter to Willard Richards, Fielding explained his instructions to the Moon brothers:

We would if we were in their place, act as if we expected to go the coming summer, but we had no thought of that being the signal for the gathering to begin, nor have we had any instruction to give such a signal and till we do *I will not be responsible for any thing that is or may be done about it.* If any go they will not say that Brother or President Fielding gave his sanction to it.[57]

At the same time, Fielding was perfectly willing to allow

40

them to go on their own, as regular emigrants, but he would not approve of their going as Saints to Zion. All of this suggests that the spirit of gathering was very much in the air by early 1840, but that mission leaders were cautions about giving official sanction until they had received permission from higher authority. Fielding even went so far as to suggest that premature emigration might be a stratagem of Satan and that some Saints had gone astray with respect to the gathering.[58]

The following month, however, saw the beginning in England of the official promotion of emigration. At a conference in Preston on April 15, it was decided that Saints wishing to go were to receive recommends from Church leaders in England. Wealthy people, however, were not to receive such a recommend unless they also assisted the poor.[59] In August the First Presidency of the Church sent a general address to all the Saints scattered abroad who were "desirous to go forward in the ways of truth and righteousness, and by obedience to the heavenly command, escape the things which are coming on the earth." The message must have struck a welcome note in the hearts of the British Saints who were already preparing to emigrate, for it declared in part:

The work which has to be accomplished in the last days is one of vast importance, and will call into action the energy, skill, talent, and ability of the Saints, so that it may roll forth with that glory and majesty described by the prophet; and will consequently require the concentration of the Saints, to accomplish works of such magnitude and grandeur.

The work of the gathering spoken of in the Scriptures will be necessary to bring about the glories of the last dispensation. It is probably unnecessary to press the subject on the Saints, as we believe the spirit of it is manifest, and its necessity obvious to every considerate mind; and everyone zealous for the promotion of truth and righteousness, is equally so for the gathering of the Saints.[60]

In particular, the newly founded settlement in Nauvoo, the desire to bring large numbers of Saints to help strengthen the position of the Church, and the plans to build a temple resulted in an open invitation for all who wished to assist. For some British Saints, it was an understatement to suggest that it was probably unnecessary to press the subject on them, for on June 6 some 41 Saints under the leadership of John Moon had sailed from England on the *Britannia*. This was the first organized group of emigrant Mormons to leave for America, although a few individuals had gone before them.[61] The pioneer emigrant company had no easy passage to America, being plagued with winds, storms, and illness, but the spirit and the devotion of these adventuresome souls is well illustrated in a letter John Moon wrote to William Clayton on July 22. Having arrived in New York harbor only a few days earlier, Moon wrote: "I feel myself glad to find my feet upon the land of Joseph after so long and tedious a journey." The *Book of Mormon* had taught them that America was a chosen land, to be inherited by the descendants of the ancient prophet, Joseph, and that they were of that lineage. Continued Moon, "Saw Long Island all covered with green trees and white houses; such a beautiful sight I never saw. I did rejoice to behold the land of Joseph: Yea, I thought, it did pay for all the hardships which I had gone through."[62]

William Clayton, meanwhile, was preparing for his own voyage. His diary provides an intimate and colorful picture of the preparations as well as the voyage itself. At first Clayton was apparently planning to send his family to America while he remained in England as a missionary, and on July 23 he was at home in Penwortham to assist them in making the necessary preparations. It is not clear why these plans were changed. A diary entry suggests that he may not have made the final decision until September 5, when his mother-in-law became so upset at having to handle all the problems alone that she prevailed upon him to go. He got special permission from Brigham Young and John Taylor to leave his missionary work. Two days later, when the company was making its final boarding, Willard Richards objected to Clayton's going, which indicates again that the decision was a sudden one. In any case, he spent the month of August with his family preparing for the voyage. On the 18th they held a public sale, probably an auction, in order to dispose of the goods they could not take with them. One indication of the problems they had in this effort is seen in Clayton's notation that he had been trying to sell John Moon's bass violin, but finding no success he had to leave it with John Melling to dispose of. They planned originally to leave on August 27, but various delays, including the fact that Elder Theodore Turley could not leave that early, kept them from actually sailing until September 8.

This emigrant company contained about 200 people and departed from Liverpool, soon to become the main point of Mormon embarkation. Theodore Turley, together with William Clayton and five other counselors, was placed in charge of the group. On September 7, Brigham Young and Willard Richards also boarded the sailing ship *North America* and spent the night with the departing Saints. The next day Elders Young, Richards, and Taylor went with the ship about fifteen or twenty miles, then returned by steamer to Liverpool. Thus the second group of emigrants officially to leave England got underway.[63]

Clayton's narrative of the Atlantic crossing does not attempt to hide either the hardships experienced by the Saints or their continued divisions and disputes. Summaries of such crossings often leave the reader with the impression that despite hardships the Saints continued to live exemplary lives and on that account all turned out well. Typical is the

43

summary in the British Manuscript History: "The company had a prosperous voyage to New York, where they arrived in the beginning of October."[64] The *Millennial Star* gave a slightly more complete report:

We have also read a letter from Elder Clayton, from New York, bringing news of the safe arrival of the "North America," with the colony of Saints which went over in her: she was thirty-three days from Liverpool to New York; the Saints were principally well; some few children had died on the passage, and one man after she came to anchor. . . . The colony were in good spirits, preparing to take passage further west."[65]

The reader of William Clayton's journal will come away with a somewhat different view of the difficulties of the voyage. As might be expected, most of the passengers had never been to sea, and immediately many became seasick, even when the ocean was relatively calm. The sick must have been shocked when the captain's mate told them to fasten their boxes, for they expected a "good rocking" that night. When the "good rocking" came, Clayton reported the effect most vividly. "This was a new scene," he said, "such sickness, vomiting, groaning and bad smells I never witnessed before and added to this the closeness of the births almost suffocated us for the want of air." It was beginning to be a far from happy voyage.

The storm lasted for several days and became so bad that one little girl was frightened out of her mind and died. Several other adults and children became ill. On Friday, September 18, Elder Turley called the company together and found that "there was some unbelief" in their midst. Another child was dangerously ill, and some believed it would not recover. Both Turley and Clayton boldly declared that they did not believe that it was the will of God that they should lose one soul, which had a cheering effect on the Saints, but that night the child died anyway. "This was a grief to our minds," Clayton pathetically reported. The next morning the mate "ordered the child to be sewed up which was soon done and it was immediately thrown overboard without any ceremony." All told, six children died and were buried at sea.

The first two weeks saw still further difficulties. Elder Turley was continually concerned with the lack of personal cleanliness displayed by the Saints, some of which went to sickening extremes. On one occasion part of the ship caught fire, but thanks to the calmness of the wind it was hurriedly put out. Then, reflecting the longing for America that characterized so many of the Saints, Clayton recorded in his diary on September 22 that "as soon as the bustle subsided the wind began to blow and we were again on our way home." They had indeed forsaken their native land, for now "home" was a strange land to which they had never been. At the same time, Clayton very honestly reflected the human mixture of gratitude and discomfiture that must have characterized all of them when he wrote, "The Lord has been kind to us for which we feel thankful but not as much as we might."

Clayton's account of the rest of the voyage reveals personal, human problems, as well as religious faith and optimism. He recorded considerable sickness caused by storms, lack of water, and other physical problems. He told of disagreements both among the Saints and between the Saints and the rest of the passengers and crew. At one time, for example, four of the young women in the company were criticized for "making very free" with some of the passengers and crew, and drinking wine with them. This caused ill feelings not only among the Mormons, but also between the Mormons who were concerned with such conduct and the crew who resented being interfered with.

At the same time, the Mormons attempted to do missionary work among the passengers, held their regular religious services, and paid attention to nightly prayers, which they believed were regularly answered. On October 8, for example, Clayton reported, "Last evening being my turn for prayer I felt to ask the Lord for a fair wind and I rejoice to see that he has answered my prayers. The wind is very favourable, near 10 mi. an hour. This is the third instance of the Lord answering my prayer for fair wind in a calm."

On the morning of October 12, the excited immigrant company had their first view of the American coast. The next day, Sunday, they cast anchor at New York harbor, and shortly after noon Clayton, Turley, and Joseph Jackson went ashore. Said Clayton, "This was another treat to us to set our feet on terra firma." The group immediately found a member of the Church, at whose home they had dinner, went to religious services, then returned to the ship. It was two days before they were allowed officially to disembark, but when they did so it was on the most friendly terms with the captain of the *North America*, who was apparently completely reconciled to them and even said that he would like to bring another group of Mormons over in the ship.

The immigrant group immediately set out for the new headquarters of the Saints at Commerce (later Nauvoo), Illinois. They traveled by boat up the Hudson River, through the Erie Canal, through Lake Huron and Lake Michigan to Chicago, then overland for a short time, then by boat again down the Rock River to the Mississippi, which took them directly to Commerce. Again, Clayton's journal provides an intimate, significant account of the migration from New York to the Mormon settlements on the Mississippi that was very likely typical of those to follow. Expressing the relief of the immigrants as they arrived in the long-sought promised land and their feeling that this, a strange country, was indeed their home, Clayton wrote:

Thus ended a journey of over 5000 miles having been exactly 11 weeks and about 10 hours between leaving Liverpool and arriving at our journeys end. We had been much exposed to cold weather and suffered many deprivations and disconveniences yet through the mercy of God we landed safe and in good health with the exception of 2 persons, one of whom died soon after landing. We were pleased to find ourselves once more at home and felt to praise God for his goodness.[66]

Clayton gives no evidence of having regretted his decision to adopt a new homeland, and, indeed, took every occasion to sing its praises. On the journey from New York to Commerce he frequently wrote in his diary of the beauty of the homes and countryside. On December 10 he wrote friends back in England that he and his group were "much pleased both with the country, and with the society there," that he was satisfied and most anxious that his English friends should come and enjoy the same blessings.[67]

But life was not to be easy in the new land. Even amongst the Saints, Clayton was to find misunderstanding and criticism, as well as uplifting experiences and choice opportunities. The last few pages of the journal provide only infrequent entries covering the next two years, but they are enough to give some candid insight into the problems and challenges confronted by Clayton and his friends. Hyrum Smith, brother of the Prophet Joseph, urged Clayton to move to Iowa Territory, where he was speculating in land. Against the counsel of other Saints who warned them that the Devil was across the river, Clayton and his family decided to settle there. They made an agreement with William Smith, another brother of the Prophet and a member of the Council of the Twelve, to purchase 185 acres of land to be paid for by giving up half the wages Clayton expected to earn on a steamboat. There is something inspiring, dramatic, and incongruous about an English bookkeeper in his twenties, with a wife and two small children embarking on an adventure as a

47

farmer on unbroken Iowa prairie, hoping to pay for his farm by working on a Mississippi steamboat. Such is the change the Mormon gospel wrought in the lives of many. The young couple purchased some equipment and livestock and on January 12, 1841, began the four-day task of moving all their luggage across the frozen river. At Montrose they first found shelter in a small rented house which had such poor ventilation that they often had to cook outdoors. Even more disappointing was the spirit and morale of the other members of the Church who had ventured into Iowa. Clayton found out what the Saints in Nauvoo meant when they told him the Devil was loose in Iowa, for he sadly reported that he found "the saints in a very bad state and having no meetings, full of envy, strife and contention." He seemed especially disappointed that they were unable to attend religious services, although they did hear Joseph Smith and Sidney Rigdon preach on two or three occasions.

Clayton's account of his efforts in Iowa is one of continuing hardship and disappointment, even though in March, 1841, Joseph Smith received a revelation stating that Iowa was to be built up and implying that it would almost rival Nauvoo in the eyes of the Lord.[68] The major settlement was called Zarahemla, a *Book of Mormon* name, and a stake was soon organized for which Clayton was appointed clerk. But the effort ultimately failed. In March Clayton began to plant his crops, only to be disappointed when a fellow church member presented a conflicting claim to the land and tried to force him off. In addition, Clayton lost his share in the steamboat which was supposed to provide an income for him. To add to his troubles, Clayton had frequent spells of illness. During one of these, some of the brethren of the Church volunteered to build a fence around his field, but they did not make it secure enough and cattle broke in and destroyed the entire crop of corn. About the same time, Joseph Smith visited Clayton. Smith became particularly concerned with his poor circumstances and continued illness. Clayton was too proud to ask for help from the Church, but after being pressed by Smith, he told of their desperate circumstances and needs. "After this," he recorded, "the church helped us considerable." Little wonder that by the end of August he decided to take the advice of Heber C. Kimball to purchase two city lots in Nauvoo and move there. He continued to work the farm for the rest of the year but on December 14 moved back across the river to Nauvoo.

Early in 1842, William Clayton was appointed to keep a record of the tithing donated for the building of the Nauvoo Temple, and with reference to this and a few other brief items this journal ends. It appears, however, that in the urban setting of Nauvoo the former British mission leader finally found his place in American society. His assignment as temple recorder was only the first of several clerical and administrative tasks. In addition, he drew close to Joseph Smith and learned to revere him most sincerely. These times were difficult for Smith, who was becoming the subject of slander and criticism. Clayton wrote to Willam Hardman in Manchester in March, 1842:

My faith in this doctrine, and in the prophet and officers is firm, unshaken, and unmoved; nay, rather, it is strengthened and settled firmer than ever. . . .
For me to write any thing concerning the character of president Joseph Smith would be superfluous. All evil reports concerning him I treat with utter contempt. . . . Joseph Smith is not the "treasurer of the Saints," and has no more to do with their money than you or me; every man just does what he pleases with his money, and neither Joseph, nor any other of the officers, ever attempt to control any one, or their property either. . . .
With regard to J. Smith getting drunk, I will say that I am now acting as clerk for him, and at his office daily, and have been since February 10th, and I know he is as much opposed to the use of intoxicating drinks as any man need be. I have never seen him drunk, nor have I ever heard any man who has seen him drunk since we came

here. I believe he does not take intoxicating drink of any kind: our city is conducted wholly upon temperance principles. As to his using snuff and tobacco, I KNOW *he does no such thing.* To conclude, I will add that, the more I am with him, the more I love him; the more I know of him, and the more confidence I have in him; and I am sorry that people should give heed to evil reports concerning him, when we all know the great service *he has rendered the church.*[69]

To some, this statement from a twenty-seven year old man who had gone through the troubles Clayton had may seem remarkable, but it was this spirit, shared by thousands, which was the popular base for the success of Mormonism.

While in Nauvoo, William Clayton had the pleasure of welcoming many immigrants from his native land, including his former president Joseph Fielding. With regard to one such group, Clayton demonstrated the tender feelings he harbored for his friends and countrymen and left a touching picture of the excitement in Nauvoo and aboard the riverboat on which the immigrants were approaching:

As we went along, we were delighted and astonished to see the number of Saints on their way to meet the boat. When we arrived, the scene was affecting; I could not refrain from weeping. I looked round, and I suppose there was not less than from two to three thousand Saints on the shore, all anxiously interested in the scene. Many were there who wanted to give the strangers (yet brothers) a hearty welcome; other waiting to ascertain if any former acquaintance was in the company—myself amongst the number; and many, whose hearts throbbed with joy, and their eyes wept tears, expecting to see their mothers, their fathers, their children, and other relatives &c., &c. While all this bustle was going on on shore, the boat was now within three hundred yards, coming directly for the shore; the confusion was so great I could but faintly hear those on the boat singing a hymn (I believe, "The Latter-day Glory.")

At this period my heart almost melted, the boat moving majestically, every head stretched out, and all eyes gazing with intensity. A few moments more and the boat was landed, and the joyful acclamations and responding welcomes would have made a heart of stone acknowledge, that whether there was any religion or not, there was a great quantity of *love*—the purest essence of religion. I soon recognized sister Davies, from Cookson street, Manchester, and a sister Martha, who lived with them; also James Burgess and family, Richard Hardman and family, Robert Williams and wife, and several others whom I knew. They soon discovered me, and we quickly felt each other's hand, and had a time of rejoicing together.[70]

During the rest of his life, Clayton participated in many of the important affairs of the Church and performed many significant functions. He continued as temple recorder and became a clerk for Joseph Smith. He was also treasurer for the city of Nauvoo. He was present when Joseph Smith received the controversial revelation pertaining to plural marriage and later demonstrated his conversion to the principle by marrying seven plural wives. Clayton moved west with the original pioneer company in 1847; his pioneer journal covering that year has become the standard account of that famous exodus. In Utah, he held such important public positions as treasurer of Z.C.M.I., Territorial Recorder of Marks and Brands, and Territorial Auditor of Public Accounts. He also served in various Church capacities, including a short mission to his native England in 1852 and 1853. In addition, he was an accomplished musician and composer. In Nauvoo he sometimes sang for Joseph Smith, and in Utah he helped organize the "Nauvoo Legion Band" and played second violin in an orchestra sponsored by the Deseret Musical and Dramatic Association. His famous hymn "Come, Come Ye Saints" is still well-loved by the Mormon people. He died on December 4, 1879, at his home in Salt Lake City.

The William Clayton journal which follows makes a significant contribution to our understanding of the human side of Mormon history. Through his eyes we see the trials and problems of a group of Saints in one of the major urban, industrial centers of England in 1840. We catch the spirit of a young, dedicated mission leader who genuinely loved the Lord and his fellow men. We see the problems that came to him and his group but also the faith and loyalty that accounted for the growth of the Church. We see the belief and dedication that led members to leave their homeland for America. We gain considerable insight into the economic and social conditions of the members and into contemporary Church administration and doctrinal practice. We get an intimate, first-hand view of one of the earliest Mormon groups to cross the ocean and a sensitive account of the effort to settle the ill-fated colony of Zarahemla across the river from Nauvoo. Clayton's sincere faith, combined with honesty in reporting, make his missionary journal a valuable source for the social history of the Mormon people.

MANCHESTER MORMONS
The Journal of William Clayton
1840 to 1842

FOOTNOTES

[1]Brigham Young and Willard Richards to the First Presidency, Manchester, September 5, 1840, in Brigham Young Papers, Historical Department of the Church of Jesus Christ of Latter-day Saints, Salt Lake City, hereinafter cited as HDC.

[2]As quoted in an excerpt from Jesse Lemisch, "Listening to the 'Inarticulate': William Widger's Dream and the Loyalties of the American Revolutionary Seamen in British Prisons," *Journal of Social History*, III (Fall, 1969), in Thomas N. Guinsburg, editor, *The Dimensions of History* (Chicago: Rand McNally, 1971), 128.

[3]*Ibid.*, 129.

[4]Orson Hyde, *A Timely Warning to the People of England*, broadside. Also appeared as an eight page pamphlet, dated Preston, August 19, 1837, and reprinted in 1839.

[5]For a general history of this and other missions to England, see Richard L. Evans, *A Century of "Mormonism" in Great Britain* (Salt Lake City: Deseret News Press, 1937).

⁶See Heber C. Kimball, Orson Hyde and Willard Richards, "Mission to England, or the First Foreign Mission of the Latter-day Saints," *Millennial Star*, III (April, 1841), 289-296, as well as various copies of the broadside in the Historical, Department of the Church. Note also that Clayton frequently refers to the distributing of "Timely Warnings" in Manchester.

⁷Hyde, *Timely Warning*.

⁸James Fielding to Joseph Fielding, Preston, August 27, 1838, in Joseph Fielding Papers, HDC. For a brief listing of some other ministers whose flocks were "robbed" by these early missionaries, see Orson F. Whitney, *Life of Heber C. Kimball: An Apostle: The Father and Founder of the British Mission* (Salt Lake City: Bookcraft, 1967), 142.

⁹Evans, *Century of Mormonism*, 53-54.

¹⁰Joseph Smith, *History of the Church*, edited by B. H. Roberts (Salt Lake City: Deseret Book Company, 1969), III, 276-277.

¹¹Richards to Fielding and Clayton, Alston, May 7, 1839, in Willard Richards Papers, HDC.

¹²Heber C. Kimball to Fielding, Richards and Clayton, Commerce, Illinois, July 25, 1839, Fielding papers, HDC.

¹³Fielding to Hannah Fielding, Manchester, March 27, 1839, Fielding papers, HDC.

¹⁴Figures for this period are probably somewhat inaccurate, but it was reported in 1838 that the membership in the mission was between 1,500 and 2,000. In the conference of April, 1840, membership in the branches represented was reported as 1,671. Manchester, however, in which there was no branch in 1838, had grown to 240 by 1840. Evans, *Century of Mormonism*, 62; *Millennial Star*, I (May, 1840), 20; Brigham Young, *Manuscript History of Brigham Young*, 1801-1844, compiled by Elden Jay Watson from Volumes 25 and 26 of the *Millennial Star* (Salt Lake City: Smith Secretarial Service, 1968), 70. Hereinafter cited as Young, *MS History*.

¹⁵If this many people had been baptized since 1838, there must have been nearly that many apostatize, for there had as yet been no migration to America and the total membership in England had not increased.

[16]Kimball to the Saints of the United States, Preston, April 17, 1840, in Smith, *History of the Church*, IV, 114.

[17]*Millennial Star*, XXVI, 7.

[18]E. J. Hobsbawm, "The British Standard of Living, 1790-1850," *Economic History Review*, Second Series, X (1957), 53-54.

[19]Asa Briggs, *The Age of Improvements* (London: Longsmans, Green and Co., 1959), 388-389.

[20]*Ibid.*, 389.

[21]This is not to say that American Mormons were "frontiersmen," but only that their general orientation was not urban or industrial. In 1951 S. George Ellsworth studied Mormon population patterns in the United States and concluded that most converts came from areas where the population density varied from eighteen to ninety inhabitants per square mile, and that most American Mormons were located in areas more rural than urban. See Samuel George Ellsworth, "A History of Mormon Missions in the United States and Canada, 1830-1860" (Ph.D. dissertation, University of California, Berkeley, 1951), 332.

[22]These figures based on congregations listed in *Millennial Star*, I (May, 1840), 20. Industrial nature of the communities was obtained by reference to Samuel Lewis, *Topographical Dictionary of England* (7th edition, 4 vols; London: S. Lewis & Co., 1848).

[23]Philip A. M. Taylor, "Why Did British Mormons Emigrate?" *Utah Historical Quarterly*, XXII (July, 1954), 260. See also P. A. M. Taylor, *Expectations Westward: The Mormons and the Emigration of their British Converts in the Nineteenth Century* (Edinburgh: Oliver and Boyd, 1965), 149.

[24]Taylor, *Expectations Westward*, 149.

[25]*Manchester As It Is: Or, Nature of the Institutions, Manufactures, Commerce, Railway, etc. of the Metropolis of Manufactures* (Manchester: Love and Barton, 1849), 12-19, 183-184; Leon Faucher, *Manchester in 1844: Its Present Condition and Future Prospects* (London: Simpkin, Marshal and Company, 1844), 26-27, 63-64. Faucher listed 169,000 people

in 1836 and said that 64 percent were operatives, but the editor of the English edition of his book said it was more like 70 to 75 percent.

[26]Faucher, *Manchester,* 16-18, 63.

[27]*Ibid.,* 65-68.

[28]*Ibid.,* 41-42.

[29]*Manchester As It Is,* 61-72, 80-99.

[30]*Ibid.,* 32.

[31]Faucher, *Manchester,* 22-23.

[32]*Manchester As It Is,* 73-79.

[33]Leslie Stepher and Sidney Lee, editors, *The Dictionary of National Biography* (22 vols; Oxford: Oxford University Press, 1960), IV, 604-605.

[34]*Manchester As It Is,* 26-27.

[35]Wilford Woodruff, "Journal," January 18, 1840, HDC; Parley P. Pratt to Brigham Young, Manchester, May 4, 1840, in *MS History,* "British Mission."

[36]Taylor, *Expectations Westward,* 2, 38.

[37]The Manchester Branch records show some 112 men and 146 women for this period. It is difficult to ascertain who was married, but an estimate was arrived at by counting the number of men and women with the same name who lived at the same address. After taking into account the possibility that many of these may have been brothers and sisters, it was estimated by the editors that there were probably about 26 married couples in the branch.

[38]Whitney, *Heber C. Kimball,* 119.

[39]Woodruff, "Journal," January 20, 1840. See also entry for January 19.

[40]Young and Richards to the First Presidency, September 5, 1840, HDC.

[41]According to notations in the Manchester Branch records.

[42]George A. Smith, "My Journal," *The Instructor,* LXXXII (1947), 323. See also Theodore Turley to Willard Richards, Stafford jail, April 14, 1840, Turley papers, HDC.

[43]William Clayton to Willard Richards, February 28, 1840, as reproduced in *MS History*, "British Mission," HDC.

[44]William E. A. Axon, editor, *The Annals of Manchester: A Chronological Record from the Earliest Times to the End of 1885* (Manchester: John Heywood, 1886), 211.

[45]Porter is a type of beer.

[46]The following story is pieced together from various entries in the diary, as well as Clayton to Richards, Manchester, November 23, 1839; Clayton to Fielding and Richards, Manchester, January 21, 1840; Clayton to Richards, Manchester, January 21 or 23, 1840; Clayton to Richards, Manchester, January 28, 1842 (all the foregoing in Clayton papers, HDC); Esshom, *Pioneers and Prominent Men of Utah*, 1965; Arthur Sydney Smith family group sheets, LDS Genealogical Society, Salt Lake City.

[47]The following story of the Lee family is pieced together from various diary entries, plus Clayton to Fielding, Manchester, January 2, 1840; Clayton to Richards, Manchester, January 28, 1840; Clayton to Fielding, Manchester, January 17, 1840 (all in Clayton papers, HDC); Fielding to Richards, January 11, 1840, Fielding papers, HDC; Woodruff, "Journal," January 18, 1840.

[48]Clayton to Richards, Manchester, January 28, 1840, Clayton papers, HDC.

[49]Woodruff, "Journal," January 18, 1840, Woodruff to Richards, February 3, 1840.

[50]Smith, *History of the Church*, VII, 146.

[51]Whitney, *Heber C. Kimball*, 152.

[52]Clayton diary, April 17, 1840; Young, *MS History*, 71-72; Woodruff, "Journal," April 17, 1840.

[53]See Romans 16:16.

[54]Smith, "Journal," 321.

[55]For detailed accounts of general Mormon migration see Leonard J. Arrington, *Great Basin Kingdom* (Cambridge: Harvard University Press, 1958); Gustive O. Larson, *Prelude to the Kingdom* (Francestown: Marshall Jones, 1947); William Mulder, *Homeward to Zion* (Minneapolis: University of Minnesota Press, 1957); Taylor, *Expectations Westward.*

[56]Clayton to Richards, Manchester, January 30, 1840, Clayton papers, HDC.

[57]Fielding to Richards, Liverpool, March 25, 1840, Fielding papers, HDC.

[58]*Ibid.*

[59]Whitney, *Heber C. Kimball*, 278.

[60]Smith, *History of the Church*, IV, 185-186.

[61]Young, *MS History*, 77; Evans, *Century of Mormonism*, 228; Clayton to Richards, Penwortham, August 19, 1840, Clayton papers, HDC. In this letter Clayton reproduced a letter from John Moon, who told of arriving in New York and inquiring after certain people who had previously emigrated.

[62]From Moon's letter to Clayton, *Ibid.*

[63]All told, there must have been approximately 300 Mormon emigrants in 1840. In addition to a few who apparently went on their own, Moon's company of 41, and Clayton's group of 200, there were 50 Scotch Saints who left on October 15. Evans, *Century of Mormonism*, 288.

[64]*MS History*, "British Mission," September 8, 1840.

[65]*Millennial Star*, I (November, 1840), 191.

[66] Diary entry, October 24, 1840.

[67]*Millennial Star*, I (February, 1841), 262.

[68]Smith, *History of the Church*, IV, 311-312; diary entry for April 6, 1841.

[69]*Millennial Star*, III (August 1, 1842), 75-76.

[70]*Ibid.*

Courtesy Manchester Public Libraries

Manchester, center of William Clayton's church activities

A Note on Editorial Procedure

The journal has been reproduced as closely to the original as possible, with exceptions noted below. Exceptions are made for purposes of readability, but a transcription of the original is deposited in the Brigham Young University Library.

Dashes at ends of sentences have been replaced by periods. In a few cases, dashes have been replaced by commas to clarify Clayton's intent. The first letter of each sentence has been capitalized even when Clayton failed to do so in the original. In those few instances where it is not clear whether or not a sentence was intended, the original has been followed strictly.

Abbreviations of clear meaning have been expanded and the word written out. Initials and abbreviations for proper names have also been expanded. Brother, sister, and days of the week have been uniformly capitalized. The ampersand is printed as "and" except in the form "&c." Words in *italic* type within brackets represent material that was not part of the original manuscript. Words or letters in roman type within brackets represent editorial reconstruction of illegible parts of the manuscript. Dates at the beginning of each entry have been standardized to include the year. Ellipses within brackets ([. . .]) represent lost letters, with the number of dots representing the approximate number of lost letters. Dashes within brackets ([— — —]) represent lost words. Material raised in the manuscript, as 1ˢᵗ has been brought in line as 1st.

References to English money will be given as Clayton used them. Thus £ is Pounds; a number followed by s or / is shillings; / followed by a number or a number followed by d is pence. See the diary, note 7, for a statement of approximate dollar equivalents.

Instead of identifying each person the first time he appears in the diary, an appendix has been prepared in which all persons mentioned in the diary who could be identified have been listed in alphabetical order.

THE DIARY

January 1, 1840[1]

Brother James Lea from Bedford[2] has called in at Thomas Miller's and I have been with him to see his wife and children. One child is sick. He states that they left Bedford on the 22nd June on account of his master wanting him to go to Leicester[3] at about two hours notice, to keep open a Inn until his master could let it. After being there sometime, his wife came to him and they remained at the Inn untill December when he determined to leave because he thought his master was trying to keep him there and he was losing ground almost daily. He wanted to be amongst the saints. He states that when he entered the Inn it was merely as steward hence the Liquors &c. was not judged[4] and he did not know anything about untill he sent his master word that he would leave. Then his master brought in a heavy Bill against him which involved him in great difficulty. He was obliged to sacrifice his goods to get to Manchester. They both seem very humble. He acknowledges having been unfaithful.[5]

1. William Clayton was at this time in Manchester where he had moved shortly after October 19, 1838. He appears to have been living at #2 Maria Street at a boarding house run by Hail Hardman.
2. Bedford is a market town in Bedfordshire about fifty miles northwest of London. The 1841-42 census showed a population of 9,178 inhabitants. It is situated in the fertile valley of the river Ouse which is navigable for barges. Its principal manufactures in the 1840s consisted of lace and straw-plat, together with some iron agricultural implements. Samuel Lewis, *Topographical Dictionary of England* (5 vols.; London: S. Lewis & Company, 1848), I, 190.
3. Leicester is a market town in the county of Leicester, located about 97 miles north-northwest from London. Its 1841 population was 48,167. Situated on the banks of the river Soar, its staple manufacture in the 1840s was worsted and cotton hosiery. Lewis, *Topographical Dictionary*, III, 57-58.
4. This was probably a reference to the Word of Wisdom which had been preached by Heber C. Kimball and those who accompanied him to Great Britain in 1837 and which seems to have been well accepted by those who joined the Church in England. Orson F. Whitney, *Life of Heber C. Kimball: An Apostle: The Father and Founder of the British Mission* (Salt Lake City: Bookcraft, 1967), 142. The revelation to Joseph Smith included in *The Doctrine and Covenants of The Church of Jesus Christ of Latter-day Saints*, Section 89.
5. Clayton's experience with James Lee is given in more detail in a letter he wrote to Joseph Fielding, the mission president, the following day: "I feel my mind rather troubled at present on account of the state of things here insomuch that I feel to write on the subject. I will mention some of the circumstances and leave you to judge wether it is necessary to write or not. I know that a little matter troubles me and perhaps I look rather to near sometimes. I rejoice at all events to know that one stands at the head of me—unto whom I can communicate matters of the least as well as of the greatest importance. When I got here last night I went down to Bro. Thomas Millers and soon found a something wrong—not with them but they knew of it. It is concerning Bro. Heath but as this cannot be attended to until next week perhaps I don't need to mention it. Neither can I say it is true. I hope not. Whilst at Thomas Millers there came in a brother from Bedford named James Lea. He told me where he came from and I put a few questions to him in order to test him and prove if possible wether he be a true saint or not. He stated that he had his wife in or about Liverpool road and 2 children and that the oldest child was very ill apparently in a dying state and he was desirous that some of the Elders should go and see it. I went out with him to have a little more conversation—and concluded to go and see the child. I ellicited the following from him. He left Bedford on the 22nd of June in accordance with his masters wish and came to Leicester. He has been there since that time. There was not Saints no meetings &c. &c. He gave way to much to worldly conversation untill he found himself growing worse

and determined to go where there were some Saints. Started off to Manchester on Sunday Morning by boat and arrived here on Tuesday night. He was searching nearly the whole day yesterday to find some Saints and I met with him as above. When I got to his wife she burst into tears of joy to see me and I think a little grief for the child which is very ill. I talked a little to them and have reason to believe that they are honest &c. They are now lodging with Bro. John Hardman. I went back to Brother Millers and saw many of the Saints but found that the meeting had been previously given up." William Clayton to Joseph Fielding, Manchester, January 2, 1840, Joseph Fielding Papers, Historical Department of The Church of Jesus Christ of Latter-day Saints, Salt Lake City, Utah, hereinafter cited as HDC.

January 2, 1840

Brother Jackson acknowledges to having told a many things to a brother from Stockport[6] which he ought not. He says he will do so no more. Brother Jackson says that brothers Broome and Bateman are about £46[7] in debt which was contracted at the time of the community. The house is 150 debt. They have tried to sell it but cannot. Broome is likely to have the Bailiffs[8] and wants Ann Criskersley to go and live with him. I have the house in her name. Ann is since gone. He did not ask our council at all.

6. Stockport is a market town in Chestershire located about 6 miles south-southeast of Manchester. In 1841 it had a population of 23,431, and was noted for its cotton and silk manufacture. It was connected directly with Manchester by the Manchester and Birmingham Railway. Lewis *Topographical Dictionary*, IV, 209-210.

7. The traditional value of the pound of the 19th century was $5.00. United States Wholesale Price Indexes for the period would yield an index figure of 35 for 1840 (1957-59 = 100). In terms of 1957-59 prices, then, the 1840 dollar would be worth approximately $2.85 and one pound approximately $14.25. U.S. Department of Commerce, Bureau of the Census, *Historical Statistics of the United States, Colonial Times to 1957*, (Washington, D.C., GPO, 1960), 115 and idem, *Continuation to 1961 and Revisions* (Washington: GPO, 1965), 107.

8. Clayton seems to mean that Broom was to be forced to sell the property to meet his debts. Apparently the attempt to get Ann Criskersley to live in the house and have it transferred to her name was a means of protecting it from sale for his debts. See note 10.

January 3, 1840

Sister Mary Powell acknowledges to having said to sister

65

Walker, "John and I am one." At the same time she had a ring on her finger. She told sister Rigby she was not married. She is determined to be married. She knows it is of God. If we attempt to hinder we shall deny her. She says we want to forbid to marry[9] and she has not a good spirit.[10]

9. The reference here is undoubtedly to a scripture much used in countering those who oppose marriage and as an indication of apostasy from correct principles. "Now the Spirit speaketh expressly, that in the latter times some shall depart from the faith, giving heed to seducing spirits, and doctrines of devils; Speaking lies and hypocrisy; having their conscience seared with a hot iron; Forbidding to marry, *and commanding* to abstain from meats, which God hath created to be received with thanksgiving of them which believe and know the truth." (I Timothy, 4:1-3) In a sense, Clayton had put himself on the horns of a dilemma by trying to counsel this sister not to marry. The reason for his counsel is not clear.

10. More details concerning Mary Powell as well as other problems of the branch are included in Clayton's letter of January 2 to Joseph Fielding. From the following excerpt one can begin to understand how personally involved Clayton became with the members of the branch over which he presided, and one can also sense the stresses that existed within the branch because of certain personal problems. "A great deal of disturbance about Sister Powell. I have heard that she is about to go and live at Little Peover with Johns Father and Mother. I suppose she has got a ring on her finger as if married. She was at Sister Rigby's and Sister Jones asked her if she was married. She says —"John and me are one" and when Jones was gone out she says to Rigby, "We are not married but I am not going to tell them &c." The saying is gone abroad that they are married. Henry Royle is giving up house "had said this weekend but I asked him to stay another week untill Paul Harris has got somewhere to live. He agreed. Another tale is going the round about some very imprudent things which were done when Sister Harris was brought to bed. I have not yet seen sister Powell. I have been after her today but she is from house. Bro. Burgess has told these things to several in the church and is going to tell Bro. Fielding all when he comes. I hope he will not be long. Bro. John Walker has been getting drunk again. Sister Holden has been falling out and scolding Sister Battersby on account of some tales which D. Poole had told her and I suppose she believes Poole. No very good sign. Sister Ann Jackson is just telling me that the old grievance between Eliza Prince and her sister Maryann has all but turned out again and they are both for leaving the church. But the most important is this—When Bro's Bateman and Boome lived together (the community) they got a great quantity of coals and flour on credit and which has not yet been paid for. The creditor is about to send the Bailifs and the way he (Bro. Boome) is going to act I don't fully approve. He has some time back been giving money to sister Ann [...]kersly and has gone so far with her that his wife was jealous but

the grievance has been settled between them and now Broome wants Anne to go and live with them and have the house and goods in her name and thus evade the Bailiffs. It is not because I object to this so much as Ann going to live that I write. I imagine I see danger in it. I have got this from Bro. Jackson and advised him to persuade Broome not to do anything untill Monday. And I do hope you will be here as early as you well can say ½ past 10. But this as you think wisdom. There are other things I can tell when you come." Clayton to Fielding, January 2, 1840, Clayton Papers, HDC.

January 4, 1840

Brother Fielding and I have been with L[11] Isherwood to her mother's and learn as follows. That Sarah and her sister has been disagreeable with each other. Sarah has been impudent and saucy with her mother. Has cleaned her shoes on the Sunday. Would not help to do any thing for her mother. She was out late at nights &c. We had a talk with her sister and brother in law. They both manifest a very bitter spirit and we have reason to believe they are more to blame than Sarah although she is much to blame. She promises to do better.

11. This could be "S" rather than "L" and refer to Sarah Isherwood but in the manuscript it does not look like Clayton's "S" at all.

January 8, 1840

Brothers Clarke, Fielding, David &c. [−] took dinner at Brother Newshers[12] and staid till 8 o clock. Had talk with Mr. Green. Prayed with Sister Battersby. Went this evening to see Sister Dewsnup and found her comfortable. Under persecution from them. To meeting at [Conner] St.[13] Had a good meeting.

12. Although Clayton wrote "Newsher" in this entry, he uses the name "Bewsher" in later entries. He probably means James Bewshaw.

13. Instead of having the members meet at one central location for regular church meetings, it appears that the city was divided into districts and meetings were held in each district in spite of the small membership. For a list of the districts in 1860 see "Manchester Branch Record of Members, 1860," Microfilm Serial No. 13656; part 43, Genealogical Society of the Church of Jesus Christ of Latter-day Saints, Salt Lake City, Utah, introduction.

January 10, 1840

Brother Fielding and I went to Stockport to enquire respecting Brother Heath. Found that Brother Nye had told them we should not come till Saturday under mistake. We saw a few of the saints and found much bad feeling against Brother Heath. My feet was sore when we got to Princes[14] at 11½ o clock. Went to see Mr. Stowell. Found him full of frayed lies, a good deal of ignorance &c.

14. Apparently Clayton and his companions walked six miles to Stockport and back.

January 11, 1840[15]

15. Although Clayton has no diary entry for this date, a letter from Joseph Fielding to Willard Richards hints at some of the problems. Fielding was in Manchester, apparently to the great satisfaction of Clayton, who had written Fielding earlier concerning some of the branch problems, and it is clear that Fielding got as deeply involved in these problems as Clayton. He reported to Richards that Samuel Heath had gone to Peover without council, that a brother Featherstone had come to Manchester to tell them his troubles, and some details on a forthcoming Church trial. He also commented on the problems of James Lee and his wife and expressed some concern that he still had nothing to do, and added "upon the whole we think they are not quite so humbel as they should be. They have suffered much. We shall not put him to work in his Office yet. Give any Council you think needful. Thank you for the Catichism I shall take to Zion with me." Fielding also noted a great anti-corn-law dinner to be held in Manchester that he expected would draw 4000 people "at a cost enough almost to build the Temple of the Lord." To this letter Clayton added a note of his own which suggests his concern for keeping in touch with his family. He asked Richards to send word to his "other half" that he might be in Burslem the following week, and since the new postage act had been put into effect she could write him every week. Fielding to Richards, Manchester, January 11, 1840, Fielding Papers, HDC.

January 12, 1840

Brother Clark preached this morning. Had a good feeling. He likewise spoke a good deal in the P M. I preached at night from Mark 16 4.

January 13, 1840

Have been with Sister Perkins this P M at Millers. After

took supper at Thomas Millers. Sarah Crooks is grieved at Sarah Perkins being hurt at a little thing. Sarah Crooks gave me 20/-10 of her own, 5 Rebekas and 5 Betsy Crooks, towards new trousers. I felt an object to taking it because they have given me considerable before this.[16] Sarah was grieved because I objected and said if I did not take it I must speak to her no more. She seemed grieved.

16. Clayton and the other missionaries were apparently devoting their full time to Church service and had to rely upon branch members to care for them. Wilford Woodruff reports that the members of the branch in Herefordshire assisted him while he was preaching in London. Matthias F. Cowley, ed. *Wilford Woodruff, Fourth President of the Church of Jesus Christ of Latter-day Saints: History of His Life and Labors as Recorded in his Daily Journals* (Salt Lake City: Bookcraft, 1964), 130.

January 14, 1840
This A.M. we received a letter from Brother Richards stating the arrival of Brothers Taylor, Woodruff and Turly requesting Brother Fielding to go. We concluded to send Brother Clark. He went by Railway.

January 15, 1840
Received another letter from Brother Richards requesting Brother Fielding to go to Preston and a letter from Brother Davids wife stating she was sick and the youngest child. Brother David went off to Preston immediately and I wrote a letter to my wife and another to Sister Morgan.

January 16, 1840
Went with Brother Fielding to bolton railway[17] from thence to Thomas Millers to dinner. Attended books[18] at meeting at night. Bought cloth for trousers 18/6.

17. The Manchester and Bolton Railway had been opened in May, 1838. From Bolton, which is located about ten miles west-northwest from Manchester, railroad connections could be made to Preston further to the northwest. Lewis *Topographical Dictionary*, I 298; III, 242.
18. Clayton is probably referring to the branch records.

January 17, 1840

Was called up this A.M. at 3 o clock to Sister Lea. I found her very ill—insensible. Prayed with her and she appeared better. Sent a letter to Fielding and Richards.[19] Went to see Brother Heath. Did not get to talk to him. Came back to Sister Lea. Found her worse. Stayed with her until $\frac{1}{2}$ past 7. Left her a little better. Went to council meeting.[20] Brothers Miller and Green took Brother Royle to Dukinfield. Agreed that Sister Duckworth[21] should go to Brother Jacksons for 2 weeks and after meeting had talk with brothers Heath and Featherstone respecting money which had been collected at Manchester for Joseph Millwood during his sickness. There was 18/— collected which Brother Green gave to Brother Heath who sent 13/—, to Jane and gave 3/— to Featherstone but did not give the other 2/— to Jane and has caused a great excitement.

19. In this letter Clayton emphasized the problems of Sister Lee, for whom he was now apparently becoming quite concerned. He had called her at 2 a.m. or 3 a.m. and found her in a very bad state, sometimes insensible and having great pain in her head and face. He prayed with her several times and annointed her head, which made her seem a little better, but when he visited her about 11 a.m. the following morning she had suffered a relapse. Still later in the day he was sent for again, and found her having hallucinations and alternately screaming, laughing and praying. He pleaded for help in his letter: "I feel to want your assistance. You must remember us and if the Lord will send Bro Turly tomorrow I shall certainly be thankful. If you have any council or advice it would be gladly accepted. . . . I suppose Bro Richards knows much about Sister Lea's afflictions perhaps he will have some advice to give." Clayton also, as usual, mentioned a few other problems in this letter, but his chief concern was for Sister Lee. Clayton to Fielding and Richards, Manchester, January 17, 1840, Clayton Papers, HDC.

20. Branch members apparently held council meetings each Friday evening in which they planned for future activities of the branch and tried to work out branch problems. See Clayton to Richards, Manchester, January 28, 1840, Clayton Papers, HDC.

21. Dunkinfield is a township about eight miles east of Manchester near Stockport in Cheshire. With regard to Sarah Duckworth, Clayton explained in a letter to Richards that she had gone to stay at the Jackson home, but Jackson's wife told her to seek other lodgings. Clayton believed that if Mrs. Jackson was turning out the poor with-

out cause she should not have the privilege of receiving the servants of God. Clayton to Willard Richards, Manchester, January 21 or 23, 1840, Clayton Papers, HDC.

January 18, 1840

Had conversation with Brother Heath who says as follows. That once he drank a little wine which was for Joseph. Mary Ann Webb did [— —] with him and David about ¾ hour and several other things. The statements made by Brothers Heath and Featherstone was very contradictory. I told him he had better remain at Manchester untill I had wrote to my brethren. I received a letter from my brethren and wrote them another back. Went to Railway and met Brothers Clark, Woodruff and Turly.[22] I rejoice to see them. Brought them to old Sister Hardmans.[23] Went to see Sister Lea and found her quite insensible. Brother Woodruff prayed and rebuked the fowl spirits. We anointed her head and gave her some oil inwardly. I then prayed and rebuked the pain.[24] After washing her forehead with rum she appeared better and we left her. We then went to Sister Perkins who had met with an accident by a fall. We prayed with her. Returned to Thomas Millers where we took supper.

22. The three probably came into Manchester on the Manchester and Liverpool Railway which had been completed in 1830, as they were coming from Liverpool. Wilford Woodruff records the meeting in his journal: "I had the happy privilege of taking Elder William Clayton by the hand and many other Saints. Elder Clayton is one of the president's council in England and a wise and worthy brother." Wilford Woodruff, "Wilford Woodruff's Journal," MSS, January 18, 1840, HDC.
23. The use of the phrase "old" sister Hardman is confusing here. The Manchester Branch Records list Alice, Mary, Margaret, Elizabeth, and Betsy Hardman all at 2 Maria Street, as well as several other Hardmans in Manchester. Alice was apparently the most prominent of the group, however, for George A. Smith reports having been taken to Alice Hardman's home. This was apparently a boarding house, for he notes the great number of people located there. It seems unusual, however, that Clayton would refer to Alice as "old" sister Hardman, for she was two years younger than he (he was nearing 26 and she was about 24). Manchester Branch "Record," 38 and George A. Smith, "My Journal," *The Instructor*, LXXXII (1947), 321.

24. Wilford Woodruff corroborates Clayton's account: "As soon as I was introduced to him [Clayton], he informed me that one of the sisters in that place was possessed of a devil. He asked me if I would not go and cast it out of her. He thought one of the Twelve Apostles could do most anything in such a case. I went with him to the house where the woman lay, in the hands of three men, in a terrible rage. She was trying to tear her clothing from her. I also found quite a number of Saints present, and some unbelievers, who had come to see the devil cast out and a miracle wrought.

"Had I acted upon my own judgment, I should have refrained from administering to her in the company of those present; but as I was a stranger there, and Brother Clayton presided over the branch, I joined him in administering to the woman. The unbelief of the wicked who were present was so great that we could not cast the devil out of her, and she raged when the company, except the few attending her, had left the house, we laid hands upon her head, and in the name of Jesus Christ I commanded the devil to come out of her. The devil left, and she was entirely healed and fell asleep." On January 20 Woodruff reported that he was called upon to visit the child of Sister Lee, who was also possessed of the devil, and was able to cast out the devil. He reported all of this in more detail in a letter to Willard Richards. Both in Clayton's diary and in the accounts of others during this period, the principle of healing through the power of the priesthood was very important. On one occasion, Joseph Smith "preached to a large congregation at the stand, on the science and practice of medicine, desiring to persuade the Saints to trust in God when sick, and not in any arm of flesh, and live by faith and not by medicine, or poison; and when they were sick, and had called for the Elders to pray for them, and they were not healed, to use herbs and mild food." Cowley, *Wilford Woodruff,* 114-115; Woodruff to Richards, Manchester, February 3, 1840, Wilford Woodruff Papers, HDC; Joseph Smith, *History of the Church of Jesus Christ of Latter-day Saints,* ed. B. H. Roberts (2d ed. rev.; Salt Lake City: Deseret Book Company, 1957) IV, 414.

See also Woodruff, "Journal," January 18, 1840, HDC. Here Woodruff reported not only this story but also his impression of Manchester on his first day there: "It is a beautiful borough Containing a population of 320,000 inhabitants considerable larger in the [—] than the City of N.Y. in the U.S.A. The Church of Jesus Christ of Latter-Day Saints in this town now numbers 164 souls."

January 19, 1840

Brother Turley spoke this A.M. I spoke a little after. The wicked spirit seemed to disturb David Crooks. I led this afternoon meeting and spoke on the necessity of the Saints dealing honestly with each other and showed the order of the church with regard to cases of poverty. I also introduced

Brother Lea to the church who forgave him his transgression and offered him the right hand of fellowship. Brother Woodruff spoke after. Prayed with a number of sick and confirmed Jane Millwood. Elizabeth Mills manifested a bad spirit. I talked to her and she appears better. Brother Woodruff preached at night. Full house. He spoke plain. Good effect. I gave [—] &c. Distributed timely warnings[25] and prayed with many sick. Went to Brother Burgess and told him plainly about tale bearing &c. Prayed with child and bless his family.[26]

There has been several dreams in the church concerning my wife during the last 10 days.[27] First I dreamt I was in the middle of a garden full of ripe fruit and after bringing some home was going again and my wife run up a hill before me and vanished out of my sight. Another night I dreamed that I was at Hodsons, Penwortham, amongst ripe gooseberrys as above. I felt like a single or unmarried person. Sister Dewsnup dreamed that she saw me at Hardmans with one child in great trouble and the child was crying for bread. I asked her to get it something to eat. While I went somewhere Sarah Crooks dreamed that one of the American brethren was talking and joking me about having a second wife and Sarah joked &c. She thought I had then a second wife. Sister C. [.]eale says today she dreamed that I was [str......] in the greatest trouble. My wife was either dead or near to dying and I had one child with me. Sister Jones dreamed same as Sister Dewsnup.

25. The tract spoken of is probably Orson Hyde, A *Timely Warning to the People of England.* . . Extant versions were printed as an eight-page pamphlet (Oxford-Hill, 1840) and as a broadside (Manchester, 1840). See comments on this in the introduction to this volume.
26. Wilford Woodruff's journal adds some detail to the activities of this Sabbath day, and comparing the two accounts provides an interesting example of the different perspective with which two people can see the same events. Woodruff told of Turley preaching in the morning, then made special observation that they got out of the

building only with difficulty because of the press of the Saints wishing to shake hands with them. In the afternoon, Woodruff said, there were "some observations from Elder William Clayton," and that he then spoke to them. Woodruff was especially impressed with the evening meeting. Clayton said he "spoke plain" and with good effect, but Woodruff said he had the spirit of God with him, had good attention from the audience, and that one woman in the congregation said she had seen a vision of Jesus pleading with the Father to "spare England one more year that the reapers might gather the grain for the harvest was fully ripe." He also told of two people wanting to be baptized and the twenty who were sick or afflicted were healed. He observed that the Saints in England had great confidence in God and His servants but that he and the other leaders needed as much faith as the apostle Paul, so that at the touch of their garments or handkerchiefs the Saints could be healed. Woodruff, "Journal," January 19, 1840.

27. During the early period of Church history, there appears to have been a great deal of emphasis given to dreams as evidence of revelation for the Church and for individuals. Contrary to the forebodings expressed in this entry, Clayton's wife lived until 1894. Smith, *History of the Church*, IV, 203; V, 515-16; Cowley, *Woodruff*, 60, 189. 60, 189.

January 20, 1840[28]

Breakfast at Thomas Millers. Dinner at Sand's and tea. Wrote a letter to Burslem.[29] Supper at Thomas Millers. Have prayed with 8 sick today. Have been much gratified with the brethrens conversation. S. Green gave me 2/— towards brethrens coach fare. Last week Sister Bewsher gave me new drawers. Have had a little talk with Brother Berry on teatotaler[s].

28. This was the last day of Wilford Woodruff's visit to Manchester, and he had made an interesting observation in his diary which suggests the concern Woodruff and others had for social and economic conditions in this industrial town as a reflection of fulfillment of prophecy. "The distress of nations is at the door in fulfillment of the word of God, while confusion is through America great trouble is manifest throughout England. Beginning in all nations. There is trouble this morning. The town of Manchester about 8000 souls is flung out of employe at the factories because of the pressure of times and the lowering of the wages and they are standing in every corner of the streets in large groups counciling what to do, and their are at the present time (I have been informed) thousands of souls in a state of starvation." Woodruff, "Journal," January 20, 1840.

29. Burslem is a market town in Staffordshire in the district known as the Potteries because of the production of china and other clay products. Josiah Wedgewood began his business there in 1756. Lewis, *Topographical Dictionary*, I, 446.

January 21, 1840

Breakfast at Prince's. Got a letter from brothers Fielding and Richards and answered it. A letter also from Brother Moore and at Walkers. Have been with the brethren to see them off per coach. Have had some conversations with Brother Berry upon the duty of the officers. Brother Woodruff laid hands on my head and spoke to this effect.[30] Dear Brother William I lay my hands upon thy head [*two unclear lines*] I pray that he will give thee a token of his love towards thee by letting his spirit rest upon thee. O God, wilt thou give me the spirit of revelation at this time that [I may] pronounce thy blessing upon thy servant. Brother, thou art of the blood of Ephraim. Thou art one of the house of Joseph. Thou art one of those who will stand upon the mount Zion with the 144,000. God shall give thee great wisdom. He shall make thee a wise counciller to council the saints of God. Thy life has been hid up with Christ in God and thou hast known it not, and I seal thee up with eternal life and while thou remainst faithful no power shall prevail against thee nor be able to take thy life. The Lord shall yet give thee many souls in Manchester over whom thou shall preside. God seal these blessings. &c &c &c. Took cocoa at Brother John Smiths after I had some conversation with Brother Arthur [*Smith*] the Deacon. I could get no satisfaction from him. He told me he had not partook of the sacrement and he was brought before the council Nov. 22. He stated that it had been told by some of the Elders to the members that his project for marriage was from hell. And if it was he was determined it should return. But he would wait untill God showed him &c. I showed him that the Lord designed his servants to council in such cases but he said he should not look to man. He should look to God. He had seen enough of men. I said every soul must be subject to the higher powers.[31] He said he should be subject to God and when God showed him that he had done wrong he would repent. I asked if Paul said so when he said let every soul be subject &c. He answered Paul said something else. He said men would rise up forbidding to marry and commanding to abstain from meats[32] &c. I said we did not forbid to marry but the scriptures forbid to commit adultry and forbid us to covet our neighbours wife &c.[33] I told him I had heard he was about to be married. He answered he had not said so. I told him I was informed it was known at all Saints Church. He said all Saints Church would not marry him. He said he should not partake anymore until God had shown him &c. I told him I could not see that we should be justified in suffering him to remain in office while he did so. He said I might take the office if I thought proper. He would not give it up untill required. Here expressed his union with the saints and his love toward the officers &c. But would tell me nothing conclusive with regard to his reasons or intentions. He said he could see a good deal. There was so much partiality in the church &c. He believed the gospel. He had no condemnation and if God showed him that he did wrong he would repent. After several other similar things passing I left him. He seems to manifest a kind of stubborness and insubordination.

We came back to Hardmans. I wrote a letter to Sarah Crooks and gave it to her. There was several of the Sisters present. Went after taking supper to Crooks St. to sleep. Found them in bed. Prayed with 5 sick.

30. This was probably a patriarchal blessing, though Clayton does not specifically say so. The patriarchial blessing was designed to prophesy of the future of the life of the individual to whom the blessing was given, give him encouragement in performing his duties, and tell him to which branch of the House of Israel he belongs. Blessings are dependent, of course, upon the worthy life of the individual. It is unfortunate that part of this blessing is so smudged in the original that it cannot be read. James E. Talmage, *Articles of Faith, A Series of Lectures on the Principal Doctrine of The Church of Jesus*

Christ of Latter-day Saints (Salt Lake City: Deseret News Press, 1899), 216; Smith, *History of the Church*, VII, 301.

31. In trying to convince Arthur Smith that he should accept the counsel of the mission leaders, Clayton was referring to Romans 13:1 "Let every soul be subject unto the higher powers. For there is no power but of God: the powers that be are ordained of God." See the introduction to this volume for an analysis of Smith's relationship to Clayton. In the early days of the Church, it was common for mature men to hold the office of Deacon, Teacher, or Priest. This contrasts with the current practice of giving these offices to all "worthy" young men beginning at age twelve.

32. I Timothy 4:1-3.

33. Exodus 20:14, Matthew 5:27-28.

January 22, 1840

Breakfast at Brother Wests. Seems comfortable. Desired Brother Davis to tell his class to pray for a revival &c. Dinner at Brother Bewsher. Sarah Duckworth came and said Brother Jacksons wife told her she must seek other lodgings &c. I have talked to her about being clean and submissive and to try to get something to do. Sister Bewsher says she can lodge with her a little while. We went to see Sister Gill and found her about as usual. We administered sacrament.[34] Took cocoa at Bewshers and came to see Sister Dewsnup. Found her some better. Went to see Brother Booth and told him concerning an accusation brought against him by Brother Jackson. He had borrowed 1/— from Brother Broome and promised to pay it back in a given time but had not done according to promise. Brother Owens had given him a suit of Cloths and he had pawned the coat and told a falsehood about it. He does not deny. There seems great grievance between him and his wife. Both are guilty. I spoke plainly to both of them shewing the consequence of their conduct and told them we should expect to see different conduct manifested for the future and should watch them more narrowly than we had done.[35] Went to meeting at Grundys. But few attended. Supper at Sister Hardman's.

34. The term "sacrament" here as elsewhere in general LDS

practice refers to the ordinance of partaking of bread and wine, or water, as instituted at the Last Supper, in remembrance of the atonement of Christ.

35. Clayton gave further details on this conflict within the branch in a letter to Willard Richards. According to the letter, Booth had been borrowing money from people at Pendleton and not repaying it. Owens had given him a suit of clothes the past Sunday but when he asked Booth what had become of the coat Booth replied that it was too long for him in the sleeves and he had therefore left it home. Apparently several people did not believe him, and a Brother Jackson (probably Joseph Jackson) volunteered to go home with him and see it, whereupon Booth said that it was not at home and it was soon discovered that it was in the pawn shop. Clayton then charged Booth with lying, which Booth did not deny, and Clayton further criticized him for such things as being idle, visiting Church members to make complaints, and talking about the doctrine of the gathering and other things which, said Clayton, they ought not to discuss. Clayton was also concerned with the internal family problems of the Booths. It was all the branch leaders could do to keep Booth and his wife from quarrelling in public, and she complained of his beating the children with ropes as well as kicking them. Clayton told them that unless they repented quickly they would be cut off the Church. Clayton to Richards, January 21 or 23, 1849, Clayton Papers, HDC. (The letter is dated January 21, but the words "or 23" are written above this date. This is probably the letter Clayton refers to in his January 23 entry.)

January 23, 1840

Breakfast at John Hardmans. Received a letter from Brother Richards and answered it. Sent one also to my wife and writ one for Mary Hardman to Nottingham. Sister Mary Hardman has dreamed about seeing my wife with her hair down upon her back all in disorder. She seemed in distress and was come to Manchester to seek me but I was gone to Burslem. No children with her. Took C[ocoa or coffee] at Brother Broomes. Find them comfortable. Went to Brother Jacksons to preach. About 9 stayed. I preached above 1 hour and Brother Clarke near 1 hour. Good attention. Some seemed affected. Gave out for another meeting. Saw sister Jackson after meeting. Seemed to have a bad feeling. Quite bitter against Sarah. Is determined not to have her only tonight. I felt it would be best to say little to her. I think kindness will do best. She had given Sarah 1/6 which had been given for her. I talked to Brother Jackson about driving his wife and cautioned him not to do so. Brother Jackson has lent Stowell the Book of Mormon. I told him he should not have done so. He said he was sorry. Sister Whiss sick. Took Supper at Jacksons and returned.

January 24, 1840

Brother Heath has called this A M and I have told him our feelings about him and that we totally disaprove of his conduct in some instances. I told him the only way to make things right was to shew better conduct in future. He is going with Brother Clarke tomorrow to Peover[36] and from there he will go to Soutwick.[37] Brother Bateman has come in and says he has given his watch for Paul Harris' debt and he owes £4 for Choutler. He has paid £2 and the man wants the other. He has heard about some work 17 miles from Manchester and wants to know if it will be wisdom to go. He can get little to do here and I can hardly say nay. I feel on account of his office. He states that Sarah Duckworth has been telling the saints about Brother Jackson and wife and is causing trouble. Took breakfast at Sister Hardman's house. Sent a letter yesterday to Brother Richards. I have received a letter from Brother Woodruff and he states they got to B[urslem] at ½ past 9 after a cold windy ride. Gives a good account of the saints there. They have baptized 22 since I was there about 1 month since.[38] Have writ a letter to Sister Dewsnup. Dinner at Walker's. Brother Walker is much troubled about his situation in work. Called at Brother Paul's. Find him much grieved at Brother Jacksons conduct. It seems Brother Jackson has spoken false concerning him. He (Paul) still says that he put nothing in the wine after I had reproved him. He has only little work. But seems humble &c. Called at Mary Ann Johnsons. Found her comfortable but very poor. Will try to do something for her. Called at Sister Whiss's. Find her better. Elizabeth poorly. Took cocoa with Elizabeth. But I would rather not because they have it not to spare. If we did not Elizabeth would be grieved. Went to Sister William Millers and saw Sister Perkins. All pretty comfortable. Came to Thomas Millers and writ 2 letters, 1 to Burslem and 1 to Brother Jackson. Sister Dewsnup came in— in deep trouble and Mary Wood says things are more comfortable at home. Took supper and came to Mother Hardmans. Have heard that Elizabeth Clayton sent for us at 8 [p.m.] o'clock. Prayed with 4 sick.

36. There are three towns near each other in Cheshire named Peover. This was probably Peover Superior, the largest of the three with 580 inhabitants in 1841. It is located 3 miles south-southeast of Knutsford. Lewis, *Topographical Dictionary*, III, 555.
37. In the 1840s there were six Southwicks in England. This is probably the one in Northhamptonshire containing 171 inhabitants in 1841 about 25 miles north-northwest of Northhampton.
38. Wilford Woodruff arrived in Burslem on January 21. He was traveling in the company of Theodore Turley who remained in Burslem for eight days then went on to Burmingham. Woodruff's work carried him in this district, called the Staffordshire Potteries, into Burslem, Hanley, Stoke, Lane End, and several other villages. He remained there until the second of March. He reported that he "baptized, confirmed and blessed many, and we had a good field open for labor. Many were believing and it appeared as though we had a door open to bring into the Church many in that part of the vineyard." Cowley, *Woodruff*, 116. The letter spoken of here is probably the one Woodruff wrote on January 23, 1840. Woodruff, "Journal," January 23, 1840, HDC.

January 25, 1840

Went to Brother Jasners to breakfast. Brothers Clark and Heath are gone to Peover. To John Hardman's to dinner. R. is very sick. John tells me of something remarkable which took place yesterday viz.. He has during the week had fears respecting Roberts Honesty and instead of leaving his waistcoat with silver in carelessly hung on a chair he has been impressed to conceal on account of suspicion. Yesterday afternoon John and Brother Lea was set together in the house and Brother Lea expressed his fears to John but they seemed stronger fully than John's. Whilst they were talking on the subject Mary came in and wanted to know what they were talking about. They would not tell her but she said she knew they were talking about Robert. She had the same feeling with them but full stronger. Soon after Sister Lea who had been busy upstairs came down and expressed herself precisely the same not knowing that they had said anything about it. She had looked round the room to see if there was anything he could take and she knew not why she felt so. She did not like it. But after all her striving against it, it still followed her. John says that Robert's conduct has been very different these last few days. He seems hasty and undependable. There had not a word been said with regard to suspicion untill the above circumstances took place. Took C[ocoa or coffee] with Brother Clayton. I have had Brother Paul and Jackson together. Find them both faulty. Jackson told me on Thursday night that Paul told him that I had told Paul all that passed at the council respecting him Friday before. Paul says he never told him anything about it. They contradicted each other and both was positive that they were correct. Jackson threatened in my presence he would bring Paul before the church for telling a lie.[39] Jackson owned to having stated several things about Paul before 2 or 3 of the members in such a manner as to hurt his character. Such as he had lost 3 or 4 pound by Paul and had given him 6/6 towards leather for new shoes and Paul had spent the money. I ascertained with regard to this that Jackson had given Paul 6/6 to buy leather and at the time said that Paul might spend 1/— for bread, he having neither money nor bread at the time. While Paul had the money Jane was brought to bed and having nothing to subsist on spent the money intending to make the shoes as soon as possible. Paul has now got the leather and begun to make the shoes. Brother Jackson also acknowledged to having said to the leather cutter to the effect that he was afraid he would not get his shoes which caused the leather cutter to say to Sister Davies one of your Latter-day Saints has turned Latter-day Sinner. Jackson accused Paul of being idle when at the shop. Paul says he went to bed once in the day time that he recollects. May have been more than once. He had to rise about from 2½ to 4 o'clock in the morning and keep the shop open until 11 at night. Jackson did not contradict this but still seemed to think he should not have gone to bed in the day time.[40] Brother Jackson manifested a bad spirit some part of the time. I told him so. Then charged him with having said to Paul he was determined Paul should have nothing to do with the office of teacher and that if it came before the church he would raise his hand against him. I showed Jackson that he could not prevent Paul having his office again but said he was determined &c. and said he would bring Paul before the church. I told him I should stop him. There was then something said between them about the money and after some conversation they mutually agreed that Paul should give 10/— besides paying for a load of coals. I then asked them if they would both agree to forgive each other and be friendly with each other and never speak of these things again. They both said yes and so did Sister Jane. I then told them if ever I heard either of them having said anything about these things I should consider them guilty. We then parted on good terms. Went from there to Brother Greens. Found them troubled about the pox. I prayed with Brother Green and wife and Henry Royle and felt to rebuke the disease in the name of the Lord. Brother Green said that Ellen Battersby went to the Doctor last night. I should have said that I had conversation with Brother Jackson after this and showed him he had been transgressing &c. and cautioned him to mind. Took Supper at Sister Hardmans. She saw several of the sisters. Saw Elizabeth Gladson. Had no conversation with her.

39. Apparently, during this period, the Church's ecclesiastical courts were still in a state of development. At the present time, charges against members are tried in Bishop's courts, with priesthood members acting as counsel for the accused. It appears that in 1840, cases were tried before the entire congregation with a majority vote of the congregation deciding the fate of the accused. (See below for the trial of Arthur Smith and Elizabeth Holding.)

40. This would mean that Jackson expected Harris to work steadily for 19 to 21 hours per day. It is no wonder that Clayton thought Jackson "manifested a bad spirit some part of the time."

January 26, 1840

Took Breakfast at Hardmans. Preached from Daniel 2 dream.[41] Spoke about 1¼ hour. Went to Bewshers to Dinner. Brother Green has told me something about Sarah Duckworth not pleasant. Received a letter from my wife, another from Brother Richards. Brothers Green and Berry spoke some time this P.M. Bother Berry speaks too much about his own works and other sects. I confirmed 2 gone to be baptised by Brother Berry. Spoke to the saints about being faithful and praying [−] [eight lines crossed out and illegible]

Sarah and Rebecca brought cocoa to the services for me. I was much grieved at the church for being talking and confused just before meeting time. Preached about 1¼ hour on the Kingdom and baptism. Prayed with 4 sick. Brother William Whitehead gave me 6 pence and Sarah Crooks gave me 1/− towards postage besides 2 oranges and some raisins. Sister Dewsnup very low. Took Supper at Sister Hardman's.

41. The second chapter of Daniel tells of a dream of Nebuchadnezzer in which he saw "A great image" with a head of gold, breast and arms of silver, stomach and thighs of brass, legs of iron, and his feet of iron and clay. A stone was cut out of the mountains "without hands" and hit the image. Daniel, in interpreting the dream said that the figure and its various parts represented kingdoms which would rise and be destroyed one after another. The key scripture for Clayton's message was undoubtedly verse forty-four: "And in the days of

these kings shall the God of heaven set up a kingdom, which shall never be destroyed: and the kingdom shall not be left to other people, but it shall break in pieces and consume all these kingdoms, and it shall stand for ever." The scripture is a favorite of Mormon missionaries, and the kingdom spoken of is equated with the Church which is to spread throughout the world and never be destroyed until Christ's second coming.

January 27, 1840

Took Breakfast at Hardman's. Brother Lea wants me to write a note for a situation and as soon as I had wrote it Brother Berry came and said he was wanted at the shop where Brother Garner works. So he went and engaged. Went to see Brother West—sick. Took Dinner at Thomas Millers. Went to see Brother Mottram and told him about manifesting a bad spirit during singing in service and also different reports which I had heard concerning him. His wife says she will be baptized as soon as her eye gets better. Is blind under Docters hands. Been at Hart Street meeting. Spoke freely and felt well. Saints seemed affected. After meeting Brother Green proposed subscription for Sarah Duckworth and Brother Arthur got up before the members and opposed him. Apparently in bad spirit. I talked a little to Sarah about her conduct. Prayed with Susan at Thomas Millers. Susannah says she will be more diligent. Supper with Sister Battersby. She fetched 1 pint porter.[42]

42. See above, note 4. Porter is a type of beer. It is interesting to note that Clayton was apparently not too strict in his personal interpretation and observance of the Word of Wisdom, at least when compared to the way it is interpreted today, but he was not hindered in his development in the Church because of it. Even in America the Word of Wisdom was interpreted variously under different circumstances in the early years of the Church. In 1834 the high council in Kirtland voted unanimously that anyone who had been taught the principle but violated it should be deprived of his position in the Church, but in March, 1838, Hyrum Smith advised members of the Church marching from Kirtland to Missouri in "Zion's Camp" "not to be too particular in regard to the Word of Wisdom." Joseph Fielding Smith, *Essentials in Church History: A History of the Church from the Birth of Joseph Smith to the Present Time* (Salt Lake City: Deseret News, 1922), 142 and Smith, *History of the Church*, III, 95.

Leonard J. Arrington, "An Economic Interpretation of the Word of Wisdom," *Brigham Young University Studies*, I (Winter, 1959), 37-49. For more information on changing interpretations of the Word of Wisdom, see Paul H. Peterson, "An Historical Analysis of the Word of Wisdom" (unpublished Master's thesis, Brigham Young University, 1972).

January 28, 1840

Received a long letter from Brother Taylor, Liverpool. Answered it and sent one to Preston to Brother Richards.[43] Got 2 letters from Bedford concerning Brother Lea. Took Dinner at William Millers &c. Spoke to Brother Berry about talking against the sectarians. Saw Sister Elizabeth Booth in a very bad state—careless. Have been to see Sister Mary Becket— is working till near 9 o clock. John Wytch married today. He nor she have said nothing to me about it as to when &c. Joked a great deal with G [—]. Supper at Sister Hardmans [—]. Brother Berry came to sleep with me.

43. In this letter to Willard Richards, Clayton again told of divisive problems in the branch, including the problem of Arthur Smith, who became upset because of a collection being taken up which he thought he should have performed. The most interesting part of this letter, however, is Clayton's attitude toward Church discipline. With regard to Smith, Clayton observed that he was not one with them, but that "I want to be just and merciful." At the same time, Clayton responded to several questions that Richards had asked in another letter. First, if a sister in transgression had been visited by the elders and had refused to give some satisfaction, either to them or to the Church, they could only be justified in bringing the case before the council. Second, transgressors ought to be suspended from fellowship until they made satisfaction to the Church if the transgression were clearly proved. Third, members under transgression ought not to have the privilege of taking the sacrament until satisfaction was made and a Church officer who knowingly administered the sacrament in such a case ought to be brought before the council. Clayton to Richards, Manchester, January 28, 1840, Clayton Papers, HDC.

January 29, 1840

Spoke to Brother Berry this A.M about being to rash in his preaching—speaking of the sects &c. Took Breakfast at Hardman's. 1 letter from Alston, 1 from Brother John Moon. Took

Dinner at Bewshers. Sent the Alston letter to Liverpool. Went to meet Brother Clark. He did not come. Preached first time at John Hardmans. About 5 strangers. Went from there to see Sister Margaret Jones—sick. Saw Sister Sarah Perkins. She says Elizabeth Booth told her that Mary Powell said the Elders are abominable liars. Took Supper with Sarah Crooks. She is troubled about Susannah again being grieved for little.

January 30, 1840

Breakfast at Hardman's. Went to see Burgess' child is very poorly. Received a letter from Liverpool and one from Preston. Sent answer to Preston[44] and a letter for my wife. Dinner at Sister Greens. Ellen Battersby fetched me a pint of porter. Sister Green is troubled. She says Brother Heath has told at Owens that Jane Millwood took 2/— of his away with her. Sister Smith is very distant with her &c. Took C[*ocoa or coffee*] at Brother Jacksons. Preached on Christs reign on earth about 1½. A full house. Supper at Brother Jacksons. Sister Battersby tells me that Arthur Smith has said a great deal to her about me. He has lost the confidence in me &c. Ellen Battersby gave me /6d, Sister Green /2d, Sister Broome 1d.

44. Clayton sent this letter to Willard Richards. He reported on the problems of James Lee, and he said that Lee was having considerable difficulty settling his financial affairs in Leicester. He also referred to several other matters including the question of emigration to the United States of one brother without the counsel of the leadership. Clayton to Richards, January 30, 1840, Clayton Papers, HDC.

January 31, 1840

Breakfast at Hardmans. Dinner at Rigby's. Saw Sister Powell and Sister Booth and Elizabeth Booth—Booths are very ill. Greaved about reports told of me. Mary Powell acknowledges to having called me or the Elders abominable liars and said that if she had plenty to give me I should go and see her often. This was said before Henry Royle and Elizabeth Booth. Elizabeth Booth cir[.....] if this was so she would come no more to this [—] Sister Powell says now—before John Wytch and Sister Booth that she was in a bad spirit when she [—]. She can see that it was a trick of the Devil she was enraged about and said cut me off. This happened on the 3rd of January [— — — — — — — — —]. I showed them the wickedness of such conduct. Sister Powell begged pardon and promised to satisfy those who had heard of her saying those things. Sister Booths were both satisfied and they all promised to mind better and guard against evil speaking. Brother Burgess's wife and child poorly. I anointed her breasts and prayed with them. Told Paul Harris that Brother Fielding said in his letter he never did say he might have his license. Brother Clark has returned from Peover January 14. Before the council meeting I took Brother Arthur Smith the Deacon alone and asked him if he was determined not to partake of the Sacrament. He said he was untill he had obtained satisfaction from God that the thing came from hell. It had been told to the members by the Elders that it came from hell and he was determined if it did it should return thither. I told if he was determined thus to act I had orders from my brethren to take his license. He said if I did he would never take the office into his hands again. He said had seen a great many things. I asked what they were. He said I shall not say. They will come from hell to and I will say no more. The following subjects brought before council: Henry Royle and John Wytch go to Dukinfield on Sunday 4 M. Clarke to Stockport. Brother Green and Thomas Miller to visit Brother Dunn who had not been seen lately. Agreed that the meeting in Bank Street be changed from Wednesday to Tuesday night for convenience of some of the members. The next subject was about the subscription made on the Monday night previous. Brother Thomas Miller stated that from what passed at the meeting on Monday night he had prevented James Mahon from making a subscription at Council of £1. I then called upon the officers to state their feelings on the subject. Brother Bateman said when his sisterinlaw came from the meeting and heard what had passed he was very much grieved and thought we were breaking the order which I had spoke upon the meeting before. Brother Green said it was by the instructions of the Elder (William Clayton) that he had done it and whatever the Elders told him to do he would do it if he knew it to be wrong and the blame should fall upon the Elder &c. Brother Arthur said Brother William has said in the council tis not meet for us to leave the word of God and serve tables.[45] The brothren had spoken against having subscriptions in the meetings. Was like Babylon but one thing was spoken or advised at one time and contradicted another. The world had taken hold of it. We had collections &c. He understood that the higher powers had nothing to do with the Deacons office but he had found it to the contrary. There had been collections before that and the Deacons knew nothing of it and the Deacon ought to have been informed of it but he was not. I then stood up and said that I had not intended it be understood that the order of money being put into the box was so exclusive as to forbid the idea of making subscriptions in cases of absolute emergency. The case alluded to was one of this nature. Sarah should have lived at Brother Jacksons 2 weeks but his wife was not willing. Sarah had been at Bewshers a few days—but Bewsher's could not do with. I had talked with Sister Bewsher about Sarah had no were to go—no bed to sleep on and something must be done immediately. The subscription was to purchase a bed and she might have Mary Ann Johnsons room and the church pay the whole rent of house. I had it not in my untill I came to the meeting and then told Brother Green just before the meeting. Brother Arthur came forward at the meeting and publickly opposed Brother Green before he asked a word about either what it was for or who had ordered him &c. Arthur manifested a bad spirit &c. Arthur acknowledged to having done wrong in opposing and asked forgiveness. Granted. I told them the money was intended to be given to the Deacon but when offered to him he refused to take it. The council was satisfied it was not a breach. I showed them it was impossible to have such a case as Jane Millward's settled from the box and must be by subscription. I then stated that the clothing had been purchased and they might please themselves wether it should be done at Powell Street or not. It was finally agreed not. Brother Bateman then said he was satisfied when he had heard both sides of the question but he believed that if any of the Elders saw him go down and baptise they would stop him and he should watch that none of the officers took the Deacons business for time to come. I then stated to the meeting the case of Arthur. I showed that it was not because he had not been diligent in his office—not been kind to me. He had done both for which I felt thankful but it was for not partaking sacrament and because he was opposed to all the other officers and was determined to follow his own views independant of council &c. He again stated his determination not to partake untill he had the matter proved by revelation &c—which proved his insubjiction. He ultimately agreed to partake of the sacrament. Brother Green stated that he had heard from Smith that he and Betsy was about to be married at all Saints and live at John Smiths and he believed the courtship was not broken up. I then stated as follows. Betsy Holden was a married woman. Her husband was a soldier. Had left England to India about 4 years since. Was 3 years since she heard from. No evidence had been given but that he was still living &c. Arthur had had a vision and it was shown to him not the person but the features and that begun the union &c. I had advised him when I first heard of it not to engaged in courtship but let it rest untill proper evidence could be obtained. I expected he would have done so but I found he acted quite to the contrary and seemed determined to pursue his own course. I asked Arthur if this statement was correct. He said it was not. I asked him to state wherein it was not and after being pressed upon he said that it was 4 years since she heard from Holden and that the features was not shewn to him but the complexion. The council then agreed that it was necessary he should make acknowledgement to the church and satisfy the church that he had broke off connexion with Betsy. He said positively he would not satisfy another individual any more about it. The council then seeing that he was determined to pursue his own course independent of council unanimously agreed to take his office from him. He said if they did he would never more take it again. The council was agreed in all their conclusions and a very solemn feeling pervaded the meeting. We separated at 12 o clock. Met at 8. Took supper at Sands. I went to see Brother Dunns child which was sick. We did not see it.

45. Clayton had apparently referred to Acts 6:2 in a council meeting. This scriptural passage tells of the ancient apostle choosing seven men to perform the various routine, temporal duties of the Church in order to relieve the apostles for larger responsibilities. Apparently Arthur Smith was jealous of his presumed prerogative, as a deacon, to take care of such temporal matters.

February 1, 1840
Took Breakfast at Sister Jane Brown's. Went to see Brother Dunn's child. I think it will die. Took Dinner at Sands. Writ a letter to Brother Fielding, Liverpool. C[*ocoa or coffee*] at Thomas Millers. Sister Perkins grieved because

her father scolded much on account of James staying out untill 12½ o'clock. Mr. Perkins got up and went to great lengths. James went away and slept at Green's. James did not intend to go to live there any more but I advised him to go back and ask forgiveness and try to do better, this partly because Sarah wanted him to stay. Went to see Elizabeth Prince. She had resolved not to come near the [–] any more. Had found herself with worldly company. Felt herself entirely drawn from us. I begged she would consider her ways. I knew she had had much said about her by some of the saints without cause &c. Her mother has been cross with her &c. She wept much. I felt to weep. [Rebecca] Partington gave me 2 oranges. Margaret Jones, Ann Jackson at Claytons.

February 2, 1840
Breakfast at Sister Hardmans. Went to Stockport. Preached the resurrection. Dinner at Brother Staffords. Talked to him about chastizing his children and training them &c. P.M. spoke about evil speaking. Showed the saints their duty. Talked about sufferings in America.[46] [B....] cut off. Preached at night on the Kingdom and restoration of earth and beasts &c.[47] Goodly company. 4 of the Manchester saints came to Stockport [– – –]. Christiana Crooks behaved bad on her return home and quite stupid and sulky. Till finally when Sister Dewsnup crossed the street to speak to her she crossed opposite and when they came back again she also went from them to the other side. I felt dis-gusted at her conduct and determined not to take any notice of her. I had considerable talk with Elizabeth Prince. I believe she has been used badly both at home and in church. She loves the Elders and believes all we have told her. She has not a friend in the church but all seemed to stand against her untill she has determined to leave the church and turn to the world again.

I reasoned a good deal with her and advised her to stand to the last and God would make it manifest who had done wrong. She acknowledges to having done wrong &c. I feel much on her account. Her mother is very cross with her and unkind. Took supper at Hardman's. My foot very sore. Felt weary.

46. The British leadership was trying at this time to dissuade members of the Church from emigrating to America until they were counseled to do so. In a letter to Willard Richards, Clayton had referred to a brother and his wife who were preparing to go to America "without council and in their present state of religion I only feel to say if *they should go* as soon as they anticipate some of them will wish themselves back again." In March, Joseph Fielding wrote to Richards saying that it would be better for the Saints to suffer in England because they would suffer in America. If they wanted to go as emigrants, Fielding said he would bless them, but he would not approve of their going as Saints to Zion. It had been just over a year since the Mormons had been driven from Missouri, and begun their struggle to erect new settlements in western Illinois. Among other things, a serious malaria epidemic in 1839 had caused much suffering. Clayton was undoubtedly referring to these struggles in this Sunday sermon. Clayton to Richards, January 30, 1840, Clayton Papers, HDC. Fielding to Richards, Liverpool, March 25, 1840, Fielding Papers, HDC.

47. The Mormons were convinced that this Kingdom which they were helping to establish would eventually engulf the world. In 1841, Parley P. Pratt, then editor of the *Millennial Star*, the Church periodical in England, wrote to Queen Victoria from Manchester: "Know assuredly, that the world in which we live is on the eve of a REVOLUTION, more powerful in its beginning—more important in its consequences—than any which man has yet witnessed upon the earth." After the destruction of the existing government, God would set up a "new and universal Kingdom, under the immediate administration of the Messiah and his Saints." *To Her Gracious Majesty, Queen Victoria,* (Manchester, 1841), 5, cited in Klaus J. Hansen, *Quest for Empire: The Political Kingdom of God and the Council of Fifty in Mormon History* (East Lansing: Michigan University Press, 1967), 3-4, 191n; see also B. H. Roberts' interpretation of this establishment in Smith, *History of the Church,* I, XXXIV-XL; Revelations 14:6-7; and note 41.

February 3, 1840

Have dreamed that I was going to baptize my father where the water was very muddy and soon as we got into it it arose almost to our heads and I could not baptize him. I also dreamed that a raging fever was making desolation in the towne. I saw carts come to the fever ward every 4 or 5 minutes with afflicted people in. Took breakfast at Hardman's.

Got a letter from my wife. Well. Fatherinlaw tempted. Dinner at Brother Black's. Went to Prestwich thence to Thatchley. Saw Brother Barlow. His wife very sick. Prayed with her and child. Returned to Prestwich. Brother Clark preached us 2 hours. Full house. After meeting I told Barlow what we had heard of him going to the churches and telling falsehood. He denied telling falshood and promised to go no more to the churches. I said if he did we should warn the church &c. I was very foot sore. Supper at Hardmans. Got home about 11¼.

February 4, 1840
Breakfast at Hardman's. Received a letter from Brother Fielding, one from Brother Richards, one from Agness Patrick. 4 went to see Elizabeth Holden but could not find her. Dinner at Thomas Millers. Went to see Brother Davies. Found him some better. Sister Rigby gave me 1/−, Sister Walker /6d, Sister Black /6d, Brother West /6d. Went to Post office to see for a letter from Agness Patrick. Will get it in the morning. Water at Thomas Millers. Talked with Sussanah Miller. [−]. She has no faith in the word of wisdom and has not kept it.[48] She has not the same degree of knowledge which the other saints have. Loves her acquaintance in Babylon &c. She seemed better when we parted. Brother Lea gave me 2/−, Sister Poole /4, Christiana Crooks 2/−. Sarah Crooks gave me a pint of Porter. Supper at Thomas Millers. Went to see Brother Burgess child. Very sick. Not very likely to recover. Let considerable matter out of my head. Brother Green rather sick. Alice Hardman sick.

48. It is difficult to determine what Clayton would have interpreted as "keeping" the Word of Wisdom, in light of his own moderate use of alcoholic beverages. (See above, note 42.)

February 5, 1840
Took breakfast at Hardman's. Went to seek Betsy Holden

again but cannot find her. Have sent a small note to her. Dinner at Brother Bewshers. Have been to the clerk at Saint Saviours who says that Arthur and Betsy was married last Sunday morning at 9 o clock. Went to Hart Street and prayed with 5 of Brother Greens family. Left Book of Covenants[49] till I return. Went to Brother Battersby to [Comet] St. Sent a letter to Burslem. Sister Perkins gave me a tea cup full of Red Wine. C[ocoa or coffee] at M. Miller. Went to Paul Harris', Mary Ann Johnson and Painer's. Brother Burgess child appears worse. Many of the Sisters at Hardman's. Sister Poole gave me 1/—, Elizabeth Mills 2/—, E[lizabeth or Esther] Crooks 2/—, Rebecca Partington 1/6, John Smith 1/—, James Mayon /8, Sarah Crooks 3/—, for Brother Richards. She gave me some raisins and some articles for my wife. Brother Sands gave me optical die for my Sarah. Sister Ellen Battersby has had an interview with Arthur and Betsy. Arthur very bitter and independent. Received a letter from Brother Heath and one from Brother Cordon. Sarah Crooks gave me an orange.

49. First printed in 1833 at Far West, Missouri, as *The Book of Commandments*, the book has gone through a number of editions and changes. The name of the book was changed to *The Doctrine and Covenants of the Church of Jesus Christ of Latter-day Saints* in 1835. The book is made up principally of revelations given to Joseph Smith.

February 6, 1840

Breakfast at Hardman's. Elizabeth Crooks came and gave me a small parcel for Brother Richards. I went to see Sister Dewsnup. Brother Gill gave me 1/— and Brother Staffords sisterinlaw 1/5 and his other lodger 1/—. We started together to the Railway by Hart Street. Sister Sands had Dinner almost ready but we had not time to wait. Ellen Battersby gave me 2 Eccles cakes. Arrived at Railway 11-40. Started about 10 minutes. Arrived Liverpool[50] about 1-40. Went to Norfolk Street and found brothers Fielding and Taylor at Mrs. Kannon's No. 43. Went from thence to see Brother and Sister Mitchell Burlington A. and from thence to Sister Arringtons where we took tea and spent the evening. After supper we returned to Kannons to sleep. We slept together.

50. Liverpool was the principal seaport in Lancashire, and is located about thirty-one miles west of Manchester on the River Mersey. In 1841 it had a population of 223,003. The town is located on the east bank of the river with the docks spoken of below on the west side of the town. One of the chief branches of its cotton trade was with the United States. It served as the port for Manchester and other textile towns. It became the major port of embarkation for Mormon emigrants. Lewis, *Topographical Dictionary*, III, 107.

February 7, 1840

Took breakfast at Kannon's. Went with Brother Taylor to see Brother Gills daughter Park Lane. Found her comfortable ready to be baptised. Returned from the Docks to Norfolk for Brother Fielding has wrote a letter to Agness Patrick and one to Brother Clark. Dinner at Kannons and then Brother Taylor gave me his blessing. He blessed me with wisdom and utterance so that I should be a wonder to myself and others. By the spirit. Ministering angels. He blessed Brother Fielding and then Brother Fielding blessed Brother Taylor. Brother Taylor afterwards give an address in tongues and interpreted.[51] We then started to go by the Docks to the Railway station. Started at 2½. Through the tunnel and then by Eugene at ⅔. Instead of stopping at Farrington went through to Preston[52] but they brought me back to Farrington by 5 o clock coach. Went to my Fathers and thence home about 5½.

51. The practice of speaking in tongues in meetings was apparently quite extensive during the early period of Church history. It was considered a sign of the true church. Smith, *History of the Church*, I, 297, 323, 383, 428. See also Mark 16:17.

52. Farrington is also spelled Farington and it is located about three miles south of Preston. In 1841, it had 2,500 people. Clayton undoubtedly wanted to stop at Farington in order to see his family at Penwortham which is close to Farington, being about one and three-quarters miles southwest of Preston. In 1841, Penwortham had 5,498

inhabitants. Just across the River Ribble from Farington and Penwortham was Preston, a city of 50,073 in 1841. Preston, where the missionaries first preached in 1837 was, like Manchester, a textile manufacturing town. Lewis, *Topographical Dictionary*, III, 610, 553, and 212. Whitney, *Kimball*, 121.

February 8, 1840

Writ a letter to Mr. James Joyne Leot[....]. Went to Preston to Brother Richards. We entered into conversation respecting a letter which Brother Richards had sent to Brother Fielding. Brother Fielding sent a letter to Brother Richards asking some questions and it seems Brother Richards had misunderstood the meaning of Brother Fielding's letter and writ rather severely &c. Brother Richards sees into the subject and purposes to write to Brother Fielding and satisfy him.[53] Took water at Brother Richard's lodgings. Went to council. Several things, part of no particular moment. When I addressed the council upon the necessity of attending to order such as seeking council from the highest officer present, the necessity of being united and upholding each other, not speaking of anything passed at the council &c. Brother Richards bore testimony to the same effect. After the council had concluded we entered into conversation with Brothers Walmsley and Miller and Halsale upon Sister Walmsleys case. We advised that it should be stated to the church that it was never intended to be understood that Sister Walmsley was a liar &c. but that she acknowledged to having circulated reports. Brother Halsale opposed the council we gave and said there was partiality in the case. Brother Richards stated last sabbath that Sister Walmsley had reported that Sisters Fielding and Richards could not agree—that two of the Elders had been to Sisters Fielding and Richards and they both testified that they could not recollect ever quarrelling but (added Brother Richards) it does not prove that they may not hereafter recollect something neither does it matter for the charge is for circulating reports—wether true or false is no matter. It seems from this statement that some understood that Sister Walmsley told lies and she was determined not to make satisfaction untill this proved. We considered it would be best to say as little as possible and let the matter drop. Brother Halsale thought we ought to state in public that Sister Walmsley's statement was true &c. and unless this was done it was partiality. He would not give his assent to it. We reasoned much upon the matter to little purposes. It was concluded that Brother Melling should state that the church was not to understand that Sister Walmsley had told a lie but for circulating reports. I fear that something else will arise out of this subject for it is almost 6 months since the circumstance took place. Sister Walmsley has manifested a bad spirit, quite rebellious, and I think she has hardly been fairly used.[54] Home about 10½

53. The problem apparently concerned a sister who was related to Fielding. It is possible that she lived in Preston as did Fielding's brother James Fielding. Fielding to Richards, Liverpool, February 11, 1840, Fielding Papers, HDC.
54. It is possible that this problem related to Jennetta Richards, Willard Richards' wife, for the question had to do with opposition to her. She was the daughter of John Richards, an independent minister at Walkerfold, Lancashire, and came from the upper-middle class. Because of this, she was used to having fine clothes. A considerable amount of dissention was created in the branch over this, probably because branch members tended to come from the lower classes. This class conflict was an extremely divisive force in the Preston Branch while Richards lived there. Richard L. Evans, *A Century of Mormonism in Great Britain* (Salt Lake City: Deseret News Press, 1937), 71-72. Claire Noall, *Intimate Disciple: A Portrait of Willard Richards: Apostle to Joseph Smith—Cousin of Brigham Young* (Salt Lake City: University of Utah Press, 1957), 125, 231-235. Fielding's wife was the former Hannah Greenwood of Preston. Smith, *History of the Church,* III, 38.

February 9, 1840

Wrote a letter to Sarah Crooks, Manchester. Preached in the A M on the ressurrection, in the P M on perfection, gifts of the spirit and how to obtain these things. Spoke upon the armour and charity.[55] After meeting went to see Sister Sumner and child. Sick. Preached at night up Daniel 7 chapter the restoration of the earth. House not full. Wet.

55. Perhaps the sermon was based upon I Corinthians 13, which ends (verse 13) "And now abideth faith, hope, charity, these three; but the greatest of these is charity," and Ephesians 6:11: "put on the whole armour of God."

February 10, 1840

Copied some extracts from "Times and Seasons."[56] Went to see Brother Cooks child. Writ a small note for Paul Chadwick. Gave me −/6d.

56. The *Times and Seasons* was a monthly religious paper, published by Don Carlos Smith and Ebenezer Robinson at Commerce (later Nauvoo) Illinois. Publication continued from November 1839 until 1845. Smith, *History of the Church*, IV, 28; VII, 454.

February 11, 1840

Went to Preston to see Brother Richards. Bought a memorandum book at Walkers for 1/6. Took at Liptrots. Went to Mechanics Institution about 4 hours. Returned home a little before 8 P.M. Saw Brother John Moon. He had been to see about preparing for Zion.[57] I told him that I could see no reason why they may not go this season, that Brother Kimball had said let the gathering alone till we come and that some of the Saints would go to Kirtland when he came. Have not been in the prayer meeting. Prayed with Father Moon.

57. After the Twelve got to England, they rescinded the original prohibition against emigration, and John Moon, Clayton's wife's cousin, led the first group of 41 to the United States on June 1, 1840. Brigham Young, *Manuscript History of Brigham Young, 1801-1844*, compiled by Elden Jay Watson from Volumes 25 and 26 of the *Millennial Star* (Salt Lake City: Smith Secretarial Service, 1968), 77; Whitney, *Kimball*, 278.

February 12, 1840

Having been writing the whole of the day. My mother came this A M to say that she thought my wife was dissatisfied on account of my being from home and it was hard for Moon's to keep her and children.[58] Brother Richards came to dinner. Went to see Brother Romney and prayed for him. Was troubled with temptation about the gift of tongues &c. Prayed with Sister Sumner.

58. At this time, Clayton had two children by Ruth Moon: Sarah L. and Margaret. Paul E. Dahl, *William Clayton: Missionary, Pioneer and Public Servant* (Provo, Utah: J. Grant Stevenson, 1964), 214.

February 13, 1840

Went to Preston. Saw Sister Morgan and then went to Brother Walmsleys. Had considerable talk with Sisters Walmsley and Fielding. Sister Walmsley promised to try to live better and let the matter rest. Saw Brother Richards and wife. Took cocoa with Sister Morgan. Conversed a good deal on the order of the church. After I returned home.

February 14, 1840

Went to see my parents. Had an conversation. Left home to Preston at 1 P.M. Started per railway at $2\frac{1}{2}$ and arrived at Manchester at 4-40. Found 2 letters from Brampton[59] for Brother Fielding. Directed them and sent them to Liverpool. Received a small note left by Brother David Wilding concerning money which I paid for his coach fare to Burslem. Received 7/— along with a note. Nothing particular at council meeting. Water at Hardman's and supper at Brother Greens. Sister Battersby is sending a soverein to Sister Wilding Preston. She said Sister Wilding is neglected. I directed letter. Brother Clark says he will go to Stockport Sunday.

59. Lewis' *Topographical Dictionary* lists eight places named Brampton. This is probably the one in Derbyshire about five miles west of Chesterfield. In 1841, it had 3,937 inhabitants. Lewis, *Topographical Dictionary*, I, 342.

February 15, 1840

Took breakfast at Hardman's. Went to Cookson Street.

Prayed with Brother Davies. Went to Brother Burgess. Had a good deal of conversation with two of Brother Burgess's brothers. William rejected our testimony. The other would seek upon it. Prayed with and anointed his wife and child. Went to Matthew Claytons.[60] Elizabeth very poorly. Prayed with her and anointed her. She received instant relief. Went to see Mary Ann Johnson and prayed with and anointed her. Came to see Brother Robert Williams. Prayed with and anointed him. Brother Clark went to Stockport. I went to William Millers. Took Water with Sarah Perkins. She is very poorly. Went to Thomas Millers. Took supper and staid till 10½. Susan very sick. Rebecca fetched a pint of Porter into the Street. Read a letter today from Brother Woodruff. Wrote on Tuesday. Have heard today that there has been 14 baptised at Manchester since last Sabbath and 4 at Stockport. E. Miller gave me a half crown.

60. This is possibly an uncle. Clayton later had a brother named Matthew, who was born in November, 1840, but died three months later.

February 16, 1840
Went to breakfast at Matthew Claytons. Elizabeth went up stairs and would not let me see. Went to the room and Brother Henry Royle preached a while and then I spoke about 35 minutes. During the service William Smith and another went to be baptised. Prayed with Sister Jones. Was sick. Went to Bewshers to Dinner. Had conversation with Sister Bewsher's cousin. She seems quite convinced of the truth. Had a considerable conversation with Arthur and told him what the church would have to do &c. He cautioned me to justly &c. He said they was intending to live together &c. His case was brought at the meeting in the P.M. I stated it from first to last and put it to the church if he must be cut off. Many held up their hands. I then put it to the contrary

100

and Sister Catherine Beates held up her hand. I called upon her to give her reason and she spake considerable but nothing to shew cause why he should not be cut off. She wanted to be merciful. I then put it again if the church would rather suspend him and Sister Usherwood and Peter Mottram held up their hand. I considered it conclusive and closed the case. Sister Holden was suspended. I spoke about 1 hour to the church. Confirmed 13—blessed 1 child, anointed 3 and prayed with 6. Tarried in the room and Rebecca Partington fetched some cocoa. She is a loving soul. Preached at night about 1-10 on the gifts of the spirit. Several given us their names to be baptised on tuesday night. Had considerable talk with Catherine Beates after meeting. Had 14 oranges and about a dozen sweet cakes given to me. Sister Bewsher gave me a pint of Porter.

February 17, 1840

Brother Cordon returned from Stockport. Took Breakfast at Hardman's. Wrote to Burslem and Liverpool. Took dinner at William Millers. Sister Perkins gave me a pint Porter. Went to Thomas Millers to Cocoa. William Miller went with me—from thence went to Prestwich.[61] William and I waited on the road for Sarah Crooks and Henry Royle. Sarah was waiting near the old church through misunderstanding. William returned and I went on alone. Arrived about 7 o clock. Waited a few minutes and Henry came in and a little while after Sarah came. The people seemed slack at coming up and we waited awhile. One of the brethren came from another house and said there was a congregation waiting for us so I went and left Henry at Eckersleys. Sarah went with me. Found a full house. I preached something more than 1 hour and the people was attentive. Some few were unruly. Had talk with some of them and think they will some be baptised.

Gave out another meeting in 2 weeks. Sarah gave me a orange and ginger losenges. Got home at 12 o clock. Supper at preaching house.

61. Prestwich is about four miles north-northwest of Manchester. In 1841 it had a population of 3,180 and was made up principally of suburban dwellings. Lewis, *Topographical Dictionary*, III, 616.

February 18, 1840
Breakfast at Hardman's. Wrote a letter for Robert Williams to his father in London. Had conversation with William Garnett. He seems to received it gladly. Anointed Sister Margaret Hardmans leg. Went to Sand's to dinner and thence to Brother Green's. Sister Green very low. Gave them each some oil inwardly and prayed with them. Had conversation with some hardened females at Sands. Took water there. Returned to Hardman's—to meet some to baptize. Had a house full of saints. Went to the water and baptised 3 females. Got my cloths changed and then Gilford came up I baptised him and changed my cloths again and another female said she would go and I went into the water a third time—5 baptised in all. Elizabeth Prince gave me a orange and 2 other sisters each one. Supper at Thomas Millers. Sister Dewsnup has left home.

February 19, 1840
Breakfast at Hardman's. Got a letter from Brother Heath. Sister Poole has been and says—Susan is jealous of Thomas.[62] He wants her out of the way. If she was to die he would be married again in 3 months &c. Thomas wanted to know who he would be married to &c. She would not tell him. He says he will not go to his work untill she does tell him and she says she will not. Thomas is very much troubled &c. Thomas has practiced kissing all in the house before he goes to bed &c. Went to Bewsher's to dinner. She gave me a

pint of Porter. Brother James was with us a little while. Went from thence to see Brother Gills wife. She is much the same. Have learned that all the family is baptised. We administered the sacrament and went to Brother John Smiths to C[*ocoa or coffee*]. Prayed with Brother John and 2 of the children. Came back to Brother Burgess and anointed and prayed with his wife. Went to Pollard Street to preach. Brother Clark talk some time after he had done two of the Owenites opposed but would not say much to them. They left the house and then I talked a little to the others. Came home and found Sarah Crooks here and Christiana who was sick. We prayed with her. [*three and one half lines crossed out*]— Supper at Hardman's. Writ a letter to H.

62. This is obviously the Miller family, with whom Clayton had spent considerable time. Apparently Elizabeth Poole had visited the Millers and then felt she should report the situation to Clayton.

February 20, 1840
Was called up this morning soon after 3 o clock to see Sister Jane Brown. She is seized with an inflamation. We prayed with her and she seemed some better. Have wrote one letter to my wife one to Brother Richards[63] and one to Sister Morgan. Dinner at Rigbys. Prayed with Brother Davies and gave him some oil. Went to old Mr. Millers and spent the P M. Very comfortable. Took C[*ocoa or coffee*]. Went to Pendleton. Sister Rebecca Partington and Susan Miller went with me. Prayed with 3. A few strangers. Preached from wheat and tares.[64] Took supper and returned by Thomas Millers. Met Brother Clark. Got home at 11-20.

63. In this letter to Willard Richards, Clayton gives some insight into the practices connected with administering to the sick. He said that Jane Brown's "mother anointed her and we prayed with her. She was some better immediately." Apparently it was not uncommon in the early church for women to participate in this ceremony by anointing with oil. Another incident reported in the letter was that Clayton had heard from a Brother Heath who was preaching and baptizing in

Congleton. Clayton's attitude toward missionary work is seen in the fact that he had cautioned Heath "not to speak of any thing but the first principles and advised him to set a very good example." Clayton to Richards, Manchester, February 29, 1840, Clayton Papers, HDC.
        64. Matthew 13:24-30. In using the parable of the wheat and tares, Clayton was obviously speaking of the wicked among the righteous on earth and alluding to the second coming of Christ and the final judgment.

February 21, 1840

Breakfast at Hardman's. Received a letter from Robert Willam's father. Went and prayed with Robert and gave him oil. Jane Brown some better. Dinner at Sister Booths and water. Conversed with several females. Blessed Sisters Booth and Knott. Went to see Sarah Perkins at William Millers. Went to see Sister Beach and prayed with her. Supper at Thomas Millers. Susan wept because she heard that Thomas had intended to buy Sarah Isherwood a new cloak. Susan is yet troubled with jealousy. Sarah Crooks gave me 1/— and some raisins.

February 22, 1840

Sent a letter to William Williams London. Breakfast at Hardman's. Went to see a sick girl in Salford.[65] Received a letter from Brother Fielding. Dinner at Brother Greens. Sister Green is troubled because Sister Smith has been reporting the case of their sickness to some of the members. Brothers John Hardman and Lea are gone to Preston. Anointed and prayed with Jane Brown's child. Jane is better. Prayed with Brother Burgess daughter. C[ocoa or coffee] at Prince's. Matthew put me some buttons on my shoes. Went to see some of the Town missions at Pollard Street. Met 2 of them. They wanted to see a sign. I proved that signs were not a sure evidence. Acknowledged. Told them the order of the gospel. They assented to it. I then said if you preach that—so—then it is a proof that you are not the servants of God. They turned from their acknowledgment. We bore testimony and asked them did they reject our testimony. Yes. So we parted.[66] Went to Thomas Millers to Supper. Susan yet grieved. Betsy Crooks very low. She has given way to her temper &c. Margaret Jones gave me two oranges and cleaned my shoes. Home about 11½. Richard Hardman gave me a few figs.

65. Salford is a suburb of Manchester located north-west of the city. Lewis, *Topographical Dictionary*, atlas.

66. Obviously, Clayton was visiting with missionaries of some other denomination. He was attempting to prove that they were wrong and he was right from the New Testament. After they asked him for a sign he quoted from Matthew 12:39-40. "An evil and adulterous generation seeketh after a sign; and there shall no sign be given to it, but the sign of the prophet Jonas; For as Jonas was three days and three nights in the whale's belly; so shall the Son of man be three days and three nights in the heart of the earth." When he spoke of the order of the gospel, he may have had reference to Matthew 7:21-23. "Not every one that saith unto me, Lord, Lord, shall enter into the kingdom of heaven; but he that doeth the will of my Father which is in heaven. Many will say unto me in that day, Lord, Lord, have we not prophesied in thy name? and in thy name have cast out devils? and in thy name done many wonderful works? And then will I profess unto them, I never knew you: depart from me, ye that work iniquity." In other words, he may have been trying to trap them into the admission that they were not true disciples of Christ because they asked for a sign. It is instructive to note that Clayton was not as impetuous as some other young missionaries in attempting to "prove" Mormonism by means of miraculous signs. See note on James Mahon in Appendix.

February 23, 1840

Breakfast at Hardman's. Went to Stockport. Preached on John 15.[67] Slender congregation. 5 of the Manchester Saints came. Dinner at Brother Staffords. Talked about 1½ hours in the P M. Preached at night on Wheat and tares. Confirmed 1 in the P.M. Had 3 oranges given me. Sarah and Rebecca came and I came along with them. Betsy Crooks and Betsy Dewsnup was shy and behaved unkind. Got home a little before 11. 2 [–] baptised at Manchester. Supper at Hardman's. My feet were very sore.

67. The chapter deals with the need to be diligent in the work, to love one another, and to bring forth good works. Some of the

petty bickering and other problems among the Saints, which is so evident in Clayton's journal, could well have led him to preach on this subject, as well as on the "Wheat and tares" in the evening meeting.

February 24, 1840

Breakfast at Hardman's. Received a letter from Sarah Flint. Wrote a letter to Brother Fielding. Went and anointed and prayed with Sister Jane Browns child. Went to see Robert Williams. Prayed with and anointed him. Dinner at Thomas Millers. Brother Clark came and is gone to Pendlebury. John Wytch to Prestwich. Went to see Wallace in Salford. Not at home. Water at Thomas Millers. Susan has been much grieved at many things. Thomas struck her this morning. He repented at it and desired that they both might begin anew. Susan has forgiven him. Margaret Jones is grieved with Betsy Crooks and is for leaving T's. Betsy Crooks is grieved at them all. She says they use her unkindly call her a hypocrite &c. She says she has made up her mind to leave the church. I feel to weep over her. Their seems to be a spirit of contention amongst them. Prayed with little Ann and Sarah Isherwood. Supper at Thomas Millers. Have advised the Saints to give up the practice of kissing.[68]

68. The practice, of course, came from Paul's admonition: "Salute one another with an holy kiss." Romans 16:16. Probably because the missionaries stressed biblical literalism and the restoration of all things, such a greeting was considered proper. It is interesting to observe that in his revision of the Bible, Joseph Smith changed this passage to read "Salute one another with a holy salutation."

February 25, 1840

Breakfast at Hardman's. Sent a letter to Sarah Flint. Went to Brother Sand's to Dinner and C[ocoa or coffee]. Went to visit also Paul Harris, B[.....] and Burgess. Went with Brother Bowman to see some of his acquaintances. Preached the gospel to them. They were kind and invited me to go again. Brother Bowman wanted advice concerning his property and I gave such as I had given me. He says he will have nothing to do with property that is not pure &c. He said a small estate was left to his father sometime since by some of his fathers relatives (brother) and when his father became entitled to it their was other relatives who had more need of it than his father had. Did his father wrong in claiming the property. I answered no—again. In the year 1825, his father began to build a range of houses in a very pleasant situation and while they were in building he was solicited through an agent to sell the houses. His mother was very much opposed to selling them and used her influence to prevent them from being sold. After repeated solicitations his father very unwillingly set a price on them £2800. The agent in a day or so returned and offered him £2700. But he being still very unwilling to part with them would not abate any thing. The agent then asked if he would not allow something as commission. His father asked what he would want. He replied it was usual to have ¼ per cent. Bowman said he did not mind that. Therefore the deed was drawn up and Bowman was desired to sign it &c. He begged they would wait and consider a few days longer—thinking the man would be willing to rue of his bargain. However at the time appointed the contract was signed and a deposit of £2 given as earnest. The purchaser had 1500 in bank and promised to pay the other in a given time. Before the time expired their began to be a great pressure in trade. Money grew scarce and property was of very little value. Said he could purchase many houses at about 12 ea. The purchaser then came and wanted to know what Bowman would accept of as the bargain. Bowman did not want the bargain to be broke as at that time. The money was of far more value to him than the property. After repeated solicitations he agreed for 400, which was given. Brother Bowman wanted to know if his father done right.

107

I told him to let it rest and if any thing was necessary to do the Lord would make it known. He next stated that he had assisted in building a chapel for Mr. Ais[....] and had 420 £ lying invested in it. He dared not to sell the chapel because he considered it as given to God. I told him if he would get all his money in and sell the chapel the Lord would not be displeased but would bless him because such places were of no use to the Lord.[69] We parted at 10. Went to Sarah Perkins to Supper and to sleep there. Sister Jones told me her trouble. I recommended mercy and charity and said she would [− −].

69. This is an interesting commentary on the direction which the Church had developed in England. Apparently the Saints were so used to meeting in homes and halls that they considered regular chapels superfluous.

February 26, 1840
Breakfast at Perkins. Sister Poole has bound my stock[70] with leather. Had conversation with Mrs. Miller (old). Told her that she should see a day when she would desire to escape out of England unless she died soon. I warned her of the jury reports &c. But she said Ninevah repented and the Lord was merciful &c. Susan is poorly. Prayed with Robert Williams. Very poorly. Prayed with Brother Green. Got a letter from Brother Woodruff Burslem. Dinner at Bewshers &c. Answered Brother Woodruff's letter. Sent 1 to Brother Carden. 1 to my wife. Brother Bewsher gave me a pair of twezers. Preached at Pollard Street to about 12 on the Kingdom &c.

70. Walking stick.

February 27, 1840
A letter from Brother Richards. Breakfast at Hardman's. Went per packet to Ashley[71] to see Brother George Woolsten-

croft. Found him in a bad state. He believes the bible is all
truth and because Brother Berry said there was errors in it
he said he had inbibed infidel principles. I told him I could
prove that there were contradictions in it and therefore could
not all be true. I referred him to Acts 9 ch. and 22 ch.[72] I
told him I had heard he could preach. Yes, he said, Jesus
Christ had sent him to preach and no man should stop him.
I said it was contrary to the order of the church. He said
he would not be led by man and he had often thought that
the order of the church was like Priestcraft &c. He said Jesus
Christ had spoke to him. Had he heard him? Yes. How did
he speak to him? In such a manner that satisfied him. I asked
him if he believed we were the servants of God. He said he
believed that sometimes Satan had sent men with a design
to do good. I answered I believed that for Satan had deceived him &c. He answered if I said that Christ had not
sent him. He would look upon me like unto the lying prophet
&c. I told him he never could be saved if he did not abide
in the church &c. He said his determination was to do the
will of God and he new he should be saved. I told him that
the will of God was that he should be subject to the higher
powers and he was not subject &c. He was subject to God
&c. I asked him what evidence he had for believing that the
order of the church was priestcraft. He referred to the Mass
book. I showed him that was no criterion—the Bible. I asked
him if he was determined to continue preaching. He said
Christ had set him to preach and he should stop him. He
would not be stopped by any man. I then told him he could
no longer hold an office in the church and must be suspended
from fellowship &c a few weeks so that if he repented he
might acknowledge it, if not he would be cut off. He seemed
to speak with great confidence and was very stubborn in spirit
of subjection. I said I wanted to do him good. He does not

believe the Book of Mormon. I walked back to the Boat about 3 miles. Took dinner with Brother James Johnson. Got back to Manchester about 4 o clock. Took C[*ocoa or coffee*] at Hardman's. Went to Thomas Millers. Susan is determined to have a less family and break up house. They would go to old Mrs. Miller. She was weary in consequence of having to much work. She could not bear it &c. I went to William Millers to meeting and spoke much on the tribulation which is at hand. The Saints seemed moved. I had great liberty in speaking. Prayed with one sister. Sarah & Rebecca brought me home. I told them what Susan was intending to do. Rebecca seemed much troubled and Sarah appeared rather tempted to get mairied. I felt to sorrow on this account. I don't want Sarah to be married. I was much troubled and tempted on her account and felt to pray that the Lord would preserve me from impure affections. She gave me an orange. I certainly feel my love towards her to increase but shall strive against it. I feel too much to covet her and afraid less her troubles should cause her to get married. The Lord keep me pure and preserve me from doing wrong.[73]

71. Ashley is in Cheshire about 13 miles south-southwest from Manchester. In 1841, it had 377 inhabitants. Lewis, *Topographical Dictionary*, I, 88.

72. Clayton was undoubtedly referring to the contradiction which is found in the two versions of Paul's conversation with Christ. Acts 9:7 "And the men which journeyed with him stood speechless, hearing a voice, but seeing no man." Acts 22:9 "And they that were with me saw indeed the light, and were afraid; but they heard not the voice of him that spake to me."

73. Later, Clayton became the scribe who, on July 12, 1843, wrote the revelation which now constitutes Sec. 132 of the *Doctrine and Covenants* on polygamy or plural marriage. Earlier, in February, 1843, "the Prophet invited me to walk with him. During our walk, he said he had learned that there was a sister back in England, to whom I was very much attached. I replied there was, but nothing further than an attachment such as brother and sister in the Church might rightfully entertain for each other. He then said, 'Why don't you send for her?' I replied, 'In the first place, I have no authority to send for her, and if I had, I have not the means to pay expenses.' To this he answered, 'I give you authority to send for her, and I will furnish you with

means,' which he did. This was the first time the Prophet Joseph talked with me on the subject of plural marriage." From sworn statement of February 16, 1874, in Andrew Jenson, editor, *The Historical Record*, VI (Salt Lake City, 1887), 224.

February 28, 1840

Was called up before six to Brother Batemans wife. She was in labour. She was delivered before I got there. A girl. Prayed with her. Took Breakfast and returned and wrote a letter to Brother Richards.[74] Went to William Millers to Dinner. Sarah Perkins gave me a pint of Porter and some Raisins. Sarah Crooks gave me 1/−. I objected but she would make me have it. Rebecca went a little on the way with me. [− − − −] I went to see Brother Owens. I had heard there was disturbance between him and wife. It was so but I was glad to find that the matter was settled between them. They gave me 1/−. I went to William Millers to C[*ocoa or coffee*] and talked to Sister Ellidge about the judgements.[75] She overherd me talk last night and was troubled and seemed short of faith. I gave scripture testimony for what I had said. I felt to prophecy last night and fully believe that the troubles are very nigh at hand. Went to see Brother Robert Williams. Anointed him and Brother Clark prayed. I prayed with. Brother Green this A.M. He is better a good deal to night. Sister Burgess says that the 2 Missionaries whom we conversed with on Saturday evening—Says that we are two of the worst devils that ever came from hell. They are coming next Wednesday evening to bring a map of America &c. At council meeting, 1 I introduced Brother Lea as a worthy member of the council. Shewed in a few words why we had kept him back &c. The council voted him in &c. 2 Stated Brother Woolstencrofts case and he was voted out of office. I applied the case—to their benifit.[76] 3 George Butterworth and wife at Edgerly disagree. Are to be visited by Brothers Thomas Miller and James Lea on sunday. 4 Brother Berry to Duk-

111

infield and Thomas Miller and Lea to Stockport. 5 Brother
and Sister Booth, Brother Bailey and Brother Mottram dont
attend class meeting. M. Becket will as soon as she gets better
of her health. Brother Featherstone proposed Adam Lee for
a teacher at Stockport. Brother Cope at Peover has got a
licence for his house. Brother Berry agreed to go to Northwich. Brother Featherstone wants the Manchester Saints to
help to pay for Brother Heaths cloths. 3-11. Meeting closed
at 11 [— —].

74. In this letter Clayton expressed his feelings about the opposition which seemed to be dogging the Church, and his statement is
very revealing of the apprehension with which Clayton looked at their
problems: "I feel that it will require no small degree of fortitude and
courage to enable us to stand faithful. We have some mighty opponents and surely Satan is seeking not only to disturb the peace of the
Saints, but to destroy body and spirit also. If my judgment is correct
in these things, we are just beginning to feel the smart. I feel as
though the Saints are about to be afflicted very much. The day of
trouble is at hand, and few indeed will there be who will escape the
affliction. Whilst we are quiet and offer no resistance to our adver-
saries, they will not trouble us much, but as soon as we resolve to
carry on the battle, then we not only feel the shots and arrows, but
the effect also, and a mighty conflict we are engaged in." Clayton to
Willard Richards, Manchester, February 28, 1840, in "British Missions,"
MSS, HDC.
75. He was probably referring to Matthew 24 which concerns the
difficulties that should arise before the second coming of Christ.
See above, February 27, in which Clayton spoke on "tribulations" at a
meeting at the Miller house.
76. He probably means that he admonished them to obedience to
the order of the Church and to the authorities.

February 29, 1840

Breakfast at Hardman's. Got 6 oz. oil and consecrated it.
Went to Crooksoon Street. Anointed and prayed with Brother
Davis. Went to Rigbys to Dinner. From thence to Newton
Water at Sister Booth's. Prayed with Sarah Ann. Called at
Brother Pauls. A little talk with Sarah Stirrup. Prayed with
Brother Burgess's wife and daughter. Went to Brother Bey-
[..], to Brother Browns to Brother Parson's to William
Miller's and Perkins. Supper at Thomas Millers. Brother Green

came to say that Elizabeth Kitley was come from Nottingham to be baptized. Sister Battersby says that Arthur wept yesterday morning because I looked distant and did not say Brother. She say's Catherine Beates has told Betsy Holden that I shall have a similar circumstance to pass through myself. Margaret Jones gave me 2 oranges.

March 1, 1840

Breakfast at Hardman's. Went to Brother Greens to meet Elizabeth Keithly. He did not come. Was tired. From thence to the room. Brother Davies preached about 35 minutes on the doctrine of Christ. I spake after about same time on infant baptism.[77] After meeting had some conversation with a man I think a Wesleyan.[78] He asked could he not be saved without baptism. Was it not awful to teach that one man could be saved by being baptized and another damned for not being. Was it essential to believe in the personal reign of Christ. Did faith always include obedience. I answered his questions and bore testimony and told him he could not be saved unless he was baptised. He said he had searched much of mans works but could get little light of the scriptures. He was in darkness, but had a hope of heaven and with that he would be satisfied. I said if he would obey the gospel he should have the light of God &c. We parted. To Bewshers to Dinner. Brother Davies was there. I talked some time in the P.M on the judgements &c. We ordained Brothers Green and Henry Royle, Elders, and Brother Sands Teacher. Brother James Royle was voted priest but he was not present. 4 was confirmed and Brother Charles Miller's child blessed. 4 sick prayed with. Brother Clark cried with a loud voice and commanded the evil spirit to depart from Sister Mary Warburton. She seemed better immediately. Sister Booth gave me —/6d. 3 baptized. Sarah and Rebecca gave me Cocoa. Rebecca gave me 2 oranges. Sarah gave me 1. Sister Birch gave me 1/—. I preached on the judgement. Prayed with a number sick. Went to see Brother Matthew Clayton. Prayed with him. Supper at Prince's. Sat with Alice and Hannah till 2 o'clock.

77. The doctrines of the LDS Church, of course, are that infants require no baptism and that they are pure and free of the sins of the world. See *Moroni* chapter 8. The Church of England and a number of other churches, on the other hand, practiced infant baptism.

78. An organization founded on the teachings of John Wesley, (1703-1791). By this time, it had become a middle-class organization, much given to sustaining the status quo. Wesley, like Calvin, had emphasized the need to work hard and do well in business. Maldwyn Edwards, *After Wesley: A Study of the Social and Political Influence of Methodism in the Middle Period 1791-1849.* (London: The Epworth Press, 1948), 87-90.

March 2, 1840

Breakfast at Hardman's. Went to see Sister Booth. Better. To Sister Jane Browns—some better. Got a letter from Brother Richards. Prayed with Brother Robert Williams and with Brother Burgess wife and [—]. Went to Brother Pauls. Sister Warburton was jawlocked. Brother Clark cried with a loud voice and rebuked the fowl spirit and immediately her mouth opened. He anointed her and I prayed. Sister Jane Harris says she has been disobedient to Paul. They have not been very comfortable together. She feels to repent and do better. We prayed with her. To Brother Owen's to dinner. I wrote him a letter to his sister in Somersetshire.[79] He gave me 1/—. Saw William Millers wife and family—Sarah Perkins and Brother Browns. Sister Brown says she enquired what time Brother Charles Miller told us about her sickness and says at the same time she began to amend. She says if she had sent a pocket Handkerchief and we had touched it she would have been well &c.[80] To Thomas Millers to water. From there to Prestwich. Alice Hardman with me. Found Brother Amos Fielding there and 2 brethren from Ratcliff. I preached 1-40 on baptism. Attentive audience. Sarah and Rebecca came to the workhouse[81] to meet us. To Thomas Millers to Supper. Home soon after 12.

79. The number of letters which Clayton wrote for Church members is a commentary on the degree of illiteracy among the lower classes in England at this time. Education was an obligation of the factory owners, but some provided schools and some did not. Michael Sanderson, "Education and the Factory in Industrial Lancashire, 1780-1840." *Economic History Review*, Second Series XX (1967), 267-278.

80. Healing by the use of a blessed handkerchief was practiced at times in the early period cf Church history. See Smith, *History of the Church*, IV, 5.

81. An institution for the employment of the indigent.

March 3, 1840

Breakfast at Hardman's. Went to see Brother Burgess wife and child. She has been disobedient. She seems very penitent. She has a cow dung plaster[82] on her breast. We promised her in the name of the Lord that if she felt to repent and begin to live faithful she should receive a blessing. We anointed and prayed with her and [—]. Went to Newton to Sister Booths to Dinner and Water. Sister White and Mary Aspin was there. To Thomas Millers to Pancake. There was too much lightness. I had little to do with it. Sarah Crooks bath my forehead with rum and gave me some mint drops. Sister Booth gave me some raisins. Sarah is anxious to know where to go to lodge. I told her I preferred Rulingtons.

82. Apparently Mrs. Burgess had either a serious infection in her breast, or caked breasts, and the "cow dung plaster" was intended to act as a poultice to draw out the infection. Such therapeutic uses of animal excretement for many ills dates back to ancient times, and was still being practiced in Europe and America even in the late 19th century. It was sometimes prescribed by regular physicians, although it was being frowned on by the early 18th century, but also survived as a common folk remedy. In American folk medicine, for example, soaking the feet in warm water with horse dung added was said to cure chilblain, cow manure was good for various kinds of infections and aches, a "Cow plaster" smeared on the face could remove freckles, and caked breasts could be cured by applying a poultice of cow manure. Theodore Rosebury, *Life on Man* (New York: The Viking Press, 1969), 138-41; Wayton P. Hand, editor, *The Frank C. Brown Collection of North Carolina Folklore* (Durham: Duke University Press, 1961) VI, 128, 143, 183, 187, 194, 197, 213, 224, 227, 231, 232, 302.

Breakfast at Hardman's. Sent a letter which came yesterday to Preston and a pamphlet written in Peover. To Brother Burgess. She is some better. We prayed with her and anointed her again and Maria. To Bewshers to Dinner. Got a letter from Brother Fielding, one from Brother John Moon and 1 from Brother Alfred Craden. Sent one to Brother Alfred. Went to Pollart Street—full house. I preached 1½ hours on baptism. Before I had got properly through one of the town Missions (3 were present) interrupted and threw the meeting into confusion. They disproved nothing but manifested a bad spirit—railing and saying the doctrine was a doctrine of damnation &c.[83] Jordan the writer was present and what he heard made him tremble. He said the devils which was in the cellar are come here. Some I think will be baptized. Supper at Hardman's.

83. Similar experiences of disruption of meetings were noted by other missionaries. Some acquired ministerial licenses in order to be able to use the force of law to resist such disruption. Evans, *A Century of Mormonism*, 52.

March 5, 1840

Went with Brother Clark to the packet[84] for Peover. To Thomas Millers. Breakfast with Betsy Crooks. Wrote a letter to my wife and another for Brother Clark. To D.C.—Smith. Dinner with William Miller. Sarah Crooks gave me orange. Sarah Perkins gave me a pint of Porter. C[ocoa or coffee] at William Millers. Preached at Pendleton—only 1 stranger. Called at Thomas Millers. Supper at Brother Jackson's. Sarah and Rebecca came to Oldham Road.

84. In addition to the River Irwell upon which Manchester was situated, the city had a number of canals which were navigable. The Mersey and Irwell Navigation, built in 1720, allowed passage to Liverpool. The Manchester, Bolton, and Buty canal built in 1791, and the Ashton-under-Line Canal constructed in 1791 allowed passage to Stockport and Fairfield. Rochdale Canal was built in 1794, and the

Grand Trunk Canal connected with the London New Quary Company was built in 1822. Lewis *Topographical Dictionary*, III, 242.

March 6, 1840

Breakfast at Hardman's. Went to see Sister Burgess. Prayed with her and anointed her breast. Prayed with Maria. Prayed with Robert Williams. Went to Sister Catherine Beates to dinner. [*sixteen lines crossed out and illegible*] She also saw in a dream. Brother Richards and Robert Williams and one of Hardmans Sons and old Richard Hardman sitting in a room together. Brother Richards seemed sick and in trouble. The room opened above their heads and she saw 12 small children dressed in white. One of them was Brother Richards child. She knew it. It came down and sat on his shoulder and bending down looked in his face. The scene closed. She says Brother Richards will not live long.[85] He is expecting a many things but in some he will be disappointed. She says she foresaw all that has taken place concerning Arthur Smith. And she prophecies bad concerning Sister Mary Wytch &c. Took tea with her. Called at Hardman's. Brother John Moon is come. Went to have conversation with Sister Mary Aspen's Sister and brotherinlaw. He is a unitarian. I proved to him that Christ was a divine being—God—&c. and preached the gospel to him. He seemed to believe. Will consider of it. Called at Thomas Millers. Took supper. Mary Aspin gave me some ascive drops.[86] Sarah and Rebecca has been at Rulingtons but they cannot take them in yet. Sarah is much troubled. She says Susan keeps hinting that she is tired of them. She cannot bear it. Gave me some raisins.

85. Richards died on March 11, 1854, at the age of 49.

86. Probably asafetida, derived from the gum resin of various Oriental plants, and occurring in the form of tear drops and dark-colored masses. It has a strong odor and taste and was formerly used as an antispasmodic. On occasion, the drug was carried in a bag around the neck to ward off diseases.

March 7, 1840

[*One line crossed out*] Went to see Sister Burgess. Anointed and prayed with her and Maria. Went to Cookson Street. Prayed with and anointed Sister Jones, Rigby's 2 children and Brother Davies. Prayed with Brother Walkers son. Dinner at Walkers. Talked to Brother Davies on the divinity of Christ. Sister Catherine Beates gave me new pocket Handkerchief. To Prince's to C[*ocoa or coffee*]. Went to Coach office for Brother John Moon's Box. Paid 1-8 for it. Received a pie from Sister Mary Miller. A letter from Brother Alfred Corden. To Thomas Millers to Supper. While here I recollected a dream which I had a few nights before. I thought I was shooting and a number of men with me. I thought some who charged lightly killed almost every shot. I charged heavy. Shook almost everything around me but stunned the bird did not kill it. Sarah and Rebecca are in trouble. They cannot go to P's. They came up with me to Sister Hardman's and engaged to come next week end.[87] They tarried till 12 o'clock. Margaret Jones gave me 2 oranges.

87. From the context, it appears that they were having difficulty finding a place to live. See above, March 6.

March 8, 1840

Sister Burgess came. Her breast is very bad. I prayed with her. Went to Prince's to Breakfast. Brother John Moon spake a while then I spoke a while in P.M. I opened meeting. Brother John spoke a little. I ordained Isaac Royle and Charles Miller Priests, Brother John Gill and James Johnson Teachers. 3 confirmed, 3 baptized by Charles Miller. Went to Kenworthy's to tea. At night Brother Moon preached on faith &c. Prayed with many sick. Sister Battersby gave me some grapes. William Whitehead gave me 1/—. After meeting went to Brother Bateman's to see Sister Street. Sarah and

Rebecca went with me. Sarah gave me 2 oranges. Brother Bewsher gave me a stick of sealing Wax. Supper at Hardman's. Used great liberty towards Alice Hardman.[88]

88. This is a rather strange and cryptic statement for Clayton to use in view of his writings about the need to control his feelings. (See February 27) It is possible that he simply means that he joked in a very familiar way with Alice Hardman. From other entries it is clear that Clayton was close to her, and after emigrating to America she became one of his plural wives. This entry may also mean that he expressed some personal feelings to her at this time.

March 9, 1840

Breakfast at Hardman's. Wrote a letter to Brother Fielding. Went to see Sister Burgess. Very bad. Prayed with her and daughter. Prayed with Mary Ann Johnson and Robert Williams. Thomas Millers to Dinner [*one line crossed out*]. Went with John Moon to Railway. Called at Paul Harris'. Prayed with him and child and Sarah Isherwood. Mary Warburton strives to hide her pipe &c.[89] Last week Sister Betsy Crooks bought a fur collar for my cloak and on Saturday put it on. Sisters Poole and Jones has left Thomas Millers this A.M. Gone to Richard Hardmans. Brother Henry Royle baptised 3 at Dukinfield yesterday. 1 baptized at Stockport. Water at Thomas Millers. Went to Pendlebury to preach on the resurrection. After preaching a socialist proposed some questions. I answered him—till he was almost speechless. He showed a mild temper &c. After I had conversation with a professor. She was very stubborn woud not believe baptism would do her any good.[90] Took Supper returned 11½.

89. Apparently she was trying to conceal the fact that she was not obeying the Word of Wisdom.

90. Latter-day Saints, of course, believe in the absolute necessity of baptism to reach the highest degree of salvation or exaltation. This view is based upon Jesus' statement that a man must be born of the water and the spirit to enter into the Kingdom of Heaven, and also his example of being baptized, "to fulfill all righteousness." John 3:5, Matthew 3:13-15.

March 10, 1840

Breakfast at Hardman's. Saw Sister Burgess. Some better. Prayed with her and daughter and Robert Williams and Richard Hardmans child. To Thomas Mayors to dinner. Went to see Sister Booth. Very ill. Prayed with her. To H's Street. Sister Smith sick. I told about circulating reports. She denies all except telling Isaac Royle and Brother Bateman that Brother Greens had the Itch. Isaac was intending to sleep their had she not told him. Prayed with her. To Brother Batemans. Prayed with Sister Street and a knee and hand. Went to Eccles.[91] Preached the gospel to a full house. Had a few words with a Wesleyan. He said Paul was not sent to baptize. I prayed with the woman of the house. She was sick. Took Water at Sister Williamsons. Supper at Hardman's. Got home at 11. Received a letter from Sister Ravenscroft.

91. Eccles is a parish four miles west of Manchester with a population in 1841 of 33,792 inhabitants. It is on the principal railroad and canal transportation leading west. The mining of coal employs a large part of the population, and cotton weaving and spinning and the manufacture of other textiles are also important industries. Lewis, *Topographical Dictionary*, II, 137-38.

March 11, 1840

Breakfast at Hardman's. To Brother Bewshers to Dinner. Brother Bewsher gave me a new pair of kid leather gloves. Went to see Sister Gill. Prayed and administered sacrement to B. to C. Sent Brother Charles Miller to preach and I went to baptize William Green. Supper at Thomas Miller's. Some lightness.

March 12, 1840[92]

Breakfast at Hardman's. Received a letter from Brother Fielding. Sent one to my wife. Went to Smiths for Timely warnings. To William Millers to dinner. To Sarah Perkins to water. Went to Leighs in Salford. Preached to him near 1 hour. He sent for an old woman named Campon. She was very stubborn and prejudiced. She said I was one of the false prophets. Leigh and wife seems to believe. Sister Mary Aspen offered me a soverein to buy a polyglot Bible.[93] But I refused to take it. She pressed much. Supper at Leighs. Sarah Crooks gave me some raisins. Mary Aspen gave me 2 oranges.

92. On July 2, 1840, Wilford Woodruff recorded in his journal an event that was said to have happened on March 12, but which Clayton never mentioned in his journal. This was a vision which Ann Booth told of having, and which Woodruff thought so remarkable that he had Mrs. Booth dictate it to him so that he could record it in his journal. The vision concerned the idea of redemption of the dead. Mrs. Booth said she saw an American apostle preaching to the spirits in prison, and then beginning to baptize them. John Wesley was among them, and after the apostle baptized him and ordained him to the priesthood he began to baptize others. While LDS doctrine of salvation for the dead does not suggest that the dead themselves are to be baptized in the spirit world, the general idea of this vision is much like the doctrine. It is interesting to note, however, that Joseph Smith did not publicly preach the doctrine until he gave a funeral sermon for Seymor Brunson, who died on August 10, 1840. He first officially informed the apostles of it in a letter of October 10. While a direct connection between Ann Booth's vision and Joseph Smith's first preaching of the doctrine cannot be established, it is worth conjecturing that Joseph may have been stimulated in his thoughts partly by some correspondence from Wilford Woodruff. Woodruff, "Journal," July 2, 1840; Smith, *History of the Church*, IV, 231; Andrew Jenson, *Latter-day Saint Biographical Encyclopedia* (4 vols.; Salt Lake City: Deseret News Press, 1901-1936), III, 331.

93. A polyglot Bible contains the text of the scriptures in several languages.

March 13, 1840

Breakfast at Hardman's. Found 4/— amongst the raisins. Was sent for to Princes. E. Dewsnup keeps bad hours. Burgess family improving. Sister Booth better. Went to Newton[94] Dinner and Water. Sister Booth and Brother Whitehead gave me 2 oranges each. Prayed with Sister Booth and read her Brother Fielding's words in his letter. Conversed with 2 females and they promised to be baptized tonight. Brought a dress to Sister Burgess. Went to see for Brother Henry Royle to bap-

tize. Could not find him. But Brother Green is gone. Sister
Sands gave me ½ a quire of papers. Agreed that Brother John
Gill should take charge of Hart Street Meeting, Brother Sands
Bank Street, Brother Thomas Miller Cornet Street, Brother
Lea Newton—the priest &c. to visit the members who cannot
attend the room on a Sunday and administer sacrement.
Brother Charles Miller to assist the Deacon. I read the offi-
cers their duty and exhorted a little. Supper at Brother
Greens. Brother Green only baptized one. Thomas Miller
gave me 1/—. I wrote a letter to Sarah Perkins. One to E.
Dewsnup. 1 to Mr. Williams London. Some trouble between
Sisters Green and Gilford and Battersby. Sister Battersby
is very low. Brother Gill gave me a pence cash.

94. A suburb northeast of Manchester. Lewis, *Topographical Dictionary*, atlas.

March 14, 1840

Breakfast at Hardman's. Sister Poole says that Ellen Battersby intends to go to her mother's. Sister Galeford complains
that B. does not do enough for G. Yet she has pawned nearly
all her cloths for them even to her Sunday dress. Got a
letter from Brother David Wilding. He says he had to sell
some of the goods out of the house to pay me that 7/— referred Feb. 14. I have given Alice Hardman 3/— to give him
back together with 50 Timely W[arnings] which he may
have the benifit. I find at Cookson Street that there is a hard
feeling against Brother Davies. Brother West says they want
another leader or else must they go to another meeting. He
says Brother Davies hints that it is their duty to support him
and is grieving the Saints minds every week. He has not said
that it is himself that he wants them to believe but says the
poor in their own class—&c. Brother West is quite bad tem-
pered over it. Seems to manifest a bad spirit trembled with
hard feelings. Sister Black and West and Walker and Rigby

quite grieved. They state that Brother Davies had said something about meeting together so much and they only meet to read the scriptures. When I had seen them all and learned all the grievances I went to Brother Davies and asked how was the meeting attended. He said very well. Not many strangers. How did the saints appear. Very comfortable. What had he been teaching of late?. On Thursday night he was speaking about the members relieving each other &c. Brother Walker had given ½ load of potatoes to Brother Barlow who lived in the country and poor old Joseph West had scarcely bread sufficient to eat and this was why he said so. I saw at once that Brother Davies had been speaking for Brother Joseph and it had been universally understood that he was hinting at his own case and Joseph said to me that there was members in the street as bad off as they (Davies) were. I then went and explained it to them all and the prejudice began to abate and they looked more cheerful. I last went to see Joseph but he would hardly speak to me. Was quite overcome with bad feelings but I begged he would be patient and I would give him some evidence that he was mistook. He would hardly listen but I showed him what passed and he began to see into it and he presently looked more cheerful but it was with difficulty that I could persuade him that it was a mistake. I trust things are comfortably settled. Came home with Brother Green and Lea to N[......] St. Brother Green was in a little difficulty concerning his club. I gave him 1d/ to set him at liberty. He is troubled about the disease which is troubling the family. I told him I thought there was something wrong and I intended to find out if possible. I told him about Sister Battersby's cloths being pawned &c. I anointed him and prayed with him and advised him to go and pray with his family. We anointed inwardly and prayed with Sister Jane Brown who was troubled with [—]. I finished writing a letter to Brother Dunns Father and then brothers Garner and Bowman came and tarried after 10 o'clock. Betsy Crooks gave me some figs. Sarah Crooks and Rebecca Partington are come to live at Hardmans. I should have gone to Richard Hardmans to see the child but did not get away. Supper at Hardman's. Sarah and Rebecca seem low.

March 15, 1840

Breakfast with Sarah and Rebecca. Preached this A.M about 1¼ on Isaiah Chapter 40.[95] To Bewshers to Dinner. Gave me 2 oranges and pint of Porter. Spoke a while in the P.M. Confirmed 3 and Brother Thomas Miller baptized 3. Christiana Crooks gave me 2 oranges and 1/—. Sarah Crooks 2 oranges. Margaret Jones 2. Sister Birch gave me 1/—. Preached at night on Isaiah 24-5,6[96] and made some remarks on a pamphlet. 1 baptized after another gave in his name for thursday night. Charlotte Grundy gave me a apple from Derbyshire. James Mahon gave me /6. Went to Prince's and found the devil busy around them. The family finds fault with Sister Dewsnup. Elizabeth called her a little wasp—a bad dispositioned girl and many other things. Elizabeth says she will never come near the church again. I did not say much to them. I thought it would be best for them to leave &c. Took C[ocoa or coffee] with Sarah and Rebecca. Supper at Prince's. Prayed with many sick.

95. He probably spoke of the coming of Christ. Verse three reads: "The voice of him that crieth in the wilderness, Prepare ye the way of the Lord, make straight in the desert a highway for our God."

96. "The earth also is defiled under the inhabitants thereof; because they have transgressed the laws, changed the ordinance, broken the everlasting covenant. Therefore hath the curse devoured the earth, and they that dwell therein are desolate: therefore the inhabitants of the earth are burned, and few men are left."
This scripture is often used by Mormon missionaries to indicate that God foresaw an apostasy from the ancient Church of Christ.

March 16, 1840

Breakfast at Hardman's. Received a letter from Brother Woodruff. He has baptized 32 in 6 days.[97] Been to see Paul Harris—sick. Got a letter from my wife. Sent a letter to Brother Fielding. 5 was baptized at Stockport yesterday. E. Booth says that those whom Brother David baptized at Bury are nearly all turned against. J. Loffe whom he lodged with reported that David was £10 in his debt. David went to ask him about it and took a man with him (not a saint). He asked for a correct statement of what he owed him. He reckoned for 3 weeks at 8/— per week 24/—. David said he had only been 17 days from the first and 3 of them 17 he spent in Manchester . The man then made out a bill for 2 weeks 1d6/—. The man who went with David paid down the money. He confirmed 8 yesterday. Water at Sarah Perkins. Prayed with Sarah and little C. Miller. Went to Narrow lane 1 mile beyond Prestwich. Preached on Revelations 20-1 to 6.[98] Full house. 1 gave his name. Several believing. Supper at preaching house. Got home at 11 o clock. Rebecca gave me some egg milk.

97. Woodruff wrote to Clayton on March 9, 1840. But this time, Woodruff had left Staffordshire and gone to Herefordshire. There he found a group which had broken away from the Wesleyan Methodists who called themselves the United Brethren. In the next few weeks, he succeeded in converting and baptizing practically all of the members of the United Brethren, including their ministers. Cowley, *Woodruff*, 116-19; Wilford Woodruff, "Journal," HDC.

98. Mormons believe that this scripture refers to the millenium, during which Satan will be bound for a thousand years and Christ will reign upon the earth. Those who have been righteous will be resurrected to meet him and reign with him. Others are to wait until after the millenium to be resurrected.

March 17, 1840

Breakfast at Hardman's. Received a letter from Brother Heath and one from Mr. R Williams stating that he had previously sent two pounds which I had not received. The letter was an order for 2 pounds which I got but could hear nothing of the other two. I sent him another letter. Dinner at Charlotte

Grundy's. She gave me 1/—. Went to see Brother Burgess Very sick. To cross. Saw Sister Williamsons to Water. From thence to Eccles in company with Elizabeth Prince. Brother's Jackson, Bowman and Walker and another gentleman took a crowded house and good attention. A few words of opposition from a professor. Home about 11. Supper at Hardmans. Brother Henry Royle baptized 1 at Dukinfield on Sunday.

March 18, 1840
Breakfast at Hardmans. Robert Williams sent me 2/6. I would have refused it but must take it. A letter from Brother Richards. Brother Green baptized 4 at Stockport last night. He brought a letter from Jane Miller. Went to pray with Brother Burgess. To Brother Bewshers to dinner. Sister Bewsher gave me 2/6. Had conversation with one of the Plymouth brethren.[99] He seemed kind and promised to have another interview. Went to Brother Gills. Took C[*ocoa or coffee*]. To Brother Booths. His wife was sick. Sent a letter to Brother Heath. Brother Lea gone to baptize 1. I went to Brother Green. Found a little hard feelings between Sisters Battersby and Galeford. Sister Galeford could not see that she had done wrong but said she would mind better. Sisters Green and Battersby wept much but seemed better satisfied. Ellen Battersby gave me a pint of porter and cheese and bread. Prayed with all the family. Rebecca Partington gave me some egg milk.

99. This movement began in 1827 and spread under the direction of Edward Cronin, Anthony Norris Groves, John Gilfford Bellett, Francis Hutchinson, John V. Parnell and John Nelson Darby. They preached the idea of the atonement of Christ, the resurrection, His intercession for man, and the Second Coming. The organization was democratic and congregational. James Hastings, editor, *Encyclopedia of Religion and Ethics* (14 vols.; New York: Charles Scribner's Sons, 1951), II, 843-48.

March 19, 1840
Breakfast at Hardmans. Went to Brother John Smiths. They

are not for leaving the house at present. Prayed with sisters. Received 1 letter from Mr. R Williams and 1 from Brother Fielding. Sister Booth some better. L. Isherwood just going to Yorkshire to see her friends. To Sister Booths Newton to Dinner. She gave me 2 oranges & −/6. Sister Mary Whitehead gave me −/5. Prayed with Sister Booth. To Thomas Millers. Prayed with and a Brother Green. Had a few words with Sister Dewsnup. She will not acknowledge that she has done wrong. I said I believed there was faults on both sides. She wept much. I advised her to go and see her parents and ask for work and if they could not find her any but desired her to go home I persuaded her to do so. Water at Thomas Millers. Sister Sarah Perkins gave me a bag for my little Sarah. Went to the post office to enquire after Robert Williams letter but could hear nothing of it. Told Robert about it and he seemed much troubled and wanted me to write immediately for more money. I said I would rather wait a while lest his father should be vexed. After I went out he began to murmur and John Hardman said it was like robbery &c. to expect more so soon. Robert gave way and rose up as if to strike John but fainted back in the chair. They came for me and I found them apparently full of the spirit of the devil. I cautioned Robert and told him if he did not be patient and humble he would die. He wept aloud. I advised him to go to bed after cautioning. Baptized 2. Supper with Rebecca. Thomas Miller gave me a crown for Brother Richards. Sarah Crooks gave me 1/− and 2/− for Betsy. Bought 1¼ tablespoons of oil for 1/6 ½ and bottle −/3. Brother Cordon returned from Peover.

March 20, 1840
Breakfast at Prince's. Ann Jackson gave me some sweets for Sarah. Sister Rigby gave me 1/6 Sister Walker 1/−. Dinner

with Sarah and Rebecca. Rebecca gave 1/6. Sarah gave me 2 oranges and Sarah gave me 10/—, towards a new pair of Boots. I was resolved not to have it. She has done so much for me but she persisted and I must take it. I received a letter also which she had wrote. Brother Thomas Mayer gave me 1/—. Sister Poole would have done to but I would not take it. We went and prayed with Burgess' family. Took the Railway at 2¼ and got home[100] about 5 o clock. Found the children rather poorly. Wife and rest of the family well. They rejoiced to see me. Dinner at home.

100. That is, to Penwortham.

March 21, 1840

Breakfast at Home. Sent 5/— to Brother Richards by John Moon. Writ 5 letters 1 to Jane Millward. Castle St. Rosen Ireland 1 to Brother Woodruff. 1 to Sister Ravenscroft. 1 to Sister Crooks and 1 to Sister Alice Hardman.

March 22, 1840

Went to Cock Pit.[101] Miles Hodgson preached. Dinner at Brother Partington's. Brother Richards occupied the P.M. I preached at night on Isaiah 46.[102] Preached 1½ hour. Full house and very attentive. 3 confirmed.

101. This building had been erected about 1801 by Lord Derby and was originally used for cock fights. It was located near the center of Preston close to the market place. Seats were arranged in a circle rising up from the floor. This was also the official meeting place of the Preston Temperance Society, which had apparently helped the Church to procure the hall. Meetings had been held there by the Church continuously since September 3, 1837. Evans, *A Century of Mormonism*, 45.
102. Possibly the sermon was on the need to worship God only and not to worship false gods. The scripture deals with this subject.

March 23, 1840

At home all day. [......]ing dogs &c.

March 24, 1840

Went to Preston. Dinner at Sister Morgans. Sister Crees gave me −/6. Spent the P M with Brother Richards. Have heard that there is some contention in the church at Blackburn.[103] At home at meeting. Spake a little while on the importance of being ready &c. E. Martin gave me 1/−.

103. Blackburn is a cotton manufacturing town located about 10 miles east of Preston. Lewis, *Topographical Dictionary*, I, 270-72.

March 25, 1840

Went to Eccleston to Sister Alice Moons Sale. They had fixed upon me to write for them. We commenced at 2 o'clock and I finished writing after 11. Dinner and supper at Moon's. The Auctioneer gave me 2/−, for copying list &c. Got home at 2 o'clock.

March 26, 1840

Brother Richards has been here this P.M. Brote me a letter from Burslem stating that Brother Turley was in prison.[104] I preached at night at Cuerden Factory. Full house. Isaiah 24-5,6. Nancy Riley gave me 1/−.

104. Turley had been confined in prison at Stafford since March 16, and was to remain so confined until May 8. Theodore Turley, "Journal of Theodore Turley," MSS, Special Collections, Brigham Young University Library.

March 27, 1840

Brother Hugh Moon gave me 2/− for timely warnings. He asked what I should charge for writing at sale. I said I should make no charge so he said no more about it. But seemed satisfied. I started at 2½ per Railway from Farrington and arrived at Manchester at 4½. Took Water at Hardmans. Saw Brother Clark. Found Sisters Alice and Hannah very low. David Wilding has grieved Alice with something. Went to council meeting. Nothing particular. 5 has been baptized at

Stockport since I left. Brother David Wilding says that Brother Green's family has the Itch. I sent a letter to Brother Fielding to know what to do &c. Sarah and Rebecca gave me supper. Sarah washed my head with rum.

March 28, 1840
Breakfast at Hardman's. Bought a new pair of Boots for 18/—. Went to Pendleton. Dinner at Sister Williamson's. Went to Brother Jennings. Met him on the road. He said his wife had not been fairly. Brother Jackson had not acted scripturally. I asked how. He answered the scriptures say if thy Brother sin against thee tell him his fault alone &c. Yes I said but a public transgression required a public acknowledgement. He said he could not find it in scrip. I answered Paul says them that sin rebuke before all that others also may fear &c.[105] He seemed rather stubborn and hard against Brother Jackson. His wife has been drunk and calling in the street in a very disgraceful manner. She had said to the effect that the LDS were L.D. devils &c. Brother Jackson wanted to cover it up and was not willing that his wife should make acknowledgement to the church. I went forward to see Sister Jackson and when I had been in a little while Brother Jackson came in. She seemed quite bitter against him because he had exposed her before the church and told all the subject in plain words. I reasoned considerable with her and she seemed to grow milder. She said she had never had so much of the spirit since she joined the church as she had when among the ranters &c.[106]   I had a good deal of talk with her and Sister Jackson. They are in a poor state. I afterwards told Brother Jackson I thought he was to rash with the saints &c. Prayed with Sister Jackson's son and returned home. Water with Sarah and Rebecca. Bought a Satin Stock for 3/6. Went to see Eliza Prince. Prayed with several at

night and after was taken very poorly. Margaret Jones gave me 2 oranges. 4 has been baptized at Dukinfield since the 24.

105. "Them that sin rebuke before all, that others also may fear." I Timothy, 5:20.

106. "The Ranters constituted the somewhat chaotic 'left wing' of a serious attempt to work out in England in the 17th century a type of Christianity conformed to apostolic, primitive Christianity, free from what the leaders of this movement called 'the apostasy,' and loosely enough conjoined and organized to allow very wide individual liberty of thought and action." Hastings, *Encyclopedia of Religion*, X, 578-579. This belief in the apostasy and the need for a restoration of primitive Christianity was similar to Mormon doctrine, and therefore may have been one reason why some people, such as Sister Jennings, were attracted to Mormonism. They were already familiar with some Mormon ideas.

March 29, 1840

Breakfast at Sarah and Rebeccas. Went to Stockport. Sarah and Rebecca went with me. [*four lines crossed out*] Brother Green preached. Dinner at Brother Stafford. In the P.M we confirmed 11 and I ordained Brother Adam Lea, Priest, Thomas Howarth, Teacher; and James Hawkins Teacher; I preached upwards of 1 hour in the evening on John 10-1 to 8. Sarah gave me 2 oranges and another sister 1. Got home at 11 in the P.M. Robert Crooks stood up previous to confirmation to shew why he suffered himself to be cut off and how he had felt since. He said he was sincere and believed it was false—through reading a tract against the Book of Mormon. He had prayed much that he might be right. But never could get peace not even as much as before he joined the church. He prayed that the Lord would let him die sooner than let him go astray &c. He was standing by the fire one night lately and was suddenly taken very ill almost lost the use of his limbs. He prayed and said if the Lord would raise him again he would go and be baptized. He found immediate relief and his former peace returned to him. He rejoiced and soon got better. He says if this church is not right there is none right in the world. He feels to love all the saints and wherever he sees them he rejoices. Those Elders which he railed the most against he feels to love the most &c. He spake to me but said he felt ashamed to do so. He seems very humble and comfortable with Sarah. He has had a deal of hard feelings against her. But all seems to be gone. After all I feel to have little hopes that he will hold out to the end. I believe he will again turn against us and be cut off &c. [*seventeen lines crossed out*].

March 30, 1840
Rebecca brought me raw egg in some red wine. Went to Thomas Millers to Dinner. Received a letter from Brother Fielding and one from Brother Woodruff. Sent one to Brother Alfred Cordon. Water at Hardmans. Went to Prestwich on Narrow lane. Preached on Revelations 14.6.[107] Several are ready to be baptized. Sarah at the preaching house. Eliza Prince and Ann Jackson came to meet us and walked behind. Eliza seemed to be in a fret. Betsy Crooks and Dewsnup went with me. 6 baptized at Dukinfield yesterday, 5 at Manchester. My feet were very sore to night. Sarah washed them and gave me a pint of warm Porter. I lent her Book of Doctrine and Covenants.

107. "And I saw another angel fly in the midst of heaven, having the everlasting gospel to preach unto them that dwell on the earth, and to every nation, and kindred, and tongue, and people." This scripture is used by Mormon missionaries as evidence of prophesy that a restoration of the gospel would be necessary. The *Book of Mormon* was the fulfillment of that prophesy, since, according to Mormon belief, it was delivered to Joseph Smith by an angel.

March 31, 1840
Breakfast at Hardman's and Dinner with Sarah and Rebecca. Went to Cookson Street. Brother Clark is gone to Macclesfield. I went to Sister Williamsons to Water and thence to Eccles.

Preached on Isaiah 24-5,6—attentive house. Got home about 11. To night Jones' Machine shop was burned to the ground. Supper with Sarah. She was waiting for me. Brother Jackson gave 1/−.

April 1, 1840

Breakfast at Hardman's. Rebecca and Alice very poorly. Went to see a lame lad. Prayed with and anointed his leg. Prayed with Brother Burgess and family and Alice. To Bewsher's to Dinner. Brother Bewsher gave me more than a pint of Porter. Betsy Crooks left me some figs. Got a letter from Brother Richards and one from Brother Heath. Went to see Sister Heath. Water with Rebecca. From thence per Railway to Patricroft[108] and to MS. Preached at Row Green to a very full house after—a Ranters travelling opposed. Nothing very particular. Preached the gospel. He said children were born in sin &c. Walked home very quick about 7 or 8 miles. Mother and Sarah[109] was waiting. Supper with Sarah. She washed my feet. She had a dream last night something like this—she thought a man brought a young man before her and said he was to be her companion. When I had told her was not true &c about eternity and he said we were of different dispositions. She was troubled and thought in her own mind she would not be in a hurry &c. [*five and one-half lines crossed out*] She gave me a new pair of slender shoes. Christiana gave me raisins.

108. Patricroft is a village about five miles west of Manchester noted for its manufacture of iron and steel. Lewis, *Topographical Dictionary*, III, 538.
109. He probably means, mother Hardman, or "old sister Hardman," not his own mother. See above, note 23. The Sarah is Sarah Crooks.

April 2, 1840

Breakfast with Rebecca. Got a letter from Brother Woodruff.

Sent 1 to my wife and one to Mr. Williams. Dinner at William Millers. Sarah Perkins gave me some raisins. C[*ocoa or coffee*] at William Millers. Prayed with S. and Charles. Supper with Sarah and Rebecca. Catherine Beates gave me fruit on Wednesday.

April 3, 1840

Breakfast at Hardman's. Have seen Brother Booth and told him respecting pledging his bible. He denies it. I warned about other things which I had heard going from house to house—abusing his wife idling &c. Dinner at Sister Booth's Newton. She gave me 3 oranges and 6 pence. Sarah Ann 1 orange. I have had some conversation with Sister Margaret Townsend. She is quite calvanistic[110] in sentiment. Will not hear of keeping all the commandments. Says I was going to Sinai &c. I read several passages and told her those opinions would be her ruin if she did not repent. She said I had no charity. She could not do with me. I should have to repent &c. I was like the Pope and many such things. She said we might cut her off. She told me I had a bad spirit. My blood boiled when she began to talk to me &c. Dinner and Coffee at Sister Booth's. Sister Mary Aspen gave me £1 *for a Bible* and some raisins. Bought a Bible and Crudens concordance[111] for 25/−. Betsy Crooks gave me an orange and Christiana gave me 1 and some mint cake. Brother Henry Royle baptized 3 at Dukinfield on the 1st. Supper with Sarah Crooks.

110. Clayton is referring to the doctrines of John Calvin, who taught pre-destination, the depravity of man, and salvation by grace alone, all of which are antagonistic to Mormon doctrine.

111. This concordance is the work of Alexander Cruden, a Presbyterian (1701-1770). Three editions of the concordance were issued during Cruden's life (1736, 1761 and 1769). Leslie Stephen & Sidney Lee, eds., *The Dictionary of National Biography*, (22 vols.; Oxford: Oxford University Press, 1960), V, 249-51.

April 4, 1840

Went to pray with Brother Davies child. To Catherine Beates to Breakfast and Dinner. Sister Catherine says her mission is nearly done in England. She thinks of going to America &c. Saw Brother Bowman and Green &c. Brother Fielding came in from Liverpool about 10. Supper with Sarah. Margaret Jones gave me 2 oranges. Betsy Crooks some drops. Rebekah is grieved at something.

April 5, 1840

Breakfast with Sarah and Rebecca. I preached on prayer and worship. Dinner at Brother Bewsher's. Gave us some Porter. Brother Fielding spake in the P M and evening on revelation.[112] Rebekah was not at the room in the P.M. Brother Green baptized 1 in the morning. I baptized 1 at night. 5 baptized at Stockport. Supper with Sarah.

112. Probably on the principle of continuous revelation, which is extremely important in Mormon theology.

April 6, 1840

Breakfast at Hardman's. Sent a letter to David Wilding. Dinner at Thomas Millers. Brother Fielding has been very sick. Water at Thomas Millers. Went to Pendlebury. Preached near an hour on the destruction of the gentiles &c. Got home at 11 o'clock. Supper with Sarah and Rebecca. They gave me a pint of Porter. Sarah washed my feet.

April 7, 1840

Breakfast at Hardmans. Got a letter from Brother Richards. Sent a letter to Alfred Cordon. Dinner with Sarah and Rebecca. Had some conversation with Sarah. It seems that the saints generally appear to envy her and feel a little jealous for some cause which they will not make known. Rebecca has seemed very much grieved at her, but

I think she is mending of it. [*twenty-one lines crossed out*]
I went with Brother Alston to Garner's and thence to the Post
office. Came home for oil and went to see the lame boy in
Islington.[113] Thence to Brother Bateman's to water. Brother
Fielding went to Eccles and I to Cookson Street. Brother Lea
preached and I said a little after. One woman ready for baptism. Supper with Sarah.

113. Lewis, *Topographical Dictionary* lists two Islington's, one
near Norfolk and one near London. Obviously neither of these is the
one to which Clayton went. This must, therefore, be either a section of
Manchester, a suburb of Manchester, or a street in or around Manchester.

April 8, 1840

Breakfast at Thomas Mayors. Wrote a letter to Brother Richards. Met Brother Fielding at Bewsher's to Dinner. Elizabeth
Mayor seems somewhat careless. She says the saints don't love
her. She has observed a great difference since her mother
died &c. Brother Bewsher gave us some Porter. Went to see
Sister Birch. She gave me an orange. To Brother Bewshers to
C[*ocoa or coffee*]. From thence I went to Worsely[114] and
preached on Revelations 20.[115] Was opposed by a Methodist,
Daniel Bradshaw. Took something to eat with Mary. She gave
me a glass of Porter. I got to Manchester about 11 o'clock
—nearly through. Sarah had some egg milk ready and she
washed my feet and I then went to bed.

114. Worsley is a town seven miles northwest of Manchester with
8337 inhabitants in 1841. It is known for its production of coal of good
coking quality, and cotton manufacture. Lewis, *Topographical Dictionary*, IV, 688.
115. Revelations 20 deals with the last judgment, the resurrection
of the dead, and the millenium, all themes that Clayton seemed to
treat regularly.

April 9, 1840

This morning Rebecca brought some red wine and a raw
egg in it. She also gave me 2 oranges. Breakfast at Hardman's.

Received a letter for Brother Fielding stating that Brother Kimball and 5 others were in Preston. They landed in Liverpool on Monday and left Parley P. Pratt at Liverpool with Brother Taylor.[116] Dinner at William Miller's. William gave me 2/6 for Brother Turly.[117] Went with Brother Fielding to the Railway from thence to Sister Bewshers to Tea. Saw Sister Plant. She expects they are about to move into Derbyshire. Went to Princes to Supper.

116. This was in connection with the important mission of the Twelve to England. On April 6, 1840, Brigham Young, Parley P. Pratt, Orson Pratt, Heber C. Kimball, George A. Smith, and Reuben Hedlock landed in Liverpool. "The ship being loaded with flour and cotton, they were packed in a small compartment with about 100 or 120 passengers, being a motley mixture of English ,Welsh, Irish, and Scotch, who were returning from America to visit their friends, or had got sick of 'Yankeedom' and were leaving for 'sweet home.' On April 8, they went to Preston by railroad, and found a multitude of Saints who rejoiced at our arrival and made us welcome." Brigham Young was so emaciated from his journey and sickness that Willard Richards did not recognize him. Young also wrote Wilford Woodruff to come to Preston and hold a conference with the Twelve who were there. Brigham Young and Heber C. Kimball had left Montrose, Iowa on September 14, 1839, with Young so sick he was "unable to go thirty rods to the river without assistance." Parley P. Pratt, Orson Pratt and Hiram Clark had left Nauvoo on August 29, 1839. Pratt lived with his family in New York until the others came. They took steerage passage to England from New York on March 9, 1840, on the *Patrick Henry* of the Black Ball line. Each paid $18 for steerage passage, and the Saints of New York furnished pillows, straw beds, and some blankets. Woodruff, Taylor, Clark and Turley had, of course, preceded them. The experience of these men in England was highly important for the Church's later development. They were to be the principal leaders of the Church of Jesus Christ of Latter-day Saints following the murder of Joseph Smith and to be principally responsible for the westward migration. Their work in England helped stimulate the tremendous growth of Church membership in that country and a subsequent huge migration to America. Brigham Young, *Manuscript History,* 50, 69-70; Parley P. Pratt, *Autobiography of Parley Parker Pratt,* editor. Parley P. Pratt, Jr. (7th ed.; Salt Lake City: Deseret Book Company, 1968), 294-300; Smith, *History of the Church,* IV. 102-03; Smith, "Journal," *Instructor* LXXXII, 320.
117. Turley was still in prison.

April 10, 1840

Breakfast at Hardman's. Received a letter from Brother Fielding. 1 from Alfred Cardon. 1 from Mr. Williams. Went to see Benson's boy. Called at Cookson Street. Dinner with Sarah and Rebecca. To Brother Thomas Owens. He and wife have been quarelling again. The boy is very disobedient. Brother Owens says he had better be cut off. His wife is upstairs but does not seem inclined to come down. Brother Owens gave me 1/—. Water at Hardman's. To council meeting appointments supplied &c. Lectured on faithfulness and true to each other. Supper with Sister Ellen Battersby. She gave me a pint of Porter. She is much troubled about the Itch &c. B[etsy] Crooks gave me some raisins.

April 11, 1840
Breakfast at Hardman's. Went to Bank and received 25/— for Robert Williams. Saw Sister Catherine Beates at Paul Harris's. She was very ill. She has brought me another fruit. Received a letter from Brother Woodruff. 1 from David Wilding. 1 from Brother Clark. 1 from Sister C. 1 from Brother Booth. Water with Sarah and Rebecca. Elizabeth Mills has been grieved on account of having lent money and clothing to some of the saints such as [—] Harris and Mary Becket and they have not returned it according to promise. Sister Hannah Walker has been sitting upstairs 4 or 5 hours. There is something matter with her but she appears to stupid to tell what is matter with her. Margaret Jones gave me 2 oranges. Supper with Sarah and Rebecca. Brother Lea gone to baptize. 7 baptized tonight.

April 12, 1840
This morning have had some conversation with Sister Hannah. She has made much trouble at the Mill and with her father. She is grieved because Alice is shy[118] with her. Has been tempted to go and live with Mather's again. She has been tempted to leave the church. Does not think of going to

meeting today. Wants Alice to speak freely to her again &c. I reasoned with her and tried to encourage her, but she is very stupid. She will have no breakfast. When I asked Alice to speak to her she seemed unwilling because she has done it so often. Breakfast with Sarah and Rebecca. Brother Charles Miller preached about 1½ hours this A.M. Had a good meeting. P.M. confirmed 4. Went to Brother M. Greens to Dinner. Had conversation with Mr. Goodson. I took a little beer. Sarah Crooks gave me a orange and a sweet cake. Preached on John 10 chapter[119] about 1¼. H. Whitehead gave me −/6. Brother Birch −/6. Sister Booth −/6. John Smith 1/−. Brother Bewsher 1/− and about 3/− besides from others. Supper with Sarah and Rebecca.

118. i.e., somewhat stingy.
119. There are a number of items he could have drawn from this chapter which would have fit into Mormon theology. The need to enter the Kingdom of God in the proper way (verses 1-2); Christ's purpose in promoting the good life for his followers (verse 10); the lost sheep on the American continent (verses 14-16); Christ's death and resurrection (verses 17-18); Christ's sonship of God (verses 27-39).

April 13, 1840

Breakfast at Hardman's. Dinner with Sarah and Rebecca. Sarah Crooks gave me 2/6. B[etsy] Crooks 2/−. Christiana Crooks 1/−. Rebecca Partington 1/6 and [−]. Brother Woodruff and Clark came in from the Potters and we started at 2¾ for Preston.[120] Found Brother Kimball and Brigham Young at home. My family well.

120. Wilford Woodruff dates this meeting on April 14, rather than the thirteenth. Undoubtedly, Woodruff and Clark were coming at the call of Brigham Young for the conference which was held on the fifteenth. Clayton means that they were arriving in Manchester from the Staffordshire Potteries (the area around Hanley and Burslem). Woodruff had actually been in Herefordshire for some time. Wilford Woodruff, "Journal," April 14, 1840, HDC.

April 14, 1840

Came this A.M. to Preston and found brothers Taylor, Parley

P. Pratt, Orson Pratt, George Smith &c at Brother Richards. Dinner with Brother Fielding. Met in council with the twelve.[121] C[*ocoa or coffee*] at George Greenwoods and again met in conference at Brother Fieldings room. I bought a voice of warning 2/6. History of the persecutions 2/6. Poems on Millennium 3/—.[122] Brother Richards ordained by the 12.[123]

121. Brigham Young says that he met with Kimball, the Pratts, Woodruff, Taylor, Smith and Richards, but he does not mention Clayton or Fielding. Brigham Young was also chosen "standing President of the Twelve by unanimous vote." Brigham Young, *Manuscript History*, 70.

122. The three works are all by Parley P. Pratt, *A Voice of Warning and Instruction to All People or an Introduction to the Faith and Doctrine of the Church of Jesus Christ of Latter-day Saints*, (2nd ed. rev.; New York: J. W. Harrison, 1839) (The First European edition, published in Manchester in 1841 was based on this edition); *History of the Late Persecution Inflicted by the State of Missouri Upon the Mormons*, (Detroit: Dawson and Bates, 1839); and *The Millenium and Other Poems: To Which is Annexed a Treatise on the Regeneration and Eternal Duration of Matter* (New York: W. Molineaux, 1840.) Up to this time, the principal tract which had been used was Orson Hyde's *A Timely Warning*.

123. Willard Richards was ordained a member of the Council of Twelve Apostles. He is the only one to be ordained to that office outside the United States. Smith, *Essentials in Church History*, 576.

April 15, 1840

Met in the cock Pit for conference. Brother Kimball was chosen president and I was chosen clerk. Total members 1677.[124] Dinner at Sister Morgans. Brother Clark appointed in the place of Brother Richards.[125] Ordained 2 priests. C[*ocoa or coffee*] at George Greenwoods. Brother Woodruff and Taylor preached at night to an overflowing congregation.

124. At the conference, various brethren represented branches and gave a report of the number in their branches. Clayton represented Manchester with 240 members, Stockport with 40 members, Peover and Macclesfield with 30 members, Middlewich with 6 members, Duckinfield with 30 members and Altrincham with 8 members. Also at the conference, it was resolved to publish a monthly periodical which was to be edited by Parley P. Pratt. Pratt, John Taylor and Brigham Young were chosen to select hymns for a hymnbook.

Heber C. Kimball, Pratt, and Young were to secure the copyright to the *Book of Mormon* and the *Doctrine and Covenants*. These books were to be printed in England because customs duties were too high to make it economical to import them. Smith, *History of the Church*, IV, 116; Brigham Young, *Manuscript History*, 70-71.

125. That is, Hiram Clark replaced Willard Richards in the mission presidency. Joseph Fielding, Clark and Clayton continued to preside over the mission until July 6, 1840, though their authority was shared with Brigham Young and the Council of Twelve. Evans, *A Century of Mormonism*, 74.

April 16, 1840

Have spent this day writing the minutes of conference. Brothers Woodruff and Richards came at night.[126]

126. Also on April 16, the Council of Twelve met to put into motion the plans made at the conference of the 15th. Parley P. Pratt was chosen as editor of the *Latter-day Saints Millennial Star*, which was to be published in Manchester. Brigham Young, Parley P. Pratt, and John Taylor were chosen as the editorial committee. The apostles decided to recommend that the gathering to America begin, but Brigham Young stipulated that no one was to go who had money unless he also assisted the poor to move. They agreed to require emigrants to obtain recommends from Church leaders in Britain. Peter Melling was selected to be ordained the first patriarch in Great Britain. Evans, *A Century of Mormonism*, 125; Whitney, *Kimball*, 278.

April 17, 1840

This day the brethren have come from Preston. Brigham Young, Parley P. Pratt, Orson Pratt, Heber C. Kimball, George A. Smith, Willard Richards, Willford Woodruff, Ruben Hadlock, Hiram Clark and Joseph Fielding. We have each had a glass of wine which my brother in law made 40 year since.[127] We spent the day together and I wrote a minute of the conference for Brother Kimball to send to America.[128] Brother Hadlock preached in my father in laws barn this night on John 15. Brothers Bradbury and Bourne from Burslem came and Brother Stafford from Stockport. They slept at our house.

127. Brigham Young and George A. Smith corroborate this. Young said that "She [Lydia or Alice Moon] presented a bottle of wine for us to bless and partake of, which she had kept for forty years, and she

said there was something providential in its preservation, for when she was married she designed to use it, but forgot until the event was over, and when her first child was married it was also forgotten, and so it passed over several events until she now had the privilege of presenting it to the Quorum of Twelve Apostles." It might be argued that the wine was used for sacrament, but there is no evidence that that was the case. The fact that it was blessed does not prove that it was, as any food or drink could have been blessed. Brigham Young, *Manuscript History*, 71; see also Smith, "Journal," *Instructor*, LXXXII, 321.

128. The minutes of the conference meetings in England were usually published in the *Times and Seasons* in Nauvoo, Illinois besides being published in the *Millennial Star* in England. They have also been reprinted in Joseph Smith's *History*.

April 18, 1840

Went to B. Budge with Brother Stafford &c. Returned home and got dinner. Borrowed 4 of my wife to pay my Coach fare. Went to Preston and took Railway at 2½. Got to Manchester 2-12—in company with Brothers Clark and Smith. Saw Sister E. Ravenscroft. She gave me a new watch guard and brought a letter from E. Bromley. Sister H. Parkinson gave me 3 oranges. Margaret Jones gave me 2. Sarah and Rebecca gave me water and supper. Sarah gave me 1 pint of Porter and told me that Catherine Beates had told her that great trouble was coming upon her and she must keep herself single for she would scarce have an inch of ground to stand upon. I felt poorly tonight. My limbs and hand ached very bad.

April 19, 1840

My head still very bad. Sarah brought me some wine and a egg in it. Breakfast with Sarah and Rebecca. Brother Clark preached this morning. To B to Dinner. Had a pint of Porter. I led meeting in P.M. Brother George Smith spake a good deal. We confirmed 9, blessed 1 child and prayed with a number sick. Sarah gave me an orange. Sarah wept this morning on account of what Sister Catherine said to her. Brother Lea baptized 4 this A.M. 5 has been baptized at Manchester this week. Sarah gave me an orange. Brother Smith gave a lengthy detail of the rise of the church to a very full house. Good attention and good feeling. A man stood up and wanted to ask questions. I told him to wait till the meeting closed. But he did not come forward. Brother Richards gave me 1/—. Sister Birch 1/—. Had conversation with Mary Darrah. She says she cannot believe the testimony. She has long seen baptism to be a duty. She asked if God was no respecter of persons why had he not sent an angel sooner &c. I talked a good deal to her. She wants to be baptised if she could believe—but she does not want to be an hypocrite. I told her she would be an L.D.S. She burst into tears and said if she thought she must not she would be miserable. I told B[*etsy*] Crooks that she should have her companion again. She is a loving young woman and desires to do right. I feel to love her much. Supper with Sarah and Rebecca.

April 20, 1840
Breakfast at Hardman's. Dinner at Sister Hedrdaker's. Went to see Bensons boy. From thence to the Railway to meet Brother Parley P. Pratt. He arrived at 4¾. Took water with Sarah and Rebecca. Spent the evening at home with a many saints. Had more conversation with Mary Darrah. She feels more satisfied and feels to love the saints. Elizabeth Gladstone gave me 2 oranges. Supper with Sarah and Rebecca.

April 21, 1840
Breakfast at Hardman's. Spent this A.M. with Brother Pratt in ascertaining the expense of printing a monthly paper.[129] Dinner at William Millers. Tea at old Mrs. Millers after which Brother Pratt and I went to Knotts Mill fair.[130] Went to see some wild animals. Brother Pratt went to preaching at Cookson Street. I remained at home. Elizabeth Gladstone gave me

an orange and Sister Mary Wood a smelling bottle.[131] Supper
with Sarah and Rebecca. Alice is poorly and seems low.

129. Undoubtedly, Clayton's previous experience as a book keeper
and his knowledge of the local prices and conditions helped him counsel Parley P. Pratt on this matter.

130. The Knott Mill Fair had been established to celebrate the
opening of the Bridgewater Canal. It was a pleasure fair which lasted
three days. The canal had been built by Francis Duke of Bridgewater
pursuant to an act of Parliament in 1760. William E. A. Axon, *Annals
of Manchester A Chronological Record From the Earliest Times to the
Eve of 1885* (Manchester and London: J. Heywod Dearsgate and
Ridgefield, 1886), 93; Wilfred H. Thompson, *History of Manchester to 1852* (Altrincham: John Sherman and Son, Ltd, 1967), 204.

131. Probably a bottle of smelling salts. Clayton had been quite
ill recently.

April 22, 1840

Spent this A.M. with Brother Parley in seeking a sutable
situation for a book establishment.[132] Brother Bewshers to
Dinner. Brother Clark is gone to Macclesfield. Went per Railway to Patricroft. Sarah Crooks went with me. Preached at
Worsley on 2 Thessalonians 1-6 to 9. Had considerable questions to answer to some very ignorant men who professed
to have a great deal of religion. I could scarce pray at the
commencement they were so noisy. They dwelt much on the
thief being saved without baptism.[133] We got home about 1
o clock. Took Supper with Hannah Walker. Sister Poole
washed my feet. Sarah Crooks gave me an orange.

132. Clayton is probably referring to the search for a place to
publish the *Millennial Star*.

133. The scripture Clayton preached from refers to Christ's Second
Coming, and the punishment of those who "obey not the gospel of our
Lord Jesus Christ." The hecklers were undoubtedly referring to
Christ's words to the thief, "And Jesus said unto him, Verily I say
unto thee, Today shalt thou be with me in paradise." Luke 23:43.

April 23, 1840

This A M. Brother Smith and Sister Ravenscroft are gone to
the Potteries. Breakfast with Rebecca. Went with Brother
Pratt to the Printers. He engaged with Mr. Thomas for 6-12

pr thousand on good paper and to print a number of prospectus's[134] gratis [*one word crossed out*]. To Brother J. at Grundy's to Dinner and William Millers to cocoa. Took a walk together to Knott Mill fair. Attended meeting at William Millers at night. Sister Jemima Whittaker went into a kind of
fainting fit she said through a blessing. Mary Darrah has
been much tempted and feels her heart quite hard. Supper
with Sarah and Rebecca. Sarah Perkins gave me a orange.

134. The prospectus for the *Millennial Star*.

April 24, 1840

Breakfast at Hardman's. Sarah Crooks is at home short of
work. Dinner at Thomas Mayors. Had some conversation
with Elizabeth. She has felt hard against the saints. They have
told falsehoods about her &c. She has not taken sacrement
but 2 or 3 time since her mother died. Took water with
Sarah. Went to see the proof sheet for prospectus and thence
to see Brother Lambert who is awfully afflicted with Small
pox. Had council meeting with the officers. Supper at Hardman's with Sarah.

April 25, 1840

Breakfast at Hardman's. Went to Cookson Street. Brother
Richards came. Dinner at Brother West's. Went again to
the printers. Brother Richards took coach for Burslem. To
Princes to Cocoa. Elizabeth Crooks very full of trouble. Had
a good deal of conversation with Mary Darrah. She had a
many objections against the work and the bible such as contradictions and Jacob and David having more wives. I reasoned with her and she was satisfied and said she would have
been baptized had it not been late. She had something against
Sarah Crooks for having taken Esther away from under the
employment of her sister without giving a weeks notice. Sarah

asked her forgiveness but she said she felt she could not. She
wanted to do. Sarah much grieved and seemed to fret. H.
Parkinson gave me some oranges. Supper with Sarah and Rebecca.

April 26, 1840

Breakfast with Sarah and Rebecca. Brother Pratt preached
on Isaiah 24 ch.[135] To Brother Bewsher's to Dinner. I opened
meeting in the P.M. Brother Pratt spoke considerable. Sarah
Crooks gave me an orange. Brother Pratt spake at night on
Jacob have I loved but Esau have I hated.[136] Sister Booth
showed a very bad spirit on account of us not speaking to
her on Thursday night. She said she came with a full determination to be cut off. She would hear no reason. Manifested
a [— —]. Supper with Sarah and Rebecca. Baptized Mary
Darrah and Mary Johnson. [one line smudged and unclear]

135. The chapter deals with the punishment of God for defiling
the covenants. Pratt was undoubtedly talking of the Apostasy from
original Christianity.
136. See Romans 9:13. The entire chapter deals with the pro-
position that birth alone does not guarantee election to salvation.

April 27, 1840

Breakfast with Sarah. To Brother Greens. [—] R to Dinner.
Went to Printing office for prospectus's. To William Miller's
to Cocoa. From thence to Prestwich. Preached on 1 Cor. 3. To
supper at Brother Briersleys. Sarah Crooks told me this A.M.
something more that she was fretting of. When she was
among the Methodists she began to keep company with
George Buchanan. But on some account she took a kind of
dislike to him. She went to Carlisle for 2 weeks and when
she came back there had been some report about her. George
came to her and humbled himself to her and when she still
resisted him he said he would leave class again &c. She felt
afraid and said if he would not leave class she would go

with him again &c. The report spread abroad that she begged of George to go with her. She was to have been called before the school for it. But she never told them any other than that which they believed. When Mary Darrah spake to Sarah on Saturday night all these things came to her mind [*ten lines crossed out*]. 1 baptized at Rudleby.

April 28, 1840

Breakfast at Hardman's. Saw Brother Josh Barrons from Bolton. Sarah is come off work poorly. Spent the forenoon with her. Took dinner with her. Sent some prospecti to Preston. Water with Sarah. She went with me to Eccles. Preached to a very full house on 1 Cor. 3. Sarah washed my feet when we got home and I took supper with Rebecca.

April 29, 1840

Alice Hardman says her mother is very unkind to her and is almost about to breakup house. Breakfast with Sarah. To Brother Bewshers to Dinner with Brother David Wilding and Pratt. Went to see Sister Jennings and found her in a bad state but she asked to be let alone a little longer. Called at the next house and there found her and 3 children sick. They have scarce any faith. He just came with medicine from the dispensary. I had some conversation and she appeared opposed in principle.[137] I went on to roe Green. Waited till after 8 o clock before any came. Preached on 1 Cor. 3.[138] Slender house. Got home about 11½. Sarah washed my feet and gave me supper.

137. There was some feeling in the Church at this time that members should not rely on physicians and medicine. In a sermon on September 5, 1841, Joseph Smith reported: "I preached to a large congregation at the stand, on the science and practice of medicine, desiring to persuade the Saints to trust in God when sick, and not in an arm of flesh, and live by faith and not by medicine, or poison; and when they are sick, and had called for the Elders to pray for them, and they were not healed, to use herbs and mild food." Smith, *History of the Church*, IV, 414.

138. There are a number of themes in I Corinthians, 3 about which Clayton could have spoken: the need to learn basics before learning the deep things of the gospel (verse 3); the need for all to labor together in the work of the Lord (verses 4-9); each man to be rewarded for his own work (verse 14); the need to keep oneself pure and unspotted from the world (verses 16-20).

April 30, 1840

Breakfast with Sarah. Went to William Millers to Dinner. Thomas Miller was sick. Sent a letter to my wife. Spent much of the day with Sarah and took water with her. Hurt my tooth and was pained all the night. Rebecca and Sarah gave me a pint of warm porter. Sarahs Birthday—23.

May 1, 1840

Breakfast with Sarah. We went to Newton. Took Dinner at Sister Booths. Sarah and I took a walk into the fields. She appeared low and fretful. Water at Sister Booths. She gave me a [— —]. Went to Council meeting—nothing particular. Supper with Ellen Battersby. She gave me a pint of Porter. Sister Sands was took very dangerously ill through miscarriage. She has been growing careless. Had hardness against me and was giving way to the world. She says she will be better.

May 2, 1840

Breakfast at Hardman's. Dinner at John Hardmans. Went to Oxford. Water with Sarah and Rebecca. Spent the evening upstairs with Sarah and Rebecca. Sarah has repaired my clothes and showed much kindness. Supper with Sarah and Rebecca. Mary Darrah is rather low. Sarah has fallen downstairs but is not much hurt.

May 3, 1840

Breakfast with Sarah and Rebecca. Went to Dukinfield. Preached at [—] on 1 Cor 3. Dinner with Sister Mary Burton. Spake on the kingdom in the P.M. Confirmed 6. Water with

Royles. Preached D on Matthew 24—this gospel &c.[139] Christiana Crooks gave me several [—]. M. Parkinson gave me 1/— yesterday. On our way home I was disgusted in some measure with the conduct of Eliza Prince. She would not keep company with us but walked behind until Ann Jacson and her missed their way. Sarah and Rebecca, A and H came to meet us. 4 baptized at Manchester 5 at Stockport—on Friday. Sarah Ann Booth gave me a small sweet cake which came from France.

139. Matthew 24:14 "And this gospel of the kingdom shall be preached in all the world for a witness unto all nations; and then shall the end come." Apparently Clayton preached on the idea that the gospel had been restored and was now going throughout the world in preparation for the millennium.

May 4, 1840

Alice Hardman and her mother is vexed at each other. Alice says her mother would soon break up the house if I was not there. Got a letter from my wife. Went to printing office to start the printer.[140] Dinner at Sister Walkers. Spent the P.M with Sarah and Alice. Water with Sarah then she went with me to Pendlebury. Preached on Matthew 24—this gospel &c. Full house. We took tea and returned. I found some oyster left by B[etsy] and Christiana Crooks.

140. During these days Clayton was very busy with the *Millennial Star,* in addition to his other duties. The first issue appeared May 27, 1840. It was in pamphlet form and 24 pages long. The price was sixpence and the editorial work was carried on at an office located at 149 Oldham Road in Manchester. Smith, *History of the Church,* IV, 138.

May 5, 1840

Breakfast with Sarah. Went to Sister Booths Newton. Sarah went with me. Dinner and Water at Sister Booth's. She gave me 3 oranges and —/6. We then went together to Eccles. Preached on Mark 16-15, 16.[141] Was much interrupted. One man asked me to lay aside my bible and preach without it. The enemies threw the meeting into confusion. Baptized 1. Supper at Harriss.

141. Mark 16:15-16 "And he said unto them, Go ye into all the world, and preach the gospel to every creature. He that believeth and is baptized shall be saved; but he that believeth not shall be damned."

May 6, 1840

Breakfast with Sarah. To Bewshers to Dinner. Came home to C[ocoa or coffee] with Sarah. She paid coach fare to Patricroft. Mary Darrah gave me an orange. Preached on Mark 16-15. Supper with Wilkinsons. Mrs. Bradford gave me a glass of porter. Sarah washed my feet.

May 7, 1840

Breakfast with Sarah. Got a letter from Liverpool saying that Brother Taylor is very sick and wants one of us to go for Sabbath. Brother Pratt says I had better. Dinner at William Millers. Went to see Eliza Prince—sickly. Sarah and I went to Mechanics Institution.[142] Supper with Sarah and Rebecca. [two lines crossed out]

142. The Manchester Mechanics Institute, opened on March 30, 1825, was located on Cooper Street, nearly opposite the present-day Town Hall. The purpose of the institute was to instruct the working classes in various vocational skills, and in "other useful arts." The founders hoped the working man would thus be "better qualified to advance himself in the world; better enabled to secure the means of support and enjoyment, and better qualified to promote the education of his children." The institute promoted lectures and evening classes, and boasted a library and reading rooms. It was apparently very successful, and it eventually moved to a new location and enlarged its facilities, finally becoming the Municipal College of Technology. It is not clear why Clayton took Sarah Crooks to the institute that afternoon, but it is presumed that they were either holding a meeting or making some other missionary contact. On the other hand, they may have wanted to just get away and talk or they may have wanted to use the reading facilities for study. At any rate, the frequency with which she accompanied him indicates the growing affection between the two. It was highly unusual, even in that day, for a missionary to spend much time alone with a young lady. On May 19, Clayton recorded that after supper with Sarah she washed his feet and they

"sat together" until two in the morning. Apparently the two were now finding it increasingly necessary to talk about their mutual concerns. Thompson, *History of Manchester*, 315.

May 8, 1840

Got a letter from my wife saying that my mother is very ill. Breakfast at Princes. Dinner with Sarah and Rebecca. Sister Walker gave me 1/— Sister Black —/6. Water at Sister Green's. Sister Grundy has been slighting Sister Green because she had Itch and did not tell her. Nothing particular at council meeting. John Bailey has been drunk again. To be visited again and if he will not repent to be cut off.[143] I spake to the officers to be faithful and set a good example—teach the church unity &c. Supper with Ellen Battersby. She gave me a pint of porter. Christiana Crooks gave me 1/— Betsy Crooks 2/— and sweets.

143. This is interesting in view of Clayton's own use of porter, beer, and wine. Apparently Clayton drew the line not at drinking but drunkenness.

May 9, 1840

Sarah is rather grieved because she thinks she is to bold &c. She remembers the liberty which has been taken with her before time and how she suffered by it. She tarried till 7 o clock. Breakfast with Hardman's. Sarah has returned from her work. Called at Jane Brown's. Alice and Jane was both weeping but would not tell me what for. H. Parkinson gave me 2 oranges. I left home at 10½ for Knotts Mill. Started by boat at 11½. Sarah came with me to Attrincham. I got to R[...]com at 5½. Set sail by steam Boat at 6 and arrived at Liverpool at 8 o clock. The days was rather wet and gloomy otherwise it was a pleasant ride. Found Brother Taylor better. Supper with Cannons. Had a pint of warm Porter at Ransons.

May 10, 1840

Went this morning at 8½ and baptized 3. Breakfast at Can-

151

nons. Preached in the Temperance Hall[144] on 1 Corinthians 3. Dinner with Brother Harrison. Brother Taylor lead the afternoon meeting. Tea with an aged man who says he is a descendant of the Waldenses.[145] He seems to be an intelligent man. I preached again on John 10. Supper with the old man.

144. In almost every place the missionaries went, they were able to use the local temperance halls because of their supposed emphasis on abstinence. The temperance hall mentioned above probably belonged to the Manchester and Salford Temperance Society, which had been formed in 1835 as the successor of the Oak Street Temperance Society. It had twelve branches, and held weekly meetings. It consisted of about 8,000 members, 500 of whom were reformed drunkards. It received financial support chiefly from members of the working class, although a few more wealthy and benevolent people also helped. *Manchester as it Is: Or, Notices of the Institutions, Manufactures, Commerce, Railway, etc. of the Metropolis of Manufactures.* (Manchester: Love and Barton, 1839), 73-79.

145. The Waldenses are members of a Protestant denomination which was situated originally in northern Italy. Its origins are uncertain, though it is one of the oldest, if not the oldest, of the continuously existing Protestant denominations. Its theology is close to that of the Calvinists. Hastings, *Encyclopedia of Religion*, XII, 663-673.

May 11, 1840

Breakfast at Cannons. Went to the Docks. Brother Taylor took me to Brother Armstrongs to be measured for a vest. He gave me 4 pence. To Brother Armstrongs to Dinner then I went to the Docks[146] and spent the P.M. Tea at Cannons. Went to preaching. I preached on Mathew 24-12.[147] Supper at Brother Mitchells.

146. The docks were located on the west side of town, on the east bank of the River Mersey.
147. "And because iniquity shall abound, the love of many shall wax cold."

May 12, 1840

Breakfast at Cannons. Went with Brother Taylor to see Sister Harrington. Took dinner and tea and returned to Brother Dumvilles. We had a church meeting for the purpose of organizing the church. Brother Taylor spake considerable on the necessity of organization the nature and design &c. He then proposed William Mitchell to be chosen as secretary for the church—Richard Harrison priest and John James priest Thomas Dumville and John Dixon T[.] which being elected unanimously Elder Taylor called upon the brethren to know if they accepted their offices which William Mitchell said he would rather have nothing to do with money matters. He was told there was no money matters—but to keep a church record —but he refused to do it. Elder Taylor then proposed Brother George Cannon who accepted the office. We then proceeded with ordination after which I spake a little on the importance of having an office and the necessity of the prayers of the Saints and concluded the meeting. Supper at Dumvills. Brother Armstrong has made me a new vest and Brother Mitchell has repaired my boots. Brother Taylor gave me 33/— for Brother Pratt.

May 13, 1840
Breakfast at Cannons. Started by packet for Manchester at 7 o clock. Got in at 3½. Water at Hardman's. Got a letter from Brother Heath. Went to see Brother Pratt and gave him his 33/—. Have heard that Brother Clark is very sick. Supper with Sarah and Rebecca. Thomas Miller gave me 1/—.

May 14, 1840
Breakfast at Hardmans. Spent the A M chiefly reading. Went to William Millers to Dinner. Sent a letter to my wife and one to Brother Heath. Called at the printers. Went at night to Prince's. E. Dewsnup has again been railing and endeavoring to prejudice them against Elizabeth Crooks. Elizabeth says she can bear it no longer and says she will be cut off. I told her we would not do it on those reasons but I would

endeavor to get things right. Took supper with them and returned.

May 15, 1840

Breakfast at Hardman's. Received a letter from Brother Clark stating his sickness. I wrote one in answer but he came soon after Dinner. Dinner with Sarah and Rebecca. Cocoa with Hannah Walker. Went to council meeting—to fill appointment. Supper with S. Battersby. Had a pint of beer. Sister Sarah Perkins sent me new comb and Elizabeth Crooks left me two oranges.

May 16, 1840

Breakfast with Rebekkah. She has left her work. Signed Brother Garncr's recommend. Dinner with Rebecca and Water with Sarah and Rebecca. Had conversation with a young man. He seems candid and open. Supper with Sarah and Rebecca. Brother Pratt gone to Stockport.

May 17, 1840

Breakfast with Sarah and Rebecca. Preached on Ephesians 4-1 to 16.[148] To Mr. Patricks to dinner. Agness was married this week to a Mr. Bilbirene. I spake again in the afternoon on evil speaking and hard feelings. There seemed to be a weight on the meeting. 2 was confirmed. I had some conversation with P. Grundy. She is grieved at Sister Green and grieved becas she has heard that we intend to remove the meeting. Preached again on the same Chapter. After meeting 2 were baptized. 2 baptized from Eccles this A.M. Had some conversation with Alice' Cousin Jane Hardman. She is a very nice young woman and does not seem to object to anything. Sister Dewsnup came and I told her what had been said about her and what I thought but she denies all and seems to justify herself but I dont feel satisfied with her spirit. I had a letter from my wife this A M. Brother Joseph Birch gave me —/6 H. Parkinson —/6 Jane Mahon —/6 and Catherine Beates —/6. Supper with Sarah and Rebecca. They gave me a pint of warm porter. 2 baptized at Pend.

148. These verses refer to the proper organization of the Church of Christ, and the purpose of the organization. "From whom the whole body fitly joined together and compacted by that which every joint supplieth, according to the effectual working in the measure of every part, maketh increase of the body unto the edifying of itself in love." (verse 16) The idea that Mormon Church organization is patterned after that of the primitive church was apparently as important a missionary topic then as it is at the present time.

May 18, 1840

Breakfast and Dinner with Sarah and Rebecca. 1 baptized at Dukinfield yesterday. C[ocoa or coffee] at Bewshers. Mary Aspen left me 2/6 and some mint drops. Brother Bewsher gave me 2/6 Elizabeth Crooks 2/— Christiana Crooks 1/— Sarah Crooks 1/6 and a cloth for Sarah. Sister Sands gave me 2/— Sister Booth 1/— Elizabeth Crooks gave me a pint of Porter. Supper with Sarah and Rebecca.

May 19, 1840

Breakfast with Rebecca. C[ocoa or coffee] with Sister Rigby. Rebecca went with me to Eccles. Preached on Ephesians 4 Chapter. Full House and behaved well. Took a little refreshment. Supper with Sarah—1 pint porter. She washed my feet. We sat together till 2 o'clock.

May 20, 1840

Breakfast with Rebecca. Went to Bewshers to Dinner. Had a pint of porter. Returned to fetch 200 stars from office. C[ocoa or coffee] with Rebecca. Brother Garner is gone to Liverpool this A.M to start for America. 3/— was sent from Brother Clark—left by a sister. Thomas Mayor gave me 1/—.

155

On Monday night Alice and Hannah went to Brother Pratts and tarried til near 11 [*nineteen lines crossed out*]. I took Railway at 5 o clock and was at home at 7. Found all Matthias Moons family except John who was gone to Liverpool but he soon returned. Had a little made wine.[149]

149. He probably means home-made.

May 21, 1840
Went to Preston in the P.M. Water at Sister Morgan.

May 22, 1840
Went to see my mother and to Factory.

May 23, 1840
Kimball came. Went to Preston. C[*ocoa or coffee*] at George Greenwoods.

May 24, 1840
Preached on Ephesians 4. Brother Kimball spake in the afternoon. 3 was confirmed. Brother Kimball preached at night. I spake a little.

May 25, 1840
Brother Fielding came and his wife. Sent for Brother Peter Melling and he having previously been ordained to the office of Patriarch he proceeded to confer a patriarchal blessing upon Thomas Moon and then upon his wife. After he got through Brother Moon proceeded to bless his children in order according to their age. I also received my blessing under his hands to this effect—that I should have a good memory—have strong faith in God—should be the means of bringing 100s and 1000s to God and to the truth of his gospel—should be preserved from the hands of wicked and ungodly men and should come forth in the kingdom of God.

156

May 26, 1840

Went with Brother Kimball to Preston. Dinner at Sister Morgans. Thence to Francis Moon's. Brother Kimball gave me a most extensive and great blessing. Returned home and proceeded to writing.

May 27, 1840

After finishing writing I went to see my mother who is a little better. Came back and got ready for Manchester. Went to Preston. Met Brother Kimball at the Railway and we started. Arrived in 1¾ hours. Called at Hardmans and took Water and then went to the office where we found Brothers Pratt, Young and Taylor. Supper with Sarah and Rebecca. Brother Kimball slept with me. I had a fit of sickness tonight. I drank 6 pints of brandy which gave me ease.

May 28, 1840

Took breakfast at Sister Pooles. Brother Kimball sent for a quart of Porter. Dinner with Sarah and Rebecca. I went to the office a little and in the P M my face began to be very bad. I had it washed with brandy and went to bed about 12 but was obliged to get up again about 1 and continued up untill 4½. I suffered a great deal.

May 29, 1840

Dinner with Sarah and Rebecca. Went to the office to help in selecting hymns.[150] At 5½ met brothers Heath, Berry and Wytch. They have been contending one against the other and has hard feelings against each other. We heard all their stories and Brother Wytch seemed to manifest in some degree a very bad spirit. I spake a little to them and advised them to be one &c. Brother Kimball and Young came to Hardman's and sung some and afterwards spake with each other in tongues.[151]

I had supper with Sarah and Rebecca. Brother Kimball went to Prince's.

150. See above, note 124. Brigham Young reported that "The committee on the Hymn Book commenced, and we continued selecting hymns until the 30th, when in company with Elders Kimball and Taylor, I went to Liverpool and preached on Sunday, 31st." Brigham Young, *Manuscript History*, May 27, 1840, 77.

151. Apparently, the practice of speaking in tongues was quite widespread in the Church during this period. In December, 1839, Brigham Young had discoursed on this subject while coming to England. "I found the Saints in confusion; they had the gift of tongues among them, and the interpretation, and they were so ignorant of the nature of these gifts that they supposed that everything which was spoken in tongues was immediate revelation from God; a false spirit had therefore crept in, and division was the result. I taught them that when they spoke in tongues the language might be from the Lord, but with that tongue they spoke things which were in their hearts, whether they were good or evil; the gift of tongues was given for a blessing to the Saints, but not to govern them, nor to control the Elders, or dictate the affairs of the Church." *Ibid.*, 60.

May 30, 1840

Breakfast at Hardman's. Dinner at P. Hams. Brother Taylor sick. He and brothers Kimball and Young are gone to Liverpool.[152] C[*ocoa or coffee*] with Sarah and Rebecca. Read the vision[153] to some of the sisters. Felt it good. Supper with Sarah and Rebecca.

152. They went to Liverpool to organize and send off the first company of Saints to emigrate from England. *Ibid.*, 77.

153. This might refer to Joseph Smith's 1832 vision of the three "degrees of glory," which is found in section 76 of the *Doctrine and Covenants,* and is nowadays often referred to as "the vision." More likely, however, it refers to the story of Joseph Smith's first vision, which, according to most accounts, occurred in the spring of 1820. The account of this vision was not widely circulated in the early years of the Church, and was not included in any missionary literature, or any publication for that matter, prior to 1840. The first printed account of this vision was published in England in 1840. It was included in a major tract by Orson Pratt entitled, *An Interesting Account of Several Remarkable Visions and of the Late Discovery of Ancient American Records.* Pratt was one of the Twelve then doing missionary work in England. It is not clear what month the tract was published, but it is apparent that whether or not it was being generally circulated in May, Clayton would have had access to early printer's copies, or

perhaps even to Pratt's manuscript. At any rate, this is probably the first time Clayton and other Manchester members had become aware of this early experience of Joseph Smith and it is significant that Clayton recorded that he "felt it good." Joseph Smith's first vision has since become a keystone in Mormon doctrine and one of the essentials of the missionary message. See James B. Allen, "Eight Contemporary Accounts of Joseph Smith's First Vision," *The Improvement Era*, LXIII (1970), 4-13, and James B. Allen, "The Significance of Joseph Smith's 'First Vision' in Mormon Thought," *Dialogue: A Journal of Mormon Thought*, I (1966), 29-45.

May 31, 1840

Breakfast with Sarah and Rebecca. Preached on John chapter 17.[154] To Bewshers to Dinner. Had a pint porter. Led the P M meeting. Brother Pratt spake some. Ordained Brother William Parr Elder. John Lee priest and William Black Teacher. Had a cake given me. Sarah Crooks tells me that she has been informed that James Mahon has a wife and 2 children living in Ireland that James was cut off from the Catholic church because of disowning her. His wife was sent for by the priest (who had got a certificate of their marriage) and she came to him but he denied her. She said if he would only own her she would not trouble him. She went back to Ireland. They separated because of poverty. James was taken ill sometime after and thought he should die. He then acknowledged the fact. These things Sarah has heard from credible witness. James is about to be married to Elizabeth Mills. Brother Pratt preached on 3 chapter 1 Peter[155]—restoration. I baptised 2 after. One was Jane Hardman. Sarah and Rebecca gave me each an orange and sweet cake and supper.

154. John 17 is the prayer Jesus offered in Gethsemane just before his crucifixion. Among other things, he prayed for strength and unity among the disciples he was to leave, and this may well have been the thrust of Clayton's sermon.

155. I Peter, chapter 3, includes counsel on the importance of wives obeying their husbands, husbands honoring wives, and general love and unity among the Saints. In view of the many family problems and squabbles among Church members in Manchester, this was an appropriate sermon for Pratt to give.

June 1, 1840

Breakfast at Hardman's and Dinner with Sarah and Rebecca. Went to Prestwich and preached on the Priesthood Hebrews chapter 7.[156] After preaching I spake to the members on the words of wisdom and afterwards ordained Brother Walker Johnson priest. Took tea and returned. Met Sarah Crooks. She seems low and poorly. Supper with Rebecca. There was some thunder and hevy rain soon as I got home.

156. This chapter deals with the priesthood. Clayton was undoubtedly using the chapter to differentiate between the two orders of the priesthood, Levitical or Aaronic, and Melchizedek.

June 2, 1840

Breakfast at Hardman's and to Sister Walker's to dinner. Went to Brother Owen's to Cocoa. Brother Owen gave me 1/—. From thence to Eccles and preached on Hebrews chapter 6 verses 1 to 3.[157] Full house. Got home before 11. Took supper with Sarah and Rebecca.

157. "Therefore leaving the principles of the doctrine of Christ, let us go on unto perfection; not laying again the foundation of repentance from dead works, and of faith toward God. Of the doctrine of baptisms and of laying on of hands, and of resurrection of the dead, and of eternal judgment. And this we will do, if God permit."

June 3, 1840

Breakfast with Elizabeth Mayor. To Bewshers to Dinner. Brother David Wilding says that Wilkinson or Worsley dare not let us preach. His master has got to hear and he is in danger of losing his work. Called at Sister Birchs. She is in much trouble on account of her husband. She gave me —/6. Supper with Sarah and Rebecca.

June 4, 1840

Have been this morning to see Mr. Hearne and enquire concerning James Mahon. He says he knows nothing about him. Breakfast at Hardman's. Dinner and Water at William Millers.

Went to Pollard St. and entered into conversation with a man untill it was time to close the meeting.

June 5, 1840

Brother Pratt spake some at the council concerning the rise of the church—the visit of angels—and many strange things &c.[158]

158. Probably Pratt was telling the story of Joseph Smith. See above note 153.

June 6, 1840

Had conversation with Mr. John Hardman about 3 hours. He seems to have much false notion and tradition &c.

June 7, 1840

Brother Pratt preached on Malachi 3rd.[159] To Bewshers to Dinner. In the P.M. confirmed 8. Brother Pratt preached at night on Revelations 17-5.[160] I baptized 1 after.

159. The chapter begins, "Behold, I will send my messenger, and he shall prepare the way before me: and the Lord, whom ye seek, shall suddenly come to his temple, even the messenger of the covenant, whom ye delight in: behold, he shall come, saith the Lord of hosts." Probably Pratt used this as evidence of the preparation for Christ's Second Coming.
160. "And upon her forehead was a name written, MYSTERY, BABYLON THE GREAT THE MOTHER OF HARLOTS AND ABOMINATIONS OF THE EARTH."

June 8, 1840

I have no reasons to believe that the reports concerning James Mahon are true but pretty clear evidence that they are false. Sarah Crooks and I went to Pendlebury. Spake on the priesthood authority &c. Sarah was taken very ill.

June 9, 1840

Went to Eccles. Eliza Prince and Ann Jacson with me. Preached on Revelations 22—If any man add &c.[161]

161. "If any man shall add unto these things, God shall add unto him the plagues that are written in this book: And if any man shall take away from the words of the book of this prophecy, God shall take away his part out of the book of life, and out of the holy city, and *from* the things which are written in this book." Revelations 22:18-19. This passage is often used by anti-Mormons to contest the validity of the *Book of Mormon*. Clayton may have tried to give the Mormon side of the argument, showing that the passage refers only to the book of Revelations and not to the Bible as a whole.

June 12, 1840

At Council meeting a number of the Saints attended. Brother Green almost got the gift of tongues. Brother Young spake in tongues.[162]

162. Brigham Young was at this time in Manchester to preach and to work on the preparation of the hymn book. On the 22nd, he returned to Liverpool to see about the printing of the *Book of Mormon*. On the 26th, he returned to Manchester and spent the next days finishing the hymn book. Brigham Young, *Manuscript History*, 77-78.

June 13, 1840

About 2 o clock this A.M. Elizabeth Crooks began in her sleep to sing in tongues. She spake and sung in about 7 languages occupying about 2 hours. During the day Betsy Pool got the gift of tongues.

June 14, 1840

Brother Young preached on Matthew 9 he that heareth these sayings.[163] In the P M Sister Pool spake in tongues then Richard Hardman James Mahon Sister Heath. We confirmed 4. Christiana Crooks and Jemima Whittaker spake in tongues. I preached on Galatians 1—though we are an angel &c.[164] After preaching I baptised, William Hardman and a young woman.

163. Clayton must have been mistaken in the scripture. The quotation which he wrote comes from Matthew 7:24-25, "Therefore whosoever heareth these sayings of mine, and doeth them, I will liken him unto a wise man, which built his house upon a rock: And the rain descended, and the floods came, and the winds blew, and beat upon that house; and it fell not: for it was founded upon a rock."

164. Galatians 1:6-9, "I marvel that ye are so soon removed from him that called you into the grace of Christ unto another gospel: Which is not another; but there be some that trouble you, and would pervert the gospel of Christ. But though we, or an angel from heaven, preach any other gospel unto you than that which we have preached unto you, let him be accursed. As we said before, so say I now again, If any *man* preach any other gospel unto you than that ye have received, let him be accursed."

June 15, 1840

Went to engage Carpenters Hall.[165]

165. Clayton went to rent Carpenter's Hall for the conference which was to have been held at Temperance Hall (the Cock Pit) in Preston. It was decided that Temperance Hall was not large enough, as the mission had grown considerably. Brigham Young and Parley P. Pratt preached at the hall for the first time on June 21, and from this time on regular meetings were held there. Rental was $500 per year. Carpenter's Hall was located on Garratt Road. It had been opened on November 12, 1838 at a cost of £4,500 by the journeyman carpenters of Manchester. Even before the Mormons began holding meetings there, it was used on Sundays by the Chartists. Smith, *History of the Church*, IV, 141; Thomson, *Manchester*, 341.

June 16, 1840

To Sister Booths at Newton. Sarah and Rebecca with.

June 17, 1840

Went again to Carpenters Hall.

June 18, 1840

Engaged the Hall—and got bills posted.

June 19, 1840

Sarah Crooks gave me 2 frocks for children and 1/–. Rebecca gave me 1/6 Christiana 1/– Catherine Beates –/6 Mary Aspen 1/– Jane Hardman 1/– Sister Mary Wood a smelling bottle. Took Railway at 5 o clock. Home about 8½.

June 20, 1840

This evening I had considerable conversation with Mr. Bland

who was once a member of the church. He was fully confounded in some of his favourite opinions and left without room to say a word. We talked about 3 hours.

June 21, 1840

This A.M Brother Whitehead preached on the restoration of all things. Went in the afternoon to Relayton to sacrement. Had a good meeting. Night went to Whittle. Preached on the power of Godliness.

June 23, 1840

Had a good meeting at night.

June 26, 1840

Left home at 9¼ and walked to Bolton. Rained all the way. Got there at 2 o clock. Took Railway and got to Manchester about 3. Was very ill. Went to council meeting but was obliged to return on account of sicknss. My sister Alice gave me 1/—.

June 27, 1840

Very poorly all day. At night Brother Green spake in tongues. The power of Satan was powerfully manifested upon some of the Sisters. Sarah gave me a pint of porter.

June 28, 1840

Brother Young preached on Romans 11-26.[166] Dinner at Bewshers. Brother Young led the meeting P M. Brother Pratt preached at night on Mark 16-15 to 19.[167] 7 confirmed. William Hardman gave me 1/— yesterday. Thomas Miller gave me 4/—.

166. "And so all Israel shall be saved: as it is written. There shall come out of Sion the Deliverer, and shall turn away ungodliness from Jacob: For this is my covenant unto them, when I shall take away their sins. As concerning the gospel, *they are* enemies for your

sakes: but as touching the election, *they are* beloved for the fathers' sakes. For the gifts and calling of God *are* without repentance." Romans 11:26-29.

167. "And he said unto them, Go ye into all the world, and preach the gospel to every creature. He that believeth and is baptized shall be saved; but he that believeth not shall be damned. And these signs shall follow them that believe; In my name shall they cast out devils; they shall speak with new tongues; They shall take up serpents; and if they drink any deadly thing, it shall not hurt them; they shall lay hands on the sick, and they shall recover." Mark 16:15-18.

June 29, 1840

Went to Hart Street. Found them all confusion—one blaming another &c. To Sister Booth's to Dinner. She gave me 1/6. Stayed at the meeting. 2 spake in tongues. I addressed them and tried to encourage them to diligen[ce]. My face was very bad.

June 30, 1840

Brothers Kimball and Richards came from Preston. We went together with Elders Parley Pratt and Young to William Millers to singing meeting.[168] Took supper. My mind was very low because I thought the brethren looked shy.[169]

168. Probably this refers to a meeting concerning the collection of hymns. Brigham Young, *Manuscript History,* 79; Pratt, *Autobiography,* 340.

169. This probably did not mean to imply that the brethren were timid in any way. Rather, Clayton undoubtedly was referring to their apparent lack of temporal means. The Twelve, like Clayton himself, were traveling without purse or scrip, and they probably appeared destitute.

July 1, 1840

Went to Sands to Dinner. Called at Sarah Perkins. Brothers Woodruff, Smith and Turley came in.[170] I received a bonnet for my little Sarah from E[*lizabeth*] Ravenscroft. Had talk with Ann Darrah. Full of sectarian notions.

170. These elders were coming in for the conference which was to be held on July 6. After they arrived, Wilford Woodruff was so impressed with a vision that was being reported by Sister Booth of Manchester that he recorded it in his journal. According to Mrs.

Booth, she had seen the vision on March 12, and it concerned the principle of redemption of the dead. Brigham Young, *Manuscript History*, 78; Woodruff "Journal," July 2, 1840, HDC; note 92 above.

July 5, 1840

Elder Woodruff preached this morning[171] and I led meeting in the afternoon. Brother Alfred Corden preached at night on first principles.

171. Woodruff preached to a large congregation of nearly 1,000 people, about half of whom were non-Mormons, according to him. Woodruff, "Journal," July 5, 1840, HDC.

July 6, 1840

This day we held our Conference in Carpenters Hall members 2513[172]—Elders 59 Priests 122 Teachers 61 Deacons 13. Elder Pratt was president I was chosen clerk. Brother Green was suspended from office for giving way to a false spirit for accusing a young female of things which he could not prove (in a public meeting) and for abusing house and congregation at Dukinfield June 28, 1840. Brother John Taylor preached at night. Ordained 14 officers and 4 others to be ordained.

172. Clayton as the presiding elder in Manchester called the meeting to order. Parley P. Pratt was chosen as president of the Conference and Clayton as clerk. At the conference Joseph Fielding and his counselors were released from the mission presidency and Brigham Young, then President of the Council of Twelve Apostles, became president. All the apostles then in Great Britain except Orson Pratt, who was laboring in Scotland, were present. At the time of the conference the mission had 41 branches and 2,513 members. Manchester had 280 members, an increase of 40 over the number in April. The hymn book on which the apostles and Clayton had been working was approved. On this day also, a number of the brethren volunteered to be missionaries, including William Clayton. Several men were ordained or approved for ordination. The Brother Green who was suspended from office was probably Thomas Green. Apparently he was later reinstated because he emigrated to the United States and was never listed as having been excommunicated. "Manchester Branch Records," 33, entry 541; Smith, *History of the Church*, VI, 146-148; Dahl, *William Clayton*, 17-18; Evans, *A Century of Mormonism*, 137-138.

July 7, 1840

Held council at the Star office. It was voted that I should go to Birmingham as soon as my family were gone to America.[173]

173. John Needham was to accompany Clayton to Birmingham. Clayton, of course, never filled this mission, but went to America with his family. See below. Brigham Young, *Manuscript History*, 78; Dahl, *William Clayton*, 18.

July 10, 1840

At council ordained John Hardman and James Rigby Deacons. Appointed John Hardman clerk of the church. Elder Pratt gone to Liverpool for America.[174]

174. Pratt had received a letter from his family in New York telling him that they were ill with scarlet fever. On the advice of the Council of Twelve, Pratt returned to New York to get them. Pratt attempted to return with his family in time for the October 6, 1840 conference at Manchester, but owing to contrary winds, he was unable to get there in time. In his absence, Brigham Young took over as editor of the *Millennial Star*, in addition to his other duties. Pratt, *Autobiography*, 309-10; Brigham Young, *Manuscript History*, 79.

July 12, 1840

Went to Stockport. Preached at night and returned by Railway.

July 19, 1840

Preached this A M in Carpenters Hall on the fall of the Gentile church and the judgements to be poured out on consequence.

July 23, 1840

Returned to Penwortham by Railway to assist my family in making preparations for America. Found them well and in good spirits. Sister Catherine Beates gave me a yellow silk Handkerchief and Sister Elizabeth Dewsnup gave me a red one. Sister Mary Wood gave me a new satin stock. Sarah Crooks has got me money for a new pair of boots 28/—. Sarah

167

Ann Booth gave me a four penny pence to remember her by.
Sister Hannah Walker gave me a Pocket handkerchief and I
feel it hard to leave the saints at Manchester yet willing because it is for the best.[175]

175. At this time, of course, Clayton did not know he would be
going to America. He was planning to leave Manchester for Birmingham as soon as his family had left for America. Birmingham was over
100 miles from Manchester, so he would not see the Manchester Saints
for some time. It was only natural that they should give him fare-
well presents after all his service to them, and this entry suggests their
closeness to each other.

September 3, 1840[176]

Since July 23—we have been engaged in making preparations
for America. On Tuesday the 18 of August we had our sale.
I was writer. We had some difficulty in getting all our money
in and especially some due from the Railway company for
damages we had after to go and did not get it untill a few
days before we started. The time had been appointed for us
to be in Liverpool on the 27th of August but the time was
prolonged untill September 4 on account of some of the saints
not being ready. It happened well it was so for we had
hardly time to settle up our business by the 4 of September.
During this time I preached ocasionally on the sabbath. The
first 3 or 4 days after I came home I spent in writing Brother
Kimballs history[177] which was lengthy. I have got a pair of
Boots which cost 27/6. On this day we have been very busy
packing up and have taken one load of Boxes to the Railway.
The brethren have collected 7/— towards carrying me to Birmingham. The parting scene was affecting. Elder Riley felt
very much he gave me 2/6. Elder Brigham Young has been
over from Manchester. On Monday we went to Longton
and returned same night. He returned to Manchester on
Tuesday. I have spent one afternoon at Sister Morgans in
company with Brother William Hardman. He made me a
present of a handsome knife. Several have been baptized while

I have been here and the work is in a prosperous state. The preaching will be held in future at Elder [..] Martins. John Melling was married to Mary Martin about 2 weeks ago. Some person on Saturday evening last threw two notes into Brother Whiteheads shop one for himself and the other for me. They both contained the same matter namely a request that we would preach from Ecclesiastes chapter 10 verse 1 signed a lover of Mormons.[178] I went over to Manchester and walked all the way and in the morning went to Liverpool. I returned home in the P.M having learned that the ship which Brother Moon's sailed in arrived in New York about the 18th of July. On Wednesday the 19th I received a letter from Brother John Moon giving an account of their voyage. They were 41 days on the water including 3 days quarantine. They had 3 storms and considerable sickness but all arrived safe and in good spirits.[179] I have endeavored to sell Brother John Moons Base Vial but without success. T. Pickering promised to buy it for the new church in Farrington but when I went to agree with him he declined taking it. I then went to William Bashale but he would not have any thing to do with it. I was obliged to leave it with Brother John Melling for sale. I have received two letters from Brother Kimball of London and one from Sarah Crooks.

176. During the summer, Clayton was quite lax in writing in his diary. He may have been traveling a great deal, and it appears that he was preparing for his family to go to America. This must have been a rather sudden decision, made either at the end of July or early in August, and the pace of events may have kept him from writing more. At this time he was planning for them to go and for him to follow later after finishing his mission in Birmingham. His decision to go to America himself was apparently rather sudden, as indicated by the entry on September 5.

177. This is probably the "History of the British Mission." Joseph Smith's *History of the Church* dates this in March, 1841, after Clayton had left England. The document is reprinted in Smith's *History* in its entirety though signed by Heber C. Kimball, Orson Hyde, and Willard Richards at Preston on March 24, 1841. It contains no information later than April 6, 1840 and deals principally with the opening of the

British Mission by Kimball and his associates in 1837 and their activities until they returned in 1838. Thereafter, the information contained in the document has to do with the mission under the presidency of Fielding, Richards, and Clayton until the return of the apostles in 1840. It seems possible that Clayton was the actual author of the history but that it was written under Kimball's direction and signed by Kimball, Hyde, and Richards when Hyde passed through Great Britain on the way to Palestine. Hyde was in England until June 20, 1841 when he left for Rotterdam to continue his journey. Smith, *History of the Church* IV, 313-21; quoting Hyde to Smith, Ratisbon, July 17, 1841.

178. The verse reads: "Dead flies cause the ointment of the apothecary to send forth a stinking savour: *so doth* a little folly him that is in reputation for wisdom *and* honour." Apparently, the anonymous author was no friend of the Mormons.

179. William Clayton copied the letter from John Moon into another letter which he (Clayton) wrote to Brigham Young and Willard Richards on August 19. Moon told of leaving Liverpool on June 6, seeing the land of America for the first time on July 17, spending three days in quarantine but still on Sunday (July 19) going into New York City and finding the Saints there. All the company arrived in New York City on July 20, which is the date Joseph Smith recorded in his history as the arrival date. Clayton to Young and Richards, Penwortham, August 19, 1840, Clayton Papers, HDC; Smith, *History of the Church*, IV, 134, 162.

September 4, 1840

We arose early this A M and packed up our beds &c, and took the remainder of our goods to Preston. All the company their came together to our house about 1 o clock from whence we started to the Farrington Railway station. Here an extra carriage had been left for us and we loaded ourselves a little after two and waited the arrival of the Train. We were 26 in number including children. The train soon came up and our carriage being attached we started off in the presence of about a dozen saints. We had a pleasant ride to Liverpool about 5 o clock. When we got here I made a bargain with a carter to take our boxes &c to Princess Dock for 1/1½. When we got to the Dock another man professing to be the owner of the cart came and demanded 1/6 pr box. We had a hard contest. He threatened to fetch a policeman &c. He then wanted 2/6. I told him that for his bad behavior I would not give him any thing more than the bargain. He refused to take it for sometime but at last he took it and went away in a rage. Several of the brethren who came had to pay extremely on account of hiring men and not making a bargain before they engaged them. I was aware of such things and therefore acted as stated above. We found Elder Turley and Young soon. All the company was confused and busy arranging their boxes. We slept in the ship this night or *lay awake*.[180]

180. Obviously, Clayton's party was not as well organized as those that came later. Later detailed instructions on such things as this were published in the *Millennial Star* and local authorities were instructed to be certain that the emigration procedures were well known. Even in this case, however, arrangements for the ship and for rail passage had been made in advance, and the Saints were not left to chance. Later, instructions were broadened to include warnings against sharp dealers of the sort which Clayton met. P.A.M. Taylor, *Expectations Westward: The Mormons and the Emigration of their British Converts in the Nineteenth Century* (Edinburgh: Oliver and Boyd, 1965), 160-75. See also Charles Dickens' description of a Mormon emigrant ship from *The Uncommercial Traveler* which is cited in William Mulder and A. Russell Mortensen, eds., *Among the Mormons: Historic Accounts by Contemporary Observers* (New York: Knopf, 1958), 334-44.

September 5, 1840

This A.M. I bought a pair of trowsers having tore my others. I engaged the cart to fetch our other luggages and during the day we got them in some measure arranged. My mother-inlaw seeing the toil and trouble there was in these things began to weep and wish me to go with them. She made her request known the Brother Young and Taylor who consented for me to go. I immediately started for Railway to Manchester where I arrived about ½ past 7. When I got to Hardmans I found Sarah and Rebecca just making preparations to leave that night. I saw there was something rather unpleasant between them and it almost broke my heart. Almost as soon as I arrived here I was taken sick on account of being so long without meat and over exerting myself. I vomited much and felt very ill. I could eat nothing. I slept at Hardmans that night.

September 6, 1840

This A M I was very sick and kept my bed till noon. Several of the saints came to see me. Went to Perkins in the P.M. Was obliged to go to bed again and remained in bed untill 10 o clock. A many of the saints came to see me. Brother Grundy gave me 2/6. Sister Birch gave me some plumbs and 1/−. Some of them wept much at parting. Sarah Crooks has got some linnen and cut it to day for shirts. Arthur Smith has been today and bought cloth for my trowsers and cut my cloths out.

September 7, 1840

Breakfast at Perkins. Sister Jane Hardman sent me a watch guard and four penny [−] box to remember her by. Brother Thomas Miller gave me a new hat. Left Perkins about 11 for Railway. Was obliged to get a cab in St. Anns Square. Was a few minutes to late at the office. Went to Mr. Thompsons where I took dinner. She gave me a glass of wine. Took first carriage at 2. Arrived at Liverpool at little after 3 o clock. When I arrived at the ship I found Elder Richards. He seemed to object to my going. This gave me some trouble. I was yet very poorly. At night preparations was made for sailing on the morrow. Ship North America captain Lower.

September 8, 1840

This A M about 8 o clock we was hauled out of dock and a steamer being attached we was tugged into the sea in the Presence of many spectators. The company cheerful. Elders Young, Richards and Taylor went with us and returned by the steamer.[181] About this time many began to be sick myself amongst the number. 2 brothers was obliged to be put back on account of being over number. We was 201 men women and children. One of those put back was Brother

Heap from Preston. I had no knowledge of having to go yet until Saturday afternoon and I did not send any letters being so sick. Brother William Hardman promised to write for me— and my brother David was at Liverpool. Soon after the steamer returned the mate came down and ordered all boxes fast as they expected a good rocking that night. It was even so. The wind blew hard the vessel rock and many were sick all night. This was a new scene. Such sickness, vomiting, groaning and bad smells I never witnessed before and added to this the closeness of the births almost suffocated us for want of air.

181. Young says that they accompanied the party about fifteen or twenty miles and left them in good spirits. Brigham Young, *Manuscript History*, 79.

September 9, 1840

This A M Elder Turley ordered all the company on deck to wash as the weather was a little more calm. We had a pleasant view of the North of Ireland as we sailed on that side. In the afternoon the wind increased and blew a gale until Saturday morning. I was in bed nearly all this time and very sick and so was many of the company. Elder Turley was sick a little. Brothers William and Robert and Nehemiah Greenhalgh, Sister Mary Moon and James Crompton was not sick. These were very kind in waiting upon those sick. During all this gale the whole of the company or nearly so was very ill and many confined to their beds. We were drifted back to the North and was 4 hours in one place and could not move. I have been told that we were in two whirlpools near to a rock and the captain expecting us to be dashed against it. We was in great danger but the Lord delivered us. On the Friday night a little girl belonging to a family in the second cabin was frightened by the storm and lost her reason. The company was composed but we were ignorant of our danger. Some of the rigging was blown away. See September 21.

September 12, 1840

The storm is somewhat abated and the company begin to brighten up a little. Myself remains very feeble.

September 13, 1840

The captain requested Elder Turley to preach this P.M. He read John chapter 1[182] and preached about ¾ of an hour. This night the child which was frightened died or rather in the morning.

182. The chapter begins: "In the beginning was the Word, and the Word was with God, and the Word was God. The same was in the beginning with God. All things were made by him; and without him was not anything made that was made." It tells of the work of John the Baptist and his testimony that Jesus was the son of God and the calling of the Twelve Apostles and Andrew's testimony that Jesus was the Messiah or the Christ.

September 14, 1840

At the request of the Captain, Elder Turley read the burial service and the body of the child was committed to the deep. The weather continues favourable.

September 15, 1840

We have had another storm and many has been sick.

September 18, 1840

Friday [— — — — —] Some of the company continue very sick especially three of the children. Some have doubt concerning their recovery. Brother and Sister Holmes of Herefordshire have given up their [—] to die. Elder Turleys mind is much grieved in consequence of these things. At night he called the saints together in order to ascertain their feelings concerning the recovery of those sick. The sequel showed that there was

174

some unbelief in our midst. He spake considerable on the subject and asked the brethren to state their feelings. One immediately said he believed Holmes's child would not recover. I said I did not believe it was the will of God we should lose one soul. Elder Turley said to the same effect. The saints then began to be more cheerful and the power of darkness was in some degree banished. We prayed with the children and desired all to hold them by faith. But after all our exertions Brother Holmes' child died same night. This was a grief to our minds—but it was so.

September 19, 1840

Saturday. Early this A M the mate came and ordered the child to be sewed up which was soon done and it was immediately thrown overboard without any ceremony. After the place was cleansed out gas was burned to sweeten the ship air and prevent disease. A head wind.

September 20, 1840

Sunday. We were not requested to preach today but Elder Turley called the saints together in the P.M and we broke bread to the company. Many seem much pleased with our meeting.

September 21, 1840

Monday. Good sail. At night Elder Turley spoke considerable on cleanliness and afterwards went round the births to see if all the company undressed. Some was found with their cloths on—and some had never pulled their cloths off since they came on deck but had done their dirt in their cloths. Others had dirt in the corner of their birth. This made the most awful smell when discovered almost to much to bear. Elder Turley undressed and washed them and ordered the place cleaned out. Some of the company are filthy indeed.[183]

Errata—See September 9th. On Thursday night during
the gale when the sailors had close reefed all the sails except about 4 and were endeavoring to Reef these there came
a gust of wind that took away 3 of the sails one maine sail.
On Friday night we lost another sail and some of the blocks.

183. With the exception of this filthy condition which was observed and corrected at this point, if the sampling made by P.A.M.
Taylor of journals and other records of trans-oceanic migration by the
Mormons is any criteria, this journey was not unlike others. Many
were plagued with bad weather, broken masts, and shortages of food.
Since most were poor people, they traveled by steerage as did Clayton
and his party. Quarters were cramped, there was sickness and death,
and it was very difficult to maintain privacy. Later, some of the
British Passenger Acts appear to have improved privacy, but there is
some question as to how well they were enforced.

One of the advantages which the Saints had over other travelers
was in the organization of the companies and the general willingness
of members of the party to help one another and to obey the authority
of the president and his counselors. This is seen in this company, in
spite of Clayton's complaint that "some are not saints who profess
to be," in the willingness to attend the sick and to clean up when it
was seen that conditions were filthy. Taylor, *Expectations*, 176-207.

September 22, 1840

Tuesday. This A M we had a calm. About 11 o clock I heard
the chief mate cry out all hands on deck and buckets with
water. It appears that some of the Sisters was sitting near
their births watching what they considered to be the reflec-
tions through a glass light until sparks of fire began to drop.
They then cried out the ship is on fire. The mate heard and
sang out as above. This caused considerable alarm and bustle
for sometime. The sailors was speedily at work and water was
poured on for sometime. It was soon discovered that there
was not much danger. The fire originated in the galley or
cooking house. The wood underneath the stove had caught
fire by some means and burned throu the deck. After the
fire was put out the Captain ordered the stove removed and
the place examined. It was cleaned out and repaired and some
improvements made. Some of the saints smelled fire last night

and told the mate but he could not discover any thing wrong. We look upon this circumstance as another attempt of the adversary to destroy us but the Lord kindly preserved us. Some of us had wished in the morning that the wind would blow but it was well we had a calm or the consequence might have been awful. As soon as the bustle subsided the wind began to blow and we were again on our way home. The Lord has been kind to us for which we feel thankful but not as much as we might. Same night also we had the painful task of casting overboard Mormon son of Paul and Jane Harris of ~~Herefordshire~~ branch. He was one of the three which has been sick for some days. He was thought to be dead sometime before he was and preparation was made to bury him. He died about 8 o clock[184] Sister Jane Harris was very sick at the same time. There are several others also very sick. We attend to prayer every evening as well as our awkward circumstances will permit.

184. It is interesting to note that the mortality rate for the Mormon groups was higher than for British emigrants as a whole. The experience of Clayton's company is some evidence that P.A.M. Taylor's speculations about the reason may be correct. Taylor says that it was because the Mormons had with them more children and old people than did other groups.

On these ships there were three classes of passage. They were: Cabin or Salon in which passengers enjoyed staterooms, abundant food and service; Intermediate or Second Cabin which might provide separate berths or enclosed berths; and Steerage which consisted of rows of bunks in a common room. Taylor, *Expectations*, 178-79, 198.

September 23, 1840

Wednesday. This A M the Captain called upon all the heads of families to give account of the number of Packages each one owned. He appeared vexed on account of some having so many boxes. Our family was one. We have reason to think that he is seeking some occasion against us from several expressions which dropped from his lips this A.M. We have had a little trouble on account of the peevish selfish actions of some of the second cabin passengers. We have some difficulty in keeping things quiet amongst us. Many things are lost and nobody finds them. Some are not saints who profess to be. But considering our situation all things have passed off pretty well through the blessing of God.

September 26, 1840
Saturday. To day being our turn to attend the sick I took it in hand. But the smoke made me very ill. My head and limbs ached much. Sister Naylor and I have had a few words concerning our boxes. They have tresspassed on our privileges a little. They are but one family and have two boxes out, we are two families and have but one. I desired them to move one about four inches but they would not. She railed a little at me and used some hard words.

September 27, 1840
Sunday. Fair wind. One of the cabin passengers read prayers out of the church prayer book. They requested us to preach but Elder Turley was not willing and I did not feel at all fit for it and so it was neglected. We had no meeting. Some sick [−].

September 28, 1840
Monday. We have had a head wind but a good days sail. Myself very sick. The infant child belonging to Brother and Sister Corbridge of Thomly died this P M and was cast overboard. At night Brother Turley spake concerning some of the company having said he had a shilling a head for all the saints and other such things. He shewed his bills and accounts to satisfy them and [−]them for their hardness of heart and unbelief.

September 29, 1840
Tuesday. This A M we have a perfect calm. The captain and some of the cabin passengers have been swimming and afterwards took a short voyage in a small boat. The weather is extremely hot to day almost to much for us to bear. Brother Samuel Bateman caught a young Shark during the calm near a yard long. The infant child belonging to Brother and Sister Green of Manchester died this evening and was buried in the deep. We have spend this P M in arranging for payment of potatoes. The whole cost is about £28 which, amounts to 3/1 per head or adult persons. Elder Turley has from time to time spoken much concerning the sisters keeping themselves from the sailors. Sister Mary Ann Holmes from Herefordshire has made great freedom with them which has been a grief to us. This night Elizabeth Wilson, Elizabeth Lambert and Eliza Prince all from Manchester and Sister Crampton from Bolton was making very free with one of the mates and 2 of the cabin passengers. Brother Cope says they were drinking wine with them. Elder Turley sent Sister Poole to request them to come away but they returned very indifferent answers and said they could take care of themselves.

October 1, 1840
Thursday. The wind began to blow [−]. During the day we crossed the fishing banks. We saw about 20 fishing boats ankered on the banks while we were crossing the banks. We had a squal. The main Top sail was torn from top to bottom and the vessel rolled much. Many were sick last night. The Captain and cabin passengers spent the night in dancing to the violin.

October 2, 1840
Friday. The wind good this A M sailing about 9 to 10 miles

an hour. We discover that the crew are mad with us and we judge it is because we are unwilling that the sisters should be so familiar with the mates and sailors. There has been some unpleasant feelings manifested from those who were in company with the mate and cabin passingers the other night. Philip the Captains brotherinlaw is proved to be an enemy to us and tells tales to the mates. He seems very kind to our face but it is to spy us. My little Margaret is very sick.

October 3, 1840
Saturday. This A M The mate says some of our company has been stealing water the last night. We don't believe they have. We have reasons to believe they have not as we had a watch appointed to see that the sailors did not come down as they have done before in the dead of night. They saw no one but must have seen them if anyone had been at the water. We look upon it as another instance of Phillips madness and seeking to injure us. About this time Elizabeth Wilson was passing the sailors cabin and one of the sailors asked her to go down and have breakfast. She would not. He then asked if she would have a piece of meat. She said she had no objections and accordingly took it. It appears the steward saw her and went and told the Captain who immediately came down and demanded it from her. He also asked who gave it her. She said she did not know. On account of this the sailors are to have a pound a day less each and they are mad and swear vengeance on the steward when they get to land. This afternoon Joseph Jackson entered into an argument with some of the second cabin passengers upon religious subjects. The Captain and some of the cabin passengers was listening The Captain went to the side of the ship and called Jackson to him to ask if he had said that he would go and take the water by force. He acknowledged to saying that he believed it right to take it as many were suffering for want of water and

also that he believed those childrens death was partly caused on account of being short of water. The Captain ordered him down and told him if he heard him say anything like it again he would bind him down in chains and feed him on bread and water. Jackson answered the Captain again that we were suffering for want of water. I rebuked him and got him to hold his peace. He said he would defend himself. The captain said he might preach his religion as much as he liked but say nothing more like that. He also said he would like to kill about a dozen of us. This myself heard. The Captain afterwards came to Elder Turley and asked if he understood the laws of mutiny. Elder Turley answered yes and the laws concerning water to. The Captain said "You must know we lost six barrels of water during the storm soon after we left Liverpool." It seems the Captain thought brother was ignorant concerning the laws but when he saw to the contrary he softened down and changed colour. He said he would bind Jackson if he heard him use the same expressions. Yes says Brother Turley and I will help you. It is more and more evident that Satan wants to destroy us or throw us into confussion. After dark the chief mate came to Elder Turley and said "some of your damb'd crew has up set the water tub." It was found to be some of the Scotch people in the second cabin.

October 4, 1840
Sunday. This A M we have a good wind. Are sailing from 9 to 11 miles an hour. We have also our full allowance of water again. We have only had 1½ quarts since September 20th. We had no meetings to day only as usual at night. My mother in law is very poorly—also Elizabeth Ravenscroft.

October 5, 1840
Monday. We are not sailing much today. I feel myself very

181

poorly. Motherinlaw and my wife yet very sick. Elder Turley and some of the cabin passengers along with the Captain have had a long argument this night concerning the ministration of the angel to Joseph. They treat it with disdain—especially the Captain.

October 6, 1840

Tuesday. This day Elder Turley went to prove to the cabin passengers the rationality of prophecy and administration of angels. They will not admit of reasonable evidence. They found themselves confounded. At night Elizabeth and William Poole spoke in tongues. He prophesied of the death of his child.

October 7, 1840

Wednesday. Early this A.M. William Poole's child died and was committed to the deep. Some at Penwortham had said it would die before it got over the waters and Betsy had been troubled on this account. I wish they would not do so for Satan takes advantage of such things to discourage the minds of the Saints when surrounded by trouble and difficulty. This A M the chief mate saw Cape Cod on the American coast. The line was heaved and found 55 fathom. They tacked about 8 o clock to near South and then found 44 fathom. We were a few hours becalmed. About 12 o'clock we was much pleased to hear the mate speak to a ships Captain. The Condor of Halifax bore down to us and they spake to each other. She was from Jamaica 24 days homeward bound. My motherinlaw yet very poorly.

October 8, 1840

Thursday. Last evening being my turn for prayer I felt to ask the Lord for a fair wind and I rejoice to see he has answered my prayers. The wind is very favourable near 10 mi.

an hour. This is the third instance of the Lord answering my prayer for fair wind in a calm.

October 9, 1840
Friday. Fair days sail. The crew are very busily engaged cleaning the ship and making preparations for landing. At night the anker chains was fastened to the anker.

October 10, 1840
Saturday. About 8 A M land was discovered by the sailors from the fire mast and in about 2 hours we had a pleasant view of Long Island. About ½ past eleven we spoke the Tuscany. New York—56 days from Gibralter. About 5 o clock the Pilot came on board. We saw the lighthouses on the Island.

October 11, 1840
Sunday. This morning early we cast anker and a little after 4 o clock I went on deck and found that we were between two Islands. We had a pleasant view of the Sailors Hospital and a many beautiful white houses and fine trees. 'Twas indeed a pleasant sight.[185] The Docter came on board about 8 o clock and about the same time the child belonging to Brother Parry from Herefordshire died. All the rest passed the docter without difficulty. The doctor ordered him to be sent on shore which was done in a small Boat. Here I may say that we struck a sand bar last night and had it not been calm we might have gone to pieces. This was off Sandy Hook.[186] After the boat returned the ship was turned land. In a short time we was on our way for New York. Considering the wetness of the morning we had a very pleasant sight of the fowls and Islands. After about an hours sail we arrived in New York exactly at a quarter before twelve. It was truly delightful to see the multitude of shipping in the Har-

183

bour. There is no docks here but a very good harbour. The buildings look elegant.[187] When our vessel came to harbour she pressed against a small schooner and stove in her bulwarks and broke some rigging. After the ship was made fast Elder Turley and me and Joseph Jackson left the ship and set our feet on land exactly at 10 minutes past 12 o clock. This was another treat to us to set our feet on terra firma although the streets was dirty in consequence of rain. In taking a slight glance I must confess I was delighted to see the superior neatness and tastly state of the buildings many painted white others brick and some have door steps painted yellow. We bought some large red apples for a cent each which was truly delicious. The streets are wide but not so well flagged and paved as in England. The first house we entered was brother Delongs where we took dinner. From here we went to meeting at the Military Hall in the Bowery.[188] The first thing that struck my attention was all the men and women I saw sitting cross legged and all the left leg over the right. Elder Adams preached on the principles of the gospel. After preaching we took bread and wine. We went to Elder Fosters and took tea with Brother Simmons. After tea Elder Turley went on business and I went to writing. We slept on board the ship. Many of the Saints went to meeting and was much pleased. We learn nothing of Brother Hardman nor the other two brethren who were turned back at Liverpool.

185. They were probably anchored between Ellis Island and Governor's Island. Assuming that the ship was parallel to the two islands facing approximately northeast, Clayton would have been able to see the southern tip of Manhattan at a distance of about one mile. The Sailor's Hospital of which Clayton wrote may have been the Seaman's Retreat and Hospital at 8 Old Slip, near the East River in the south side of Manhattan just northeast of the Battery. John Doggett, Jr. *The Great Metropolis: Or New York In 1845* (New York: S. W. Benedict, 1844), 196.

186. Along with the southern end of Long Island, Sandy Hook forms a natural shelter for the harbor of New York. It is 18 miles

from the city and supports a lighthouse. In 1845 the water at Sandy Hook was 27 feet at high tide and 21 feet at low tide. *Ibid.*, 54.

187. New York in 1840, of course, looked a great deal different than it does today. The famous skyline was absent as well as the Statue of Liberty. In front of South Street along the East River, Clayton would have seen a "dense forest of masts." In 1840, the city had a population of 312, 710. *Ibid.*, 54-56.

188. Bowery Street stretched northeastward from Division at what is now Chatham Square to Union Square. It is in the district generally known as the lower East Side. Just which building Clayton referred to is not known. The United States Arsenal was located near Union Square, but in 1823 it was converted into a juvenile reformatory known as the House of Refuge. This may have been the building to which Clayton has reference, though it was partly burned in 1839. Doggett, *Great Metropolis*, 133-34; Federal Writers' Project, *New York City Guide* (New York: Random House, 1939), 108-24; James Hardie, *The Description of the City of New York* (New York: Samuel Marks, 1827), 196-204, 208; J. H. French, *Gazetteer of the State of New York: Embracing a Comprehensive View of the Geography, Geology, and General History of the State and A Complete History and Description of Every County, City, Town, Village and Locality* (Syracuse: R. P. Smith, 1860), 436-37.

October 12, 1840

Monday. This P.M a lighter came to the ships side into which we put our luggage. We slept on board the North America again.

October 13, 1840

Tuesday. Having finished loading our luggage those of the company who were present went on board a steamer (the Congress) and sailed to the Albany basin. We bid adieu to the North America at 12 o clock. The Captain seemed very friendly and said he should wish to bring another company of us over. He enquired if we had a church in New York and where they meet. Elder Turley introduced him to Elder Foster. I gave Elder Adams 25 letters for England for which I paid 25 cent. The agreement which Elder Turley made with the proprietors of the Congress was that we should sail this day but they have broke their bargain and Elder Turley is much troubled. We slept on board the Congress. I feel struck to see the horses and carts even to see the light harness and small carts and light loads drawn by them. The drivers all ride. The fruit is quite delicious to English people. I slept in best cabin.

October 14, 1840

Wednesday. About 9 o clock this A M   H.C. Greenhalgh died after being ill 8 or 9 days. The city coroner came and sat over him. I was one of the jurors. Verdict—died from unknown cause. A coffin was provided and he was taken into the city to be buried. At 5 o clock P.M. we had a very beautiful sight. 7 steam boats all left the harbour at once. It seemed as though the harbour was on a move. We left about 20 minutes after 5. The company in good spirits. As we left New York we had a pleasant view of the North part of the city. The buildings chiefly white and very neat. The several spires towering towards the sky bore a majestic appearance. On one part there was a large lot of wood which we was told was provided for [poor] folks against winter. We had not gone far before it began to grow dark and we could only discover by moonlight the lofty rocks on earth since the river which is Hudson river especially the west side which was indeed beautiful with here and there a beautiful white house scattered on the banks. Before we started from New York we learned that the Mary Kingsland was arrived in New York and that Brother H[ardman] and the other families was arrived. Some one went over to get them along with us but it found impossible. We left Brother Richard Tell at New York. He got work there and was likely to do well.

October 15, 1840

Thursday. This morning I arose to behold again the beautiful white houses and banks on the river's side. We passed the village Cantskill[189] which looked very beautiful and a little further we passed a village called Colonel Youngs village. He settled in this place and established a foundry and got a number of workmen along with him where they now have houses built which forms the village. As we proceeded we saw many fields of grain which was cut. We saw in one field a great numbr of pumpkins quite yellow and pretty. On one farm we saw about 140 cows and oxen and sheep in different places. After proceeding sometime we passed the beautiful town of Hudson[190] on the East side of the river. This seems to be a town of about ten thousand inhabitants. Stil passing along we continued to be delighted with the houses and in some places we saw fruit on the trees. As we got higher up the river the land appeared to grow richer but yet very rocky. Close to the banks of the river about 14 miles from Albany we passed a coal wharf which is a scarce thing in this country. The fuel is almost all wood and this article is exceeding plentiful. About ½ past 5 we arrived at Albany.[191] We left a boat with a number of passengers here. This is a large town on the west side the river containing perhaps 40 thousand inhabitants. We could see the court house and prison and the different churches interspersed here and there. Here is also a pleasand harbour for a few shipping. The coast is almost covered with timber. We saw a large Iron foundry and workshops of different kinds. We soon left Albany and at 7 o clock arrived at the city of Troy[192] where we now are stopped for the night. We also passed the City Athens[193] a while before Albany.

189. Clayton is probably referring to the village of Catskill which is on the Hudson at the mouth of Catskill Creek. Catskill is located about one hundred miles up the Hudson from Manhatton Island. French, *Gazetteer*, 332; Robert J. Rayback et al, eds., *Richards Atlas of New York State* (Rev. ed.; Phoenix, New York: Frank E. Richards, 1965), 2.

190. Hudson is located about 5 miles north of Catskill. It lies on the east bank of the Hudson an a bluff above the river. French, *Gazetteer*, 246-47; Rayback, *Richards Atlas*, 2.

191. Albany lies on the west bank of the Hudson River about 130 miles north of New York City and is the eastern terminus of the Erie Canal. It was important as a grain and lumber market and is the capital of the state of New York. French, *Gazetteer*, 159-62; Rayback, *Richards Atlas*, 2.
192. Troy is about 8 miles north of Albany.
193. Athens is almost directly across the Hudson River from Hudson. Rayback, *Richards Atlas*, 2.

October 16, 1840

Friday. This A M Elder Turley bought a sheep ready dressed for 1½ dollars. This was divided amongst some of the company. We got our luggage off the steamer by 10 o clock and soon after we were tugged to the canal. We were obliged to hire another boat into which some of us got with much difficulty. It is evident Mrs. Benbow wants one boat for their company and they have made choice of one with a best cabin. This has caused a little feeling. Elder Turley had again considerable trouble with the proprietor and had to pay more than he ought at last. About ¼ to 4 we left West Troy.[194]

194. They were traveling on the Erie Canal, which ran north from Albany, parallel to the Hudson, to the Mohawk River. It crossed the Mohawk and ran along the north side of the river until it recrossed east of Schenectady. From there it paralleled the south bank of the Mohawk to Rome, where it turned southwest to Syracuse. At Rochester an 802 foot long aqueduct carried the canal across the Genesee River. From there the canal went into a generally westerly direction to Lockport where five double locks raised it fifty feet to the level of Lake Erie. The total vertical lockage of the canal was 645 feet and the canal plus its improvements down to 1862 cost $36,252,000. It was 363 miles long and had 71 locks. *Ibid.*, 49-50.

October 17, 1840

Saturday. We are now passing through a very pleasant country. Many fruit trees loaded with fruit and loads scattered on the ground. I took up a large handkerchief full. There are a great quantity of pigs kept in this region. We have passed the upper aqueduct which is a stupendous work. Soon after this we arrived at the beautiful town of Schenectady[195] seated close to the canal or rather the canal passed through it. Here there is a Railway. We buy our milk at the grocery shops for 4 cents a quart.

195. Schenectady is on the Mohawk and is a trade and railroad center. In 1840 it had a population of 6,784. The railroad about which Clayton wrote was probably the New York Central. Schenectady had extensive engine houses and repair shops. French, *Gazetteer*, 598-99.

October 18, 1840

Sunday. We are now standing still as the owner of the boat is religious and will not allow it to run on Sundays. Some of our people went to washing as we had not had the privilege of washing since we left England. Last night William Greenhalgh's family came into our boat. Not having room to sleep in the other ones. I and several others went to the top of a very large hill and George Foster and I went up the topmost tree from whence we had a pleasant view. As we returned we met Elder Turley and some of the sisters going up the hill to pray. We returned with them and united our hearts together.

October 19, 1840

Monday. We passed a town called the little Halls.

October 20, 1840

Tuesday. About 2 o clock this A M we passed Utica[196] in the midst of heavy rain. One of our horses fell into the canal and was near being drowned. A horse belonging to another boat was drowned a little before. We passed the city of Rome.[197]

196. Utica lies on the south bank of the Mohawk River and is the north terminus of the Chenango Canal. It was a center for both agriculture and textile manufacturing. Its population in 1840 was 12,782. *Ibid.*, 468-69.
197. Rome is located on the Mohawk River and had a population in 1858 of 7,083. *Ibid.*, 466.

October 21, 1840

Wednesday. Before sun rise this A.M we passed Syracuse[198]

a place where a great quantity of salt is daily made. I got to day a 2 Dollar Bill which I cannot pay also a coin for a quarter dollar which only pays for 17 cents. At night we passed a very pretty town called Montezuma. I have wrote a letter which I intend to send from Buffalo to Brother John Moon. 10000 Bushels of salt per day.

198. Syracuse is located in Onondaga County. The salt works of which Clayton wrote were an important industry. At the time, they were operated by an evaporation process. *Ibid.*, 479-80, 488-89.

October 22, 1840

Thursday. William Poole paid my 2 Dollar Bill loning 12½ cts. We have passed the city of Palmyra[199] and soon after viz about 11 o clock Elder Turley and myself left the silver Arrow[200] and took packet for Tonnewonta[201] fare 4.12 each. About ½ past 7 we landed at Rochester[202] which appears to be a place of considerable business of different kind. Here we changed packets and in about 15 minutes started off again.

199. Located in Wayne County, Palmyra was the former home of Joseph Smith and it was near there that Smith discovered the plates from which the *Book of Mormon* was translated. Also nearby the Church was organized in 1830.
200. The *Silver Arrow* was apparently the name of the canal boat upon which they were traveling.
201. Tonawanda is on the Erie Canal at the confluence of the Niagara River and Tonawanda Creek. It is near Buffalo. French, *Gazetteer*, 293.
202. Because of the falls of the Genesee River near Rochester, this city became an important manufacturing town . The staple manufacture of the city was flour. Its population in 1840 was 20,191. *Ibid.*, 402-04.

October 23, 1840

Friday. About 11 this A.M. we passed the town of Lockport.[203] At this place there are 5 locks which raise the canal 60 feet. These locks as well as above from 1 to 2 miles of the canal westward is cut out of solid rock and present a stupendous appearance. The wind arose very high and in our place opposite the river from the lake drive us against the shore.

Several were thrown down and somewhat frightened. As we passed along the side of the river we saw the large drifts of sand like mountainous drifts of snow. We arrived in Buffalo[204] about 6 o clock and soon met with some of the brethren from the first boat the J D. Hawks. We went to her and found that 3 children had died since we left them. Sister Benbow manifested a bad spirit as she has often done and has given Elder Turley many slight cants. After this we went to meet the second boat Chatauqua which had been detained at the second bridge on account of the canal being high. In this boat all were pretty well but had been short of provisions. The first boat arrived here about 9 this A M and the captain immediately ordered the company to get their luggage out of the boat which they did to great disadvantage into a wharehouse. They had to pay 5 cents for this privilege.

203. The name of the city came from the fact that there were a greater number of locks on the canal than at any other point. Water power from the locks was put to good use in manufacturing. *Ibid.*, 454.

204. Buffalo, a city in 1840 of 13,213 population, was the terminus of the Erie Canal. Located on Lake Erie, it became an important commercial center. *Ibid.*, 284-88.

October 24, 1840

Saturday. We got the luggage of two boats weighed and engaged to Chicago on board the Wisconsin [*one word crossed out*] at 10 Dollars each person. Some went on board same day. We waited at night on the other boat untill 2 o clock Sunday morning but did not come. Then I bought a pair of mittens for 5/6 York money. On this day Elder Turleys mind was much cast down in consequence of being obliged to leave some of the poor in our company at Buffalo. While he was reflecting upon the best manner of accomplishing this and when almost heartbroke the President Elder of the stake at Kirtland[205] Kellog came by and Turley knew him. After they had saluted each other he made his case known to Elder

191

Kellog who immediately advised to take the company to Kirtland as they would winter more comfortable there than in Commerce.[206] This was total deliverance to Elder Turleys mind and a relief of his burden. The reason why some must be left here was a want of money. Elder Turley had been given to understand that we might go from Buffalo to Chicago for 5 Dollars a head and had it been so all the company would no doubt have gone through. But when he enquired the fare it was found to be 10 Dollars a head instead of 5 and there was no privilege of altering it for there was only one boat appointed to go this season. The Wisconsin had lately come in and was not to go any more only short voyages. Elder Turley went to the captain and endeavoured to charter the boat but to no purpose. After some time consulting between Elders Turley and Kellog it was concluded that all who wanted and could raise means should go to Commerce and the remainder to Kirtland which proved highly satisfactory to the majority of the company. The weather was at this time very cold as a large quantity of snow had fallen and whitened the streets. One boat load of the company went on board the Wisconsin expecting we should go on that boat. The other boat load having nowhere to go Mr. Proper's partner kindly offered them the Counting House to sleep in which they gladly accepted and immediately went there.

205. Kirtland is a village in northeastern Ohio about 160 miles northeast of Columbus. Parley P. Pratt, Peter Whitmer, Jr., and Ziba Peterson went to Kirtland on a mission in 1830 and converted Sidney Rigdon, a Campbellite minister, and most of his congregation. Early in 1831, Joseph Smith and his family moved to Kirtland. A branch was organized there and Kirtland was headquarters of the Church from 1831 until 1838 when Joseph Smith left.
206. Commerce was the name of the village formerly located on the site of Nauvoo. It was on the Mississippi River about 220 miles above St. Louis and slightly above the Keokuk rapids. Thomas Baldwin and J. Thomas, *A New and Complete Gazetteer of the United States* (Philadelphia: Lippincott, Grambo & Company, 1854), 762. See also Robert Bruce Flanders, *Nauvoo, Kingdom on the Mississippi* (Urbana: University of Illinois Press, 1965), passim.

October 25, 1840

Sunday. This A.M. Elder Turley and my self went to meet the Silver Arrow which we came in sight of after walking about 3 miles. When we went on board the saints rejoiced greatly. They had had some very ill treatment from the captain and crew since we left them and we found them with scarce room to stand. We arrived in Buffalo about 12 o clock. I spent the remainder of the day in making up accounts for those who were going to Kirtland. Whilst I was doing this Sister Elizabeth Poole's son Edward fell into the canal and was near drowned when got out. This Mother fainted and was very ill some time. This evening the Greenhalgh's concluded either to go to Kirtland or stay at Buffallo which grived me much.

October 26, 1840

Monday. The weather was very wet and cold. It was concluded that the Wisconsin Steamboat should not go. Consequently the company had to embark on board the Illinois captain Blake.

October 27, 1840

Tuesday. This A M the Boat should have left Buffallo but could not on account of storm. The Greenhalghs have took a house and two of them got work. I have bought a cap for 12 Dollars and a pair of Boots for 4 a Rifle for 16 powder 71. We also bought Saw and plane.

October 28, 1840

Wednesday. The weather continues stormy at night. We moved amongst the shipping to the end of the Creek. The other brethren [— — —].

October 29, 1840

Thursday. About 1 this A M we left Buffallo for Chicago. The names of those who are gone to Kirtland are Thomas

Green and family, Josh West and family. Alice Whiss and family. M. Blake and wife. Josh Jackson and wife from Manchester. T. Featherston. Martha Shelmerdine and Jane Fyldes from Stockport. J. Crompton and wife from Bolton. Josh Hutchinson and family. John Craig and family. Ralph Thompson and family from Cumberland. George Slater and family from Penwortham. Samuel Bateman and family from Pendlebury. Thomas Hooper and family from Herefordshire. George Naylor and family from Bolton. Jane Harris from Manchester. These all had their names on a recommend except Thomas Hooper whose conduct has been very bad. This company generally appeared chearful and rejoiced in the prospect of soon having a place of rest. Some was inclined almost to wish they had not left England rather than be left short of Commerce. We proceeded on our way pretty well until we arrived at Fairport[207] partly to take in wood and part on account of strong wind. Here some of us went on shore and had we time Elder Turley and myself would have gone to Kirtland as we were then only 11 miles from that place. Sometime in the night we started forwards again.

207. Fairport is a village in Lake County, Ohio, on Lake Erie at the mouth of the Grand River. It is 165 miles northeast of Columbus and about 25 miles east-northeast of Cleveland. It had a large harbor and lighthouse. Baldwin, *Gazetteer*, 321; Melville Bell Grosvenor, ed., *National Geographic Atlas of the Fifty United States* (Washington: National Geographic Society, n.d.), 10.

October 30, 1840
Friday. We had a place sail at night we anchored at the mouth of the river between lakes Erie and Huron.[208]

208. This was probably at the mouth of the Detroit River which flows south-southwest from Lake St. Clair to Lake Erie. Grosvenor, *Atlas*, 11.

October 31, 1840
Saturday. This A M about 7 o clock we arrived at Detroit.[209]

This is a very pleasant looking place of about 20000 inhabitants. Here we took in some more passengers which crowded us up very much. We left Detroit after taking on wood and proceeded up lake St Clair[210] where we saw many hundreds wild ducks. Some amused themselves by shooting at them with their Rifles.

209. Detroit is on the west bank of the Detroit River about 302 miles west of Buffalo. The city was founded by the French in 1760 as a military post. It was noted in 1840 for manufacturing and commerce and had a population of 9102. Baldwin, *Gazetteer*, 322.
210. Lake St. Clair is northeast of Detroit. The Detroit River flows from it into Lake Erie and the St. Clair River flows from Lake Huron into St. Clair. Grosvenor, *Atlas*, 10.

November 1, 1840

Sunday. We are on lake Huron in the P.M. we called at Pesqu Isle[211] to take in wood. Here I picked us some curious pebble stones. The lake is bounded by gravel of the whitest and hardest kind. At night we arrived at Mackinau[212] where we again took in wood.

211. Presque Isle was in 1840 part of an unorganized frontier area of Michigan. As late as the 1850 census, the region furnished no returns because there were so few inhabitants. It is located about 205 miles north-northwest of Detroit in Lake Huron. Baldwin, *Gazetteer*, 958; Grosvenor, *Atlas*, 10.
212. Mackinac, Michelimackinac, or Mackinaw was the capital of the county on the island of the same name in Lake Huron. It is 320 miles by water north-northwest of Detroit. Fort Mackinaw is above the harbor. Baldwin, *Gazetteer*, 638.

November 2, 1840

Monday. We are on lake Michigan[213] and for some time could not see land. We called at the Manitou Islands[214] to take in wood. Here I took up some more pebbles. Some of the company shot a few rabbits and small birds. We continued here some hours on account of strong head wind.

213. Lakes Huron and Michigan form a long horseshoe around the southern part of Michigan.
214. The Manitou Islands are about 240 miles north-northeast from Chicago in Lake Michigan. Grosvenor, *Atlas*, 10.

November 4, 1840

Wednesday. About ½ past 1 this A M we arrived at Chicago.[215] Very early in the morning we moved our luggage from the boat and Elder Turley went to seeking teems to go to Dixons[216] ferry as that was considered to be the best rout. We engaged two teems for our family but after loading both and weighing one we found it necessary to have another. I went back to were the boat landed and after a little time met with another. We got loaded about 2 o clock and proceeded on our way. After leaving Chicago we entered a wide prarie which was to us a new scene. We traveled about 12 miles and rested for the night. We made our fire and cooked our victuals out of doors. We slept on the floors of the tavern. We had no beds—but some bedding.

215. In 1840, Chicago was a city of 4853 inhabitants, having been settled only in 1831 and not incorporated until 1836. Baldwin, *Gazetteer*, 231.

216. Dixon was a village (1850 population 1,073) and the capital of Lee County. It was on the Rock River about 110 miles west of Chicago. The Rock River rises in Fond du Lac County, Wisconsin and flows south and southwest to Illinois, which it enters at Beloit. From there it flows southwest through Dixon to the Mississippi at a point south of Rock Island. *Ibid.*, 326, 1002.

November 7, 1840

Saturday. This day we arrived at Dixon after travelling about 100 miles. We saw a wolf on one prairie and many prairie hens. At one house we saw a wild cat which had been shot in the woods. It was as large as a common sized dog. We have several times had one of the teems fast in the sloughs. During this journey brothers Cope and Benbow went with their teems foremost and thus secured to themselves the best accommadations and provisions &c. We was obliged to submit to it and take what we could get. When our teems viz our 3 and Copes 14 and Benbows 2 and Walter Cran 1 arrived at Dixon the others being considerable behind we made inquiry as to the probability of boats going down the river. We was told that some boats had gone a week previous but it was not likely that any more would go this season. We then asked if there was any boat we could buy but of this we could get no satisfaction. We were advised to take our teams and go over to Fulton[217] and there take steamboat. To this I objected on account of Turley not being arrived. S. Cope was disposed to go and would not unload his waggon. I engaged a house for the whole company at a Dollar 24 hours. We went to the house and unloaded our waggons myself being determined not to move until the others arrived. I paid the teamsmen 75 dollars for the 3 teams but desired them to wait till morning to see what course Elder Turley would pursue. It appears that at this place I offended Brother Cope from what he said afterwards. In the building was 3 rooms one a small room which would scarce hold our folks. Into this we moved our boxes and laid down our bedding (no beds). During this time Mr Copes brought some of our luggage in saying they would go in their for they had as much right as any one else or something like this. But when they saw us lay our bedding down they took their things out apparently much grieved. But I would not submit to move out as we had submitted to the worst fare all the way from Chicago and I had took the house and considered myself at liberty to go into any part I choosed.

217. Fulton was a village in Whiteside County, Illinois on the Mississippi about 42 miles west of Dixon. *Ibid.*, 410. Grosvenor, *Atlas,* 10.

November 8, 1840
Sunday. This morning Walter Cran engaged his team and started for Fulton. Mr. Cope wanted to do likewise and asked my intentions. I told him I would not move any further untill the remainder of the company arrived. He seemed a little

vexed and would rather have gone on. In order to pacify him
and others I started back with our teams to meet the others.
We met them about 7 miles from Dixon. I gave Turley a
statement of things as I had found them and that I believed
it was possible to go down Rock river. Brother Cope still
desired to go by land to Fulton. I told him I had no disposi-
tion to go and leave the poor behind (as was evident we
should have to do if we went that way). He then manifested
anger and said he had not either &c. We arrived back about
2 o clock.

November 9, 1840
Monday. This day Elder Turley purchased a boat bottom
for 75 Dollars and engaged 2 men to fit it up ready for sailing.

November 13, 1840
Friday. During this week the boat has been got ready myself
and many of the brethren assisted. We got our luggage on
board to start but it being late and beginning to snow it
was decided not to move untill morning. While loading the
boat Brother Cope and I had a few words again. I had fixed
some of our boxes in one corner of the boat and Cope brought
his and was determined to have them fixed up to ours so that
we could get no more of ours up to them. I told him what
I had intended to do. He was vexed and said—"Your nasty
scamp I pay as much as you." We had not many more words
but seemed much vexed. I told him to use his pleasure and
I would be satisfied.

November 14, 1840
Saturday. This A M Brother Cope declined going with us in
the boat and would not pay his share according to his agreement. I paid down one half of the expenses and we got

loaded and prepared to start. We left Wood got at Dixon and started about 10 o clock. We went about 12 miles and tarried overnight at Stirling. The weather was very cold.

November 20, 1840

Friday. This day we passed over the rapids. The greater part of us walked while the boat went over. It stuck fast once but was not damaged. Soon after this we entered the Mississippi river which caused us to rejoice much.[218]

218. They probably entered the Mississippi from the Rock River at Rock Island, some 130 miles north of Nauvoo. Their rejoicing would come, of course, because of the prospect of much easier navigation from there to their destination.

November 21, 1840

Saturday. This night we had to camp at a wood there being no houses near. We had some rain. Elder Turley and some others camped in the wood. He spake much to them and called upon those who had had quarrels to forgive each and manifest it. Many acknowledged their faults and asked forgiveness. Some spake in tongues and William Poole interpreted. It was a time of rejoicing.

November 22, 1840

Sunday. We arrived at Burlington[219] this evening and as we anticipated landing at Commerce on the morrow many of us washed ourselves and changed our cloths. Many of our family slept on a carpet on the floor.

219. Burlington, Iowa was in 1840 a commercial city and the seat of Des Moines County. It had been the capital of Iowa until 1839 and was about 45 miles from Keokuk, 250 miles above St. Louis, and about 35 miles from Nauvoo. Baldwin, *Gazetteer*, 163; Grosvenor, *Atlas*, 10.

November 23, 1840

Monday. This A M Elder Turley and my self had some unpleasant words in consequence of his taking the boat rond some Islands which appeared to me and others to be considerable out of our course. I spake to him about it but he would not listen. I then turned my conversation to C. Price. Elder Turley then said if I did not cease to agitate the minds of the company he would put to shore and leave the boat. This was said in an unpleasant spirit. In the P.M we got the boat fast on a tree and lost considerable time. After Elder Turley had tried his own way to move the boat a long time but in vain I begged of him to let me have my plan. After much request he partially consented and finding it likely to answer he yielded to my plan and the boat was soon loosed. We sailed untill after dusk almost determined to go to Commerce that night. But seeing a light on shore we made towards it and hearing a man we asked how far we were from Commerce. He said 9 miles. At which report we concluded to stay for the night.

November 24, 1840
Tuesday. This A M Elder Turley having been in company with a man from Commerce said that if any choose to walk that man would conduct them at which William Poole myself and several others went along with him by land to Commerce where we arrived at about 12 o clock. We called at the Upper stone house and found Sister Garner from Manchester. They had arrived about one week previous having been 6 months on their way. We then went to Sister Hyrum Clarks[220] and on our way called at Francis Moon's. After we had been here a little while we perceived Elder Turley and some others coming. Knowing then that the Boat had arrived we returned to the boat and after taking a little dinner we proceeded according to the appointment of Committee to move our luggage to a new house on the banks of the Mississippi

river. Thus ended a journey of over 5000 miles having been exactly 11 weeks and about 10 hours between leaving Liverpool and arriving at our journeys end. We had been much exposed to cold weather and suffered many deprivations and disconveniences yet through the mercy of God we landed safe and in good health with the exception of 8 persons one of whom died soon after landing. We were pleased to find ourselves once more at home and felt to praise God for his goodness. We did not get all our luggage unloaded that night and having no fire we concluded to take the invitation of Brother Henry Moore and stay overnight at his house. He kindly gave us our breakfast the following Morning. We slept on the floor. On the morning of the 25th we proceeded to unload the remainder of our luggage. Brother Thompson lent us a small stove. The house being small for 14 of us viz William Poole and family. Richard Jenkinson and wife. Mary Ware and my father in laws family and my family; we was some crow'd but we were pretty comfortable. We made our bed on hay on the floor and was obliged to move them every morning for the room. After a few weeks we made our beds upstairs and fill them with oak leaves. In a few days after we arrived at Nauvoo Elder Hyrum Smith came for me to go on board the Steam Boat Nauvoo. I spent one day on it and it was then concluded not to sail her any more this season. We remained at this house 7 weeks during which time we made enquiry concerning some land and after much consultation I went to Hyrum Smith for council. He said he had some land to sell in Iowa Territory for 3 dollars an acre and he counciled us to go. We finally concluded to move over the river into the Territory. The saints frequently told us that the devil was over the river &c but this did not hinder us from going. I agreed with William Smith for 185 acres of land and was to pay for it out of my wages on the Steam Boat which

he ensured to [–]. I was to give him ½ of my wages untill it
was paid up. We also bought a Waggon of him for 60$ pay-
ing ½ down the rest with the land. We bought a Yoke of
oxen and chain for 55$ and 3 Hogs for 8$ of Mr. Thomas
Grover. We did not attend many meeting while on this side
the river. We heard Joseph[221] speak twice and Sidney Rigdon once. We attended singing meetings frequently and
often had to sing "Gentle Gale" for Joseph and others. On
January 12th 1841 we began to move our luggage over the
river on the Ice which occupied 4 days in the whole. I had
previously taken a house a little from Montrose[222] at 18 pr
month. This house smoked very bad and we had oftentimes
to be without fire and cook out of doors. We found things
in some measure as was told viz the saints to be in a very bad
state and having no meetings, full of envy, strife and contention and in a very bad state. Soon after we arrived here
the weather began to be extremely cold and having no wood
for fire it seemed as though we must be froze to death. We
were still 31 in number and all could not get to the fire.
When the weather moderated we went to cutting logs and
hauling them for building also making rails. We got our
house part raised by the 8th of March William Poole assisting us. At this time William Poole moved over the river to
seek employment and left us. We continued to labour pre-
pareing rails and house &c untill about the 16 of March when
we seemed to be all at once put under a cloud of trouble. In
the night I was taken sick and could not go to work for a few
days. ~~Same day~~ We had a hog we set much store on and was
very desirous to keep him to breed from. On the 15th he got
out of the penn and did not come home at night. On the morning of the 16th he came home cut[223] which was a sad grief
to us. (~~We afterwards learned partially that the person
who cut the Hog was Doctor Patten of the High Council~~) Not
true. On the same day about 5 o clock while I was set doing a

202

little something in the house a person called and said the new house was all on fire. I immediately sprang up and started off. Just as I got to the door I saw a waggon going that way and I got into it. Having 2/4 miles to go we was sometime before we arrived. When I got there I found the lady who lived at Bosiers house had carried water from the house about a quarter of a mile and put the fire partly out. I soon put all the fire out and ascertained that the house had not sustained much damage but a large rope which cost $2.50 also a pair of Bed cords was entirely burned to ashes which in our circumstances was a considerable loss to us. We have during the winter had this chimney on fire 3 times. First on a cold day when William Poole killed his hog. He made to large a fire and the chimney was turned on.

220. Clark had left his family in Nauvoo when he left for his mission in England.

221. I.e. Joseph Smith, prophet and founder of the Church.

222. Montrose, Iowa was, in 1850, a village of about 800 people located about 12 miles above Keokuk on the west bank of the Mississippi across from Nauvoo. Baldwin, *Gazetteer*, 738.

223. That is, castrated.

March 19, 20, 1841

I commenced planting seed for the first time in this land. On the latter day while I was busy in the garden a person named William Miller (who said he had a claim upon the land we bought from Hyrum Smith) came up and with him a constable and another man. The constable drew from his pocket book a paper and read it to me which was a notice to quit the land signed William Miller.[224] I felt some astonished at this but not many words passed between us. Miller said he had been to Brother Ripley who was somewhat saucy and told him he must fight it out—and that was the way he intended to do it. A few days after I took the notice paper to the river to Sister Smith who advised me to take no notice of it but to proceed with our business, I however felt it would be wisdom to wait a while as we expected Hyrum at home in a few weeks.

224. The land upon which Clayton had settled was what Robert Flanders has called "a land purchaser's nightmare." It was part of the land set aside for half-breed offspring of whites and Sac and Fox Indians. The right to transfer the land was granted by Congress in 1834, and large groups of speculators had purchased the scrip which allowed conveyance of the land. Isaac Galland and others were active speculators in the land. Flanders, *Nauvoo*, 28-29.

March 24, 1841

Wednesday. This night the constable brought me a summons to appear before Justice Spain to answer to William Miller for trespass on his premises.

March 26, 1841

Friday. I went over the river to see Brother Ripley and ask his council. I called at the store and made Joseph acquainted with the circumstance who ordered Brother Thompson to write a few lines to Bishop Ripley in his name requesting him to take the matter into his own hands and appear with me before the justice. I saw Brother Ripley who said I need trouble myself no further he would see to it. I would here state that during the past few months I have had much trouble concerning the boat which was made at Dixonville. I have repeatedly endeavored to see Mr. Benbow who ownes one half of it and settle with him but have yet been disapointed. He has been for council to Brother Law and has divided the boat and taken away his share. Soon as I learned this I also went to Brother Law for council who advised me to get 2 men to value the portion of the boat which fell to us and then charge the whole company with the whole of the difficiency. This I immediately attended to and made out bills for all our own family taking an equal share of the loss. Some of the accounts I took in and the first man who complained was

John Blezard. He did not believe it was a just debt and did not intend to pay except others did &c. His conduct since has fully proved that he does not intend to pay for he has been insolent both to myself and Lydia and her mother who have been to ask repeatedly for the money. But hitherto we can get no satisfaction wether he will pay or no.

March 28, 1841

Sunday. This day we met at Montrose. Uncle John Smith presided. He called upon all who had hardness and who had transgressed to confess and repent. He stated that about 12 months ago he had appointed them a person to take charge of the meeting and administer the sacrement which he had only attended to once since that time. After many had confessed he called upon myself and Brother Nickerson to break bread and administer which was done and we hope it will be continued faithfully hereafter.

March 30, 1841

Tuesday. This day I made a contract for a cow with Abner Tibbetts for 20 dollars value to be cut out in cord wood at 75 cents pr cord. She calved on the morning after and seems to answer pretty well.

April 2, 1841

Brother Nickerson settled with William Miller for his claim on the land and we can now pursue our improvements.

April 6, 7, 8, 9, 1841

These four days I attended Conference. *See over.[225] On the 7th I was organized with the High Priest quorum and set with them during the conference. I was much pleased with the order of the meeting. When any case was to appear before the church it was first put by the Bishop to the quorum of the

Lesser Priesthood. Then by the president of the Elders to that quorum—then the 70 then High Priests—then High Council and lastly to the presidency. If any objection arose it had to be tried by that quorum who objected but a majority of the quorums decided the matter. The names of the official characters are as follows—Joseph Smith first president Sidney Rigdon and William Law councillor. Brother Law was appointed councillor at this conference in the stead of Hyrum Smith who was appointed a Prophet Seer and Revelator according to a Revelation given January 19, 1841.[226] Brother Law was objected to by our quorum but honourably elected after investigation on account of the ill health of Sidney Rigdon. John C. Bennett was appointed in his stead until Brother Rigdons health improved. Names of the 12 or traveling high Council.[227] Brigham Young, Heber Chase Kimball, Parley P. Pratt, Orson Pratt, Orson Hyde, William Smith, John Taylor, John E. Page, Willford Woodruff, Willard Richards, George Albert Smith and Lyman Whight was appointed in the room of D. W. Patten deceased. Standing High council[228]—Samuel Bent, Henry G. Sherwood, George W. Harris, Thomas Grover, Newel Knight, Lewis D. Wilson, Aaron Johnson, David Fullmer, Alpheus Cutler, William Huntingdon Senior, William Alread, Leanord Sowby was appointed this conference. Presidents of the High Priest quorum —Don C. Smith, councillors Noah Packard, Amasa Lyman. President of Elders quorum—John A. Hicks, councillers Samuel Williams, Jesse Baker. Quorum of seventies[229]—Joseph Young, Isaiah Butterfield, Daniel Miles, Henry Heremond, Zerah Pulcipher, Levi Hancock and James Foster. Lesser Priesthood Priests[230]—Samuel Rolphe, Stephen Markam, Hezekiah Peck counselors. Teachers—Elisha Everett, James W. Huntsman, James Hendrick. Deacons—Phineas R. Bird, David Wood, William W. Lane. Bishopric[231]—Vincent Knights, councilors Samuel H. Smith and Shadrac Roundey. Newel K. Whitney, coun[selors] Jonathan H. Hale, William Felshaw. George Miller, councillors Peter Haws and John Snider. Isaac Higbee, coun[selors] Graham Coultrin and John S. Higbee. Alanson Ripley had his Bishopric taken from him for frequently being drunk and not fit for business. President of the stake William Marks,²³² councillors Austin Coles and Charles C. Rich.

225. This was the eleventh annual conference of the Church. The first day was taken up by an elaborate morning parade of the Nauvoo Legion, and by religious service in the afternoon in connection with laying the cornerstone of the Nauvoo Temple. General conference meetings were held on April 7, 8, 9, and 11. The minutes of the conference are found in Joseph Smith's history. It is obvious that at this stage in the development of Nauvoo, conditions were favorable and the Saints were prospering. In spite of several cases of minor dissention in the conference, things went along very well. The (°) and words "see over" were above the lines and refer to the entry for April 6, on the next page of the diary. Smith, *History of the Church*, IV, 326-343.

226. The revelation mentioned contains a great deal of information on the organization of the Church and plans for the development of Nauvoo. *Doctrine and Covenants*, Section 124. Hereinafter cited as *D. and C*.

227. Or, Council of Twelve Apostles. It is interesting to note that all of the group who were in England at the time followed the lead of Brigham Young and the Council of the Twelve to Utah after Joseph Smith's death and all of the others failed to do so or were excommunicated.

228. These were the members of the Nauvoo Stake high council. Their authority during this period was much greater than it has subsequently become. In a revelation given March 28, 1835, it was revealed that: "The standing high councils, at the stakes of Zion, form a quorum equal in authority in the affairs of the church, in all their decisions, to the quorum of the presidency, or to the traveling high council." *D. and C.*, 107:36; Smith, *History of the Church*, IV, 12.

229. The First Council of Seventy was selected to act, under the direction of the Council of Twelve, in promoting the missionary work of the Church. *D. and C.*, 107:34.

230. "There are, in the church, two priesthoods, namely, the Melchizedek and Aaronic, including the Levitical Priesthood." High Priests, seventies, and elders are members of the higher or Melchizedek Priesthood and priests, teachers, and deacons are in the lower or Aaronic Priesthood. The Melchizedek Priesthood was to concern itself with spiritual matters and the Aaronic with temporal matters. *D. and C.*, 107.

231. Bishops are local religious leaders equivalent to pastors,

ministers, or parish priests. The city of Nauvoo was divided into various wards over which bishops presided. In March, 1841, the city was divided into four political wards by the City Council, and these divisions were apparently coterminus with the ecclesiastical wards. Four bishops were thus called to serve over the congregations in these districts. Smith, *History of the Church*, IV, 305.

232. The stake organizations were approximately coterminus with the counties. William Marks presided over the stake in Hancock County, Illinois (the area around Nauvoo); and John Smith presided over the stake at Lee County, Iowa. During the same period, a stake was functioning in the area around Kirtland, Ohio, but in December, 1841 it was disbanded. *Ibid.*, IV, 476.

April 6, 1841

The Nauvoo Legion[233] was drawn up to exercise and afterwards proceeded to the Temple ground to lay the corner stones. The first Presidency proceeded to lay the South East corner stone. (The High Council laid the South West corner in the name of the travelling High Council. The President of High Priest quorum the North West and the Bishops the North East. See Times and Seasons April 15). Before the ceremony of laying the corner stones President Rigdon delivered an address for the occasion in his usual powerful manner.[234]

233. The Nauvoo Legion was a military organization authorized by section 25 of the Nauvoo City Charter, and in an ordinance of the Nauvoo City Council of February 8, 1841. The Illinois legislature granted unusual power to the Nauvoo Legion by allowing certain legislative authority to be vested in its commissioned officers, and by granting the mayor of Nauvoo authority to call out the militia to enforce city laws. The legion, which attained an estimated 5,000 members, thus became practically independent of the state and aroused the anxiety of non-Mormon citizens in the surrounding area. The city charter was repealed in January, 1845, which also legally terminated the Legion. See Hamlin Gardner, "The Nauvoo Legion, 1840-1845—A Unique Military Organization," *Journal of the Illinois State Historical Society*, LIV, No. 2 (Summer, 1968), 181-97.

234. See Smith, *History of the Church*, IV, 329-31, for more elaborate details of this impressive ceremony, and Joseph Smith's explanations of the religious significance of the laying of each cornerstone. Similar ceremonies had been held at Kirtland, Ohio, in 1833 and at Far West, Missouri, in 1838.

April 8, 1841

Thursday. President Rigdon delivered a discourse on baptism for the dead, showing the propriety and absolute necessity of such an ordinance. After preaching a many were baptized for their dead relatives and many for the remission of sins.[235] At this conference a Revelation was read (given January 19, 1841) containing instructions to build the Temple and a boarding house called the Nauvoo house and many other important items.[236] A short revelation was also read concerning the saints in Iowa. The question had been asked what is the will of the Lord concerning the saints in Iowa. It read to the following effect—Verily thus saith the Lord let all those my saints who are assaying to do my will gather themselves together upon the land opposite to Nauvoo and build a city unto my name and let the name of Zarahemla be named upon it. And all who come from the east and West and North and South who have desires let them settle in Zarahemla that they may be prepared for that which is in store for a time to come &c.[237] Brother Joseph when speaking to one of the brethren on this subject says you have hauns Mill for a sample.[238] Many of the brethren immediately made preparations for moving in here but on account of its being so late in the season President John Smith advised to get through with planting and then proceed to move in.

235. The doctrine of baptism for the dead was probably new to William Clayton, but at the same time most impressive and welcome. Although the idea that the worthy dead might receive the gospel in the spirit world had been suggested in earlier teachings of Joseph Smith, the actual practice of baptism for the dead was not expounded until August, 1840 at the funeral of Seymour Brunson. (Brunson died August 10, 1840). From then on the doctrine apparently developed rapidly, and baptisms for the dead were performed in the Mississippi River. At first the practice seemed limited to dead relatives, and there was no restriction, as there is today, on men or women being baptized for members of the opposite sex. (See entry for May 9 where William Clayton was baptized for a grandfather, 2 grandmothers, and an aunt.) On January 19, 1841, a revelation required that a temple be built for this and other purposes, and in the April 8 conference session described above not only Sidney Rigdon but also John C. Bennett and Joseph Smith gave sermons on the subject. According to a *Times and Seasons* report, Rigdon spoke "with an eloquence peculiar

to the speaker," and Joseph Smith also "threw considerable light on the doctrine which had been investigated." The situation seemed ready-made for a movement down to the river where many would be baptized for their dead relatives, although that incident is not recorded in the official minutes of the conference, or in Joseph Smith's history.

Clayton noted that many were also baptized for remission of sins. This probably has reference to the practice, which was not uncommon, for members of the Church to renew their covenants through re-baptism, even though they were still members of record. William Clayton was re-baptized, for example, on May 9. B. H. Roberts, *A Comprehensive History of the Church of Jesus Christ of Latter-day Saints,* (6 vols.; Salt Lake City: Deseret News Press, 1930) II, 69-77; Smith, *History of the Church,* IV, 231; *Times and Seasons,* April 15, 1841, 387-88.

236. Section 124 of the *Doctrine and Covenants,* originally given January 19, 1841. It was appropriate that this revelation be read at this conference, for it commanded the building of the Nauvoo Temple, the cornerstones of which were laid on the first day of the conference. The baptismal font was completed first and dedicated November 18, 1841. From then on it was used for baptism for the dead. The temple was dedicated in the spring of 1846, and later abandoned as the Mormons moved to the West. In 1849 it was burned by an arsonist and in 1850 a hurricane blew over the remaining walls. The Nauvoo House was begun in the spring of 1841 and was never finished. The revelation contained many details concerning its size, its purpose, the organization of the building committee, and the sale of stock in the venture.

237. This revelation is recorded as section 125 of the *Doctrine and Covenants.* According to Joseph Smith's history, it was originally given on March 20, 1841 in reply to the question, "What is the will of the Lord, concerning the Saints in the Territory of Iowa?" In addition to the ideas recorded by Clayton, the revelation called for the Saints to "build up cities unto my name." The village of Nashville, not far from Zarahemla, was to be one of them. This would suggest that Joseph Smith had great hopes not only for Nauvoo, but for successfully extending the territory of the Mormon kingdom to the west bank of the Mississippi.

Actually the Lee County, Iowa settlements had a hectic history, and finally failed. A few comments later in Clayton's diary reveal some of the disappointments he experienced, and his own decision to move back to Nauvoo. The very beginning of settlement was probably a portend of bad times to come for the land was purchased from Isaac Galland, a speculator of highly questionable character, whose own title to the land was unclear and who gave customers stock in his venture in place of deeds to the land. He apparently even hoodwinked Joseph Smith. The Saints who settled in Lee County soon ran into difficulty with others who claimed the same land. In addition, they had problems among themselves which led the high council to vote to disfellowship anyone who took a brother before the law. Their effort to keep the "law of consecration" also failed and they had to be instructed by Joseph Smith not to attempt it any longer. The stake was finally discontinued in 1842. Only about 30 houses were built on the site of Zarahemla. Smith, *History of the Church*, IV, 311; Flanders, *Nauvoo, passim.*; Andrew Jenson, *Encyclopedic History of the Church of Jesus Christ of Latter-day Saints* (Salt Lake City: Deseret News Publishing Co., 1941), 366-67, 971-72; "Records of Members and Minutes of the Branch Established in the Territory of Iowa 5 Oct. 1839," LDS Ward Records, Genealogical Society of the L.D.S. Church, Salt Lake City, Microfilm Serial No. 2624, hereinafter cited as Iowa Branch Records.

238. The Haun's Mill Massacre was one of the most tragic stories in the history of Mormon persecution in Missouri. On October 30, 1838, the little Mormon settlement was attacked by about 240 mobsters who brutally massacred seventeen men and boys and severely wounded fifteen other people. It is interesting that Joseph Smith should have referred to Haun's Mill when discussing the reason for settling Zarahemla. It may be that by 1841 Joseph had determined that the only way to keep the Saints from experiencing troubles similar to those in Missouri was to build a strong, almost fortresslike establishment of the Saints on both sides of the Mississippi that would be able to withstand the onslaughts of all who came, and that he had no doubt but what some would try to drive them out again. The establishment of the almost autonomous Nauvoo Legion, and of an independent rifle company at Zarahemla (see entry for April 24) lend support to this interpretation. See Roberts, *Comprehensive History*, I, 480-83; Smith, *History of the Church*, I, 183-86; Andrew Jenson, *Historical Record*, VII, 671-84; Jenson, *Encyclopedic History*, 320-322.

April 16, 1841

Alice Moons family arrived from Pittsburgh State of Pennsylvania.

April 25, 1841

*See over[239]

Brother Clark arrived with a company of saints amongst whom was my sister Alice.

239. The (*) and the words "see over" were written on the side of the page and indicate that Clayton was recording these things some time after they happened, and inadvertently left out a few dates. The "see over" refers to the entry for April 24, which is located in the diary on the other side of the page, following May 9.

May 1, 1841

We finished cutting the 26 cord of wood for corn. Same day Brewetts company arrived amongst whom was Seth Cook and family.

May 2, 1841

Elders William Law and Hyrum Smith preached at Zarahemla. On the 6th my wife was taken poorly about 4 o clock A M. Her mother was on the other side the river. As soon as it was light she wanted me to go and fetch her. I went and got Brother Davis' skiff and went a cross as hard as I could and was about 2 hours away. When she got back she was delivered of a daughter who are both doing very well. She got up on the 8th and continued to mend without interuptin. The child is named Henrihetta Lucretia Patten Clayton.

May 9, 1841

Joseph preached on his side on baptism for the dead (see Record.)[240] Afterwards a number was baptized both for remission of sins and for the dead.[241] I was baptized first for myself and then for my Grandfather Thomas and Grandmother Ellen Clayton, Grandmother Mary Chritebly and aunt Elizabeth Beurdwood.

240. This possibly refers to a record which Clayton knew was being kept of Joseph Smith's activities—perhaps Joseph's own history, but no mention is made of a sermon on this date (which was a Sunday) either in Joseph Smith's published history, or in the *Times and Seasons*.
241. See above, note 235.

April 24, 1841

I was requested to attend meeting of the High Council at President John Smiths.[242] I was appointed one of the number in the place of Erastus Snow who is gone preaching. At this council Willard Snow was appointed to get up a company of independent Rifle men.[243] I have joined this company.

242. John Smith, an uncle to Joseph Smith, was made president of the stake in Iowa when it was organized in 1839. In the official minutes it was first called a "branch," but a high council was organized the same day (October 5th). In most Church histories it is referred to as a stake.

In addition to William Clayton's appointment on April 24 as a member of the high council, several other new appointments were also made. It is interesting to notice that the High Council itself selected its own new members as well as the two new counselors to President John Smith.

William Clayton was also appointed as clerk of the high council of Iowa on July 12, to replace George W. Gee, who said he had too much to do in keeping records of the Church. It appears that Clayton did not long function in this capacity, however. Smith, *History of the Church*, IV, 352, 382; Iowa Branch Records, July 12, April 24, 1841.

243. This was apparently a militia group which was to function in Zarahemla in a manner similar to the Nauvoo Legion across the river.

May 16, 1841

I went over the river to hear Joseph Election and Eternal judgement (see Record).[244]

244. A sketch of this sermon is found in *Times and Seasons*, II No. 15, 429-30, and in Smith, *History of the Church*, IV, 358-60. On this occasion Joseph Smith's sermon occupied more than two hours of the morning. In the afternoon Hyrum Smith and John C. Bennett also addressed the Saints.

June 30, 1841

We have continued to labour very hard in splitting rails up to the present time. The wether now begins to be very hot almost more than we can bear. We are yet very far short of completing the fence and in danger of having the corn spoiled by cattle every day.

July 1, 1841

Early in the morning I was taken very sick with vomiting and purging which held me 5 or 6 hours very severely. I could not go to work. I felt a little better on friday and saturday. On Sunday I went over the river and saw Brother Kimball and went with him to Sister Pratts where we took a little dinner.

July 5, 1841

I attended the celebration of American liberty at Zarahemla.[245] We was called to drill at 8 in the morning and continued until about 4 o clock at which time the company went to dinner which was set out in a field on account of so many being present. The provisions was done before all had had dinner. I was shure without and felt bad for want of meat. *turn over.[246]

245. The Independence Day celebration was held at Nauvoo on Saturday, July 3. Since the Mormons would not hold such a celebration on Sunday, the Zarahemla Saints probably held their own celebration on Monday, the 5th, in order to avoid conflict with the colorful and impressive Nauvoo ceremonies. In Nauvoo, Joseph Smith reviewed the Nauvoo Legion and gave an "eloquent and patriotic speech" in which he expressed his high regard for America's national welfare and declared: "I would ask no greater boon, than to lay down my life for my country." See Smith, *History of the Church*, IV, 382; *Times and Seasons*, Vol. II, No. 18 (July 15, 1841), 479.

246. This refers to the August 8 entry, which is on the other side of the page in the original journal, following August 17.

August 14, 1841
Alice Moon died.

August 17, 1841
Up to the present time I have been very sick after the 5th. As stated above I went to work on the 6th but was not able to do much. On the 7th I was seized with the bilious fever and after a few days suffering took an Emetic which gave me relief. Soon as I began to amend I was seized with the Ague and Fever and shook every day.[247] After about 10 days shaking I was advised by Dr. Rogers to take some Pills. I objected but Sister Taylor had bought some Quinine[248] and I finally for her sake concluded to take it. These Pills broke the Ague for about 10 days during which time I had another attack of the Bilious Fever and took an Emetic which gave relief. After about 10 days relief from the Ague I was seized with it again and had it every day for about 2 weeks. At this time we were near all sick and had been except Lydia and on this day Thomas Moon died ¼ before 11 A.M. after

about 2 weeks sickness. On this day also the brethren went to haul Rails and put up a fence around our field but did not complete it on account of being short of Rails. Soon after there were many cattle in the field especially Mr. Copes sometimes to the number of 35 in one day. The brethren again went to haul more Rails and complete the fence but did not make it secure consequently cattle continually were eating up the corn untill they destroyed the whole both the corn and fodder. On the 19th Dr. Culbertson came and said he would cure us of the ague and charge nothing for his trouble. Accordingly 5 of us took each a dose of Calomel and Caster Oil. Afterwards I teaspoon full of Bitters every hour for 8 hours.[249] This broke our ague for sometime. On the 20th our infant child Henrihetta Lucretia Patten Clayton died after being sick and having chills some time. During the last 2 days she suffered much at times and especially in the last hour of her life. When dead she was as pretty as I ever saw in my life. She died about 10 minutes after 3 P.M. This was a grief to us but we afterwards saw the hand of God in it and saw it was best to be so During this time.

247. The extensive community illness in this and later entries in which most of Clayton's family suffered and his infant child died, was not an uncommon experience for western settlers in the first half of the 19th century. The ague, in fact, was so common that some frontiersmen hardly recognized it as a disease, and someone with a sense of humor could even write to eastern friends to "come out and have a shake with us." The ague was a form of malaria that produced alternate chills and fevers, and apparently attacked many frontier communities. A Michigan pioneer, for example, wrote in 1838 that three persons were sick to every well one in his county, and the well ones were simply between the sweating stage of one ague attack and the coming of the chill of another.

The experience of the little settlement of Zarahemla in this year (1841) was not unlike the severe epidemics which swept over settlers at Nauvoo in 1839, 1840, and 1841. Originally Nauvoo was swampy and unhealthy. Malaria was endemic in the region, and hit the Mormons as soon as they began to settle in 1839. In that year a number of miraculous healings were reported. The following summer, however, the epidemic was worse, and many died. It reached calamitous proportions in 1841 (the same year Clayton reported the above epidemic in Zarahemla), when so many died that Sidney Rigdon preached a "general funeral sermon" for them all. Avery O. Craven, *A Frontier Cycle* (Detroit: Wayne State University Press, 1958), 4-6; Roberts, *Comprehensive History*, II, 18-22; Flanders, *Nauvoo*, 53-54.

248. Quinine came into wide use as a remedy for malaria after 1830. The need became so great that the cost was extremely high. As late as 1846 an Indian doctor drove cattle to market at $7.50 a head in order to buy quinine at $8.00 per ounce. A Michigan settler reported that they would rather go without bread and water than without quinine. Craven, *A Frontier Cycle*, 10-11.

249. Calomel was one of the most common "cure-alls" in this period of time. Composed of mercurous chloride, it was a white, tasteless powder used as a purgative. One Philadelphia physician gave his patients as much as four tablespoons of calomel per day and he is credited with helping to build up a popular demand for such dosing. It was soberly reported that it reached such a point that some rugged pioneers actually ate bread and calomel instead of bread and butter.

An all-purpose remedy simply known as "bitters" was another of the old reliables. It was one of many home remedies commonly carried by pioneers, and handed down from one generation to another. The bitterness of the remedy seemed to be a guide to its value. To brew a batch of bitters, one stewed and crushed various berries, leaves and barks, distilled the mixture, then combined it with whiskey, brandy, or, as a last resort, cider. Pepper pods might be added to give increased sting (and thus increased confidence in the brew). It was taken not only as a remedy for specific ills, but also as a spring tonic. The "high alcoholic content made it popular among good churchmen throughout the year for real and anticipated troubles." From this description it appears that Clayton partook of the full course of frontier remedies. Richard Harrison Shyrock, *Medicine in America: Historical Essays* (Baltimore: The Johns Hopkins Press, 1966), 206; Craven, *A Frontier Cycle*, 8-9.

August 8, 1841

President John Smith and several other brethren came and for the first time during our sickness we received the sacrement. Afterwards President Smith asked particularly concerning our circumstances and being pressed I told him that had not a privilege of having many things which we greatly needed. After this the church helped us considerable. Being advised by Brother Kimball to buy 2 city lots and move into the city of Zarahemla (according to a previous revelation) on the 30th I went over to President John Smiths and bought two.

September 11, 1841

Lydia Moon Senior was taken suddenly ill and remained very sick 3 or 4 weeks. On the 18th Richard Jenkinson died appearantly suffering much. About this time we suffered severely on account of having no fire in the house. The chimney was blown down in March and was not built up again untill George A. Smith one of the twelve and Brother Montague came on the 29th with a load of wood and afterwards built up the chimney for which we felt thankful. The wether was wet and having no fire in the house our clothing were damp and we took cold. Consequently on the 21st I began to shake every day again. On the 28th Brother Tanner brought us some Beef. Oct. 6 Ellen Jenkinson died. She was never baptised nor believed in this work while she lived. We had about 1 acre of Potatoes planted and the time now came that they should be dug. We sent over to William Pool to come and help us also to Edd Whittbe. They both promised to come but were sick at the time. They did not come after they got better. Seeing this and after waiting untill the frost had destroyed about one half I began to dig them myself. I dug in the morning untill the Ague came on and afterwards as long as I could bear. I was soon reduced so that I was not able to dig any longer and then my wife and her sister Lydia dug the remainder and gathered about 1½ acres of corn which we had on the farm we rented. About the middle of November I came over to Nauvoo and there Brother Kimball councilled us to move over the river into Nauvoo which we did on the 14th of December.²⁵⁰ We were still sick and occasionally shaking. We moved into a very bad house and suffered much from cold. We remained here 6 weeks and then moved to were we are now living viz lot South of the burying ground. During the 6 weeks above mentioned I proved that William Pool (who had always professed to be my friend) had been striving to cause a separation in the family viz to cause mother Moon to turn me out of doors and in order to accomplish this he had told Margaret many reports one of which was that I was the sole cause of her fathers death.

250. This may have been due partly to Clayton's illness, which was apparently quite severe. The fact that such a family would be advised to leave Zarahemla, however, must have been rather disappointing to others, in light of their call by revelation to settle there, and this was undoubtedly a tacit admission that the settlement was not achieving the success anticipated.

February 10, 1842

Brother Kimball came in the morning to say that I must go to Joseph Smiths office and assist Brother Richards. I accordingly got ready and went to the office and commenced entering tithing for the Temple.[251] I was still shaking with the Ague every day but it did not much disable me for work.

251. In being assigned to collect tithing for the temple, William Clayton was involved in what to Joseph Smith was an essential project: the completion of the temple which was financed largely through the collection of tithing from members of the Church. Even those who lived away from Nauvoo were required to contribute tithing for the temple. This could be contributed in cash, produce, or labor, and some men donated every tenth day of work to quarrying rock or performing some other kind of work. Donations to the temple were required before Church members could take part in temple ceremonies, including the use of the baptismal font in order to perform baptisms for the dead. (This, of course, is not unlike the general requirement today that Church members must be tithe payers in order to obtain a temple recommend. The difference was that in Nauvoo the tithing was specifically earmarked for the temple.) William Clayton, then, was now assigned the task of keeping a record of the tithing paid, partly to determine worthiness to use the temple. An interesting document signed by William Clayton, recorder, is preserved in the museum on Temple Square in Salt Lake City. Dated February 6, 1846, it certifies that Howard Egan is entitled to the privilege of the baptismal font, having paid property and labor tithing in full to April 12, 1846.
On this date William Clayton began what was to become many years of service as a recorder and scribe. He acted as scribe for Joseph Smith until the prophet's death in 1844, and then became scribe for Brigham Young and other leaders of the Church. Flanders, *Nauvoo*, 201-05.

February 12, 1842

Saturday. I was able to continue writing all day although I had the ague but not severe.

February 13, 1842

Sunday. We had a Singing meeting at Brother Farrs. Brother and Sister Kimball was present.

February 17, 1842

Thursday. I dined at Sister Hydes with Brother Joseph Smith, Heber Kimball, Wilford Woodruff, Brigham Young and Willard Richards. At night saw W & S.

February 18, 1842

Friday. Pained with tooth ache all day—heard Joseph read a great portion of his history.[252]

252. Refers to Joseph Smith's history which was being published in the *Times and Seasons*, and which has since been edited by B. H. Roberts and published in six volumes. Joseph Smith was in the habit of reading portions of his history to friends and associates.

APPENDIX

*Alphabetical list of identifiable persons
appearing in the Diary:*

Mary Aspin was baptized February 23, 1840. She lived on Oldham Street and later emigrated to the United States. Manchester Branch, "Record of Members," Microfilm Serial No. 13656; part 3, Genealogical Society of the Church of Jesus Christ of Latter-day Saints, Salt Lake City, Utah, 1.

Thomas Bateman was baptized on March 17, 1839, and lived in Pendleton. He later emigrated. *Ibid.*

Catherine Bates was baptized January 13, 1839, and later emigrated. *Ibid.* Clayton consistently misspelled her name as **Beates**.

Ellen Battersby was baptized on March 16, 1839. She lived on Hart Street and later emigrated to the United States. *Ibid.*, 6.

John Benbow was one of the converts of Wilford Woodruff in Herefordshire. Joseph Smith, *History of the Church of Jesus Christ of Latter-day Saints*, ed. B. H. Roberts (2d ed. rev.; Salt Lake City: Deseret Book Company, 1957) IV, 150-51.

William Berry represented branches at Northwich and Altrincham in the July, 1840 conference. Smith, *History of the Church,* VI, 148. No Berry is listed in the Manchester records.

Ellen Bewsher is really **Ellen Bewshaw,** but Clayton consistently misspelled the name. She was baptized April 27, 1839 and lived on Hart Street. She emigrated to the United States on March 1, 1844. Manchester Branch, "Records," 6.

James Bewsher is really **James Bewshaw.** He was baptized on April 27, 1839. He lived on Hart Street and emigrated to the United States on March 1, 1844. He was a coachman by profession. *Ibid.;* Wilford Woodruff, "Wilford Woodruff Journal," January 19, 1840, HDC.

Joseph Birch was baptized March 22, 1840 and lived on Chatham Street in Chorlton on Medlock. He was excommunicated August 10, 1845. Manchester Branch, "Records," 7.

Jane Black and **Mary Black** were baptized respectively March 16, and November 17, 1839. It is not clear which is meant in the entry of February 4, 1840. Both lived on Cookson Street and later emigrated. *Ibid.,* 6-7.

Thomas Booth was baptized November 22, 1838. He was excommunicated from the Church April 10, 1842. *Ibid.,* 5.

James Bowman was baptized March 1, 1840. He lived on Davy Street in Hulme, and was eventually cut off. *Ibid.,* 7.

William Broom lived at 2 Maria Street and later emigrated to the United States. According to the record he was not baptized until August 22, 1841 but Clayton refers to him as Brother Broom in the diary. *Ibid.,* 10.

Jane Brown lived at #2 Maria Street, near where Clayton lived. She was baptized December 9, 1838 and emigrated in 1852. *Ibid.,* 5.

James Burgess. No date is given in the branch records for his baptism, but he lived on Pollard Street and later emigrated to the United States. *Ibid.*

George Cannon and his wife, **Ann Quayle Cannon,** lived in Liverpool in 1840. George was the brother of John Taylor's wife, and upon arriving in Liverpool in January, 1840, Taylor visited these relatives whom he had never before met. He made his home with them during his Liverpool stay. They were the parents of George Q. Cannon, who was twelve years old in 1840, and who later served for twenty-one years as first counselor in the First Presidency of the Church. Beatrice Cannon Evans and Janath Russell Cannon, editors, *Cannon Family Historical Treasury,* (George Cannon Family Association: 1967) 32-35, 113.

Hiram (sometimes spelled Hyrum) **Clark** arrived in Preston, Lancashire, England on December 7, 1839. He was one of the group called to go to England with some of the Twelve Apostles in 1839. He was born September 22, 1795 in Wells, Rutland County, Vermont. He later served as president of the Hawaiian Mission and as a missionary to California. Smith, *History of the Church,* IV, 7, 45; Andrew Jenson, *Latter-day Saint Biographical Encyclopedia,* (4 vols.; Salt Lake City: Deseret News Press, 1901-1936) IV, 339.

Alice Clayton was born March 28, 1816 and died April 27, 1859. She was the second child (after William), and first daughter of Thomas Clayton and Ann Critchley. Paul E. Dahl, *William Clayton: Missionary, Pioneer and Public Servant* (Provo, Utah: J. Grant Stevenson, 1964), 215.

Ann Critchley Clayton (1793-1848) was William Clayton's Mother. *Ibid.,* 213.

David Clayton (1818-1849) was William Clayton's brother. *Ibid.*

Margaret Clayton, William's daughter, was born April 24, 1839. *Ibid.,* 214.

Ruth Moon Clayton was the daughter of Thomas Moon and first wife of William Clayton. She was the mother of Margaret and Sarah.

Sarah L. Clayton, William's infant daughter, was born August 1, 1837. *Ibid.*

Thomas Clayton, William's father, was born in 1783. William was finally influential in persuading his parents to be baptized, and they later emigrated to America. Thomas died in St. Louis, Missouri, in 1849. *Ibid.,* 7, 213.

Alfred Cordon presided for the Church in the Staffordshire Potteries region. Zora Smith Jarvis, *Ancestry, Biography and Family of George A. Smith,* (Provo, Utah: Brigham Young University Press, 1962), 70; George A. Smith, "My Journal," *The Instructor,* LXXXII (1947), 322.

Christiana Crooks was baptized May 4, 1839, and excommunicated February 14, 1845. Manchester Branch, "Records," 16.

Elizabeth Crooks was baptized April 14, 1839. She emigrated to the United States in March, 1843. *Ibid.*

Esther Crooks was baptized at age 19, May 2, 1839. She was excommunicated February 4, 1845. *Ibid.*

Robert Crooks became an elder, was excommunicated, and then rebaptized on January 31, 1847. He was again cut off April 14, 1848. *Ibid.,* 17.

Sarah Crooks was baptized on March 29, 1839. Her relation with Clayton, while apparently never passing the platonic stage, was very close, as the reader of numerous entries will observe. *Ibid.,* 60.

Benjamin Davies was baptized on March 16, 1839, and John Davies was baptized on June 23, 1839. Both lived on Cookson Street and later emigrated. It is not clear which is meant in the entry for January 22, 1840. *Ibid.*, 22.

Sarah Duckworth. The Manchester Branch Records show her as having been baptized January 21, 1831. This is probably a mistake, however, for the Manchester Branch did not open until 1838. She was probably baptized in 1839. She lived on George Leigh Street. She spent the last part of her life in a workhouse, and was dead by 1852. *Ibid.*

John Dunn was baptized in December, 1839. He became an elder before he emigrated in January, 1852. He lived at 3 Heron Street in Charleton on Medlock. *Ibid.*

Joseph Fielding was born in March 1797 at Honeydon, Bedfordshire, England, the son of John and Rachel Fielding. He emigrated from England and located near Toronto, Canada in 1832. He and his two sisters, Mary and Rachel, were converted by Parley P. Pratt in May, 1832. He had returned to England in 1837 with Heber C. Kimball, Willard Richards, and others to help in opening the British Isles as a new field for missionary service. In April, 1838, as Kimball prepared to return to the United States, Fielding was chosen as president of the Church in England, a position equivalent to that of mission president today. He served in that position until his release on July 6, 1849. Richard L. Evans, *A Century of Mormonism in Great Britain* (Salt Lake City: Deseret News Press, 1937), 66-67; Smith, *History of the Church*, II, 492n.

John Galeford was baptized on February 23, 1840. He lived on Hart Street and later emigrated. Manchester Branch, "Records," 33.

William Garner was baptized June 16, 1839. He later emigrated. *Ibid.*

John Gill was baptized July 14, 1839. He later emigrated. *Ibid.*

Mary Gill was baptized September 29, 1839. She later emigrated to the United States. *Ibid.*

Elizabeth Gladstone was baptized March 21, 1839. She lived on Bradford Road and was eventually excommunicated. *Ibid.*

Thomas Green was baptized on March 16, 1839. He lived on Hart Street. He emigrated to the United States. *Ibid.*

Thomas Grover was born in Whitehall, New York, on July 22, 1807. He and his wife Caroline Whiting joined the Church in 1834 at Freedom, New York. He moved to Kirtland and later to Nauvoo and served missions in various areas for the Church. Grover moved to Utah in 1847, served on the gold mission, and settled in Davis County. He served in the territorial legislature and was probate judge of Davis County. He died on February 20, 1886. Jenson, *LDS Biographical Encyclopedia*, IV, 137-42.

James Grundy has no baptism date listed in the branch records, but he became a priest and lived in Bank Street. Manchester Branch, "Records," 33.

Alice Hardman was the first female baptized in the Church in England. Her family ran the Maria Street boarding house where Clayton stayed in Manchester. She later emigrated to America and in 1844 she became a plural wife of William Clayton. They had four children. Dahl, *William Clayton*, 215.

Jane Hardman was baptized on May 31, 1840. She lived on Halliwell Street and later emigrated. Manchester Branch "Records," 38.

John Hardman was a member of the branch who lived on Colton Street. He was a teacher in the priesthood and later emigrated to America. *Ibid.*

Mary Hardman was part of the Maria Street Hardman family with whom Clayton boarded. She was baptized on

November 25, 1838, and later emigrated to America. *Ibid.*

Richard Hardman was a branch member who lived on Colton Street. He was probably a member of the family of John Hardman, perhaps a son. He was baptized in 1838 and later emigrated. *Ibid.*

Jane Harris, a member of record who lived on Oldham Street, was probably the wife of Paul Harris. *Ibid.*

Paul Harris was a member of the Manchester Branch who was baptized November 22, 1838. He lived on Oldham Road and emigrated later to the United States. *Ibid.*

Samuel Heath was baptized on December 23, 1838. He emigrated to America later. *Ibid.*

Elizabeth Holding was baptized February 3, 1839, and lived on Granby Row. She eventually married Arthur Smith, in spite of the trouble mentioned in the diary. In some entries, Clayton refers to her as B. Holden, but he has obviously misspelled her name. Since the Church records list Elizabeth Holding as marrying Smith, this is obviously the same person. *Ibid.*

Sarah Isherwood was baptized July 23, 1840. *Ibid.*, 46.

Ann Jackson was baptized April 7, 1839, and lived in Pendleton, a suburb of Manchester. *Ibid.*, 22.

Joseph Jackson was baptized April 7, 1839, and lived in Pendleton. *Ibid.*, 48.

Thomas Jennings was baptized May 16, 1839, became a priest, lived at Pendleton, and was excommunicated November 15, 1850. *Ibid.*

Mary Ann Johnson lived on Loom Street. She was baptized on March 11, 1839, and later emigrated. *Ibid.*

Margaret Jones, whom Clayton baptized on November 28, 1838, lived on Maria Street then moved to Ashley Lane. *Ibid.*

William Jordan was a prominent Manchester journalist.

His third son, Thomas Hudson Jordan was more famous, but William apparently had a considerable reputation. Frederick Bouse, *Modern English Biography*, (6 vols.; London: Frank Case and Company, Limited, 1965) IV, 795.

Elizabeth Keitley is probably the real name of **E. Keith-ly** mentioned on March 1, 1840. She was baptized January 21, 1839, and later cut off. Manchester Branch, "Records," 53.

Hiram Kellogg was elected in May, 1841, as president of the high priests' quorum in Kirtland. Smith, *History of the Church*, IV, 362.

Heber C. Kimball was born June 14, 1801, at Sheldon, Vermont. He was an early convert to the Church in New York and become a member of the first group of Twelve Apostles. After moving successively to Ohio and Missouri, he became head of the first mission to England in 1837. He returned to Missouri, and again to England in 1840. He was first counselor to Brigham Young until his death in 1868. Orson F. Whitney, *Life of Heber C. Kimball: An Apostle, The Father and Founder of the British Mission* (Salt Lake City: Bookcraft, 1967).

Elizabeth Knott was baptized May 5, 1839. She lived in Newton, a suburb of Manchester. She was eventually excommunicated. Manchester Branch, "Records," 53.

William Law and **Wilson Law** were active in Nauvoo affairs. Wilson became brigadier general of the Nauvoo Legion, and William became a counselor in the First Presidency. Later, they helped form the nucleus of the group opposing Joseph Smith in Nauvoo which led to the printing of the *Nauvoo Expositor* and Smith's subsequent assassination. Smith, *History of the Church*, IV, 296, 282.

Ann Lee was baptized in January, 1840. Manchester Branch, "Records," 56.

James Lee is recorded as having been baptized in January, 1840. No place or date of baptism is given. This is the only name similar to Lea listed in the branch records. There is some confusion, however, since Lea (or Lee) was apparently already a Church member on January 1. *Ibid.*

James Mahon was baptized August 18, 1839. While yet a priest, he was assigned to accompany Elder John Leigh on a mission to Arden, Chesire, in October, 1840. He later became an elder and emigrated. While living in Manchester, Mahon apparently became involved in some interesting controversies. When he was about to be married to Elizabeth Miller, he was accused of having deserted a wife and two children in Ireland. Clayton investigated, however, and was satisfied that the accusation was false. (See diary, May 31, June 4 and June 8, 1840.) Mahon later apparently had the experience of speaking in tongues, (see June 14, 1840), but on October 1, 1840 he rashly accepted a challenge to prove publicly that he could do it. The critics of the Mormons were gleeful when, according to the report, "he then spoke what he declared to be Hebrew, but the teacher of languages, who was the referee, declared that there was not a word of Hebrew in his jargon." Smith, *History of the Church*, IV, 217; William E. Axon, editor, *The Annals of Manchester: A Chronological Record from the Earliest Times to the End of 1885* (Manchester: John Heywood, Deansyote and Ridgefield, 1885), 211.

Elizabeth Mayer was baptized January 1, 1839, and lived on Jersey Street. Manchester Branch, "Records," 60.

Thomas Mayor was baptized June 5, 1839. He lived in Chapel Court. *Ibid.*

Peter Melling was the first patriarch ordained in England. Evans, *A Century of Mormonism*, 130.

Charles Miller was baptized July 31, 1839. He eventually became a high priest. Miller lived on Edward Street and emigrated to the United States. Manchester Branch, "Records," 60.

There are two **Susan Millers,** but no **Susannah** listed in the Manchester Branch Records, one baptized November 29, 1838, and the other April 5, 1839. The first lived on Blakely Street and emigrated; the second lived on Edward Street and was cut off February 14, 1845. The Susan Miller referred to in some entries seems to be the wife of Thomas Miller. *Ibid.*

Thomas Miller of Manchester was baptized on June 5, 1839. He emigrated to the United States sometime before 1852. *Ibid.*

Elizabeth Mills was baptized November 25, 1838. She was excommunicated on November 27, 1842 and rebaptized on December 23, 1842. *Ibid.*

Alice Plum Moon (1779-1841) married Clayton's wife's uncle, Mathias. This couple also had a daughter named Alice (1818-1857). "Three generation family group sheet," submitted by LaVerne Ward, in the Genealogical Society, Salt Lake City, microfilm copy in the Brigham Young University Library. Whether Clayton is referring to the mother or the daughter in the entry for March 25, 1840 is not clear in his diary. The apparent reason for Clayton's being asked to write by the Moons was to keep an inventory of goods being sold as they were preparing to emigrate. On Saturday, June 6, 1840, John Moon led a company of forty emigrants, which included Hugh Moon, his mother (Alice Plum Moon), and seven other family members. Alice Plum Moon had nine children, which means that on this date the entire family emigrated to America. Smith, *History of the Church,* IV, 134.

Francis Moon emigrated with the John Moon group to America somewhat earlier than Clayton. Evans, *A Century of Mormonism,* 54; Smith, *History of the Church,* IV, 134.

John Moon was probably Ruth Moon Clayton's first cousin, though the records are somewhat confused. He was born on July 2, 1809 and died July 12, 1850. A number of members of the Moon family of Eccleston, Lancashire, joined the Church during the period when Heber C. Kimball and Orson Hyde first opened the mission. A number of them, John included, labored as missionaries in England before emigrating to the United States. Evans, *A Century of Mormonism,* 54; "Third and Fourth Generation Family Group Sheets of the William Moon, Mathias Moon, and Thomas Moon Families," Genealogical Society, Salt Lake City, Microcopy in Brigham Young University Library.

Thomas Moon (1783-1848) was the father of Ruth Moon Clayton. *Ibid.*

Henry Moore emigrated with the first company of Saints from England. Smith, *History of the Church,* IV, 134.

Peter Mottram was baptized March 29, 1839, and lived on Broughton Street. He was a deacon, but was later cut off from the Church. Manchester Branch, "Records," 60.

Moses Chapman Nickerson became a counselor to President John Smith at the same time Clayton was chosen to be on the Zarahemla Stake high council. Smith, *History of the Church,* IV, 352.

Owenites were disciples of **Robert Owen** (1771-1858). Owen was born in Newton, Montgomeryshire, and after his early years in London and elsewhere he went into business at Manchester in the manufacture of cotton yarn. He was very successful, but his sympathy for the men in his and other factories led him to believe that to most businessmen the machinery was more important than the workmen. He had business dealings in Glasgow where he met Anne Caroline Dale, whom he later married. He and his associates purchased the New Lanark mills belonging to her father. Owen tried to improve the condition of his workers and establish schools for the children under twelve. He opposed the views of Thomas Malthus on the necessity for wages to remain at a subsistence level and thought the laissez-faire economics of the classical school absurd. He believed men could be improved in their environment. His views that the hours of children's work in mills should be limited led to the passage of the so-called Factory Act of 1819. He was convinced that religion, in general, posed a great obstacle to progress, possibly because of the general support religionists gave to the status quo. A believer in the labor theory of value, he also believed machinery displaced laborers. He proposed the establishment of communitarian villages around industries with three to four hundred families in each village. In an attempt to implement his ideas, he purchased the Rappite village of Harmony, Indiana in 1825. The experiment failed, but he spent the remainder of his life in Britain and the United States promoting his views. Leslie Stephen and Sidney Lee, editors, *The Dictionary of National Biography*, (22 vols.; Oxford: Oxford University Press, 1960) XIV, 1338-1346.

Thomas Owens was baptized on March 29, 1839. He became a teacher in the priesthood before he emigrated and lived on Broughton Road. Manchester Branch, "Records," 69.

Rebecca Partington was baptized July 17, 1839. She later emigrated. *Ibid.*, 72.

Agnes Patrick was baptized January 13, 1839. She later moved to Sheffield. *Ibid.*

John Patten was appointed to the high council of the stake in Iowa Territory on October 5, 1839. Smith, *History of the Church*, IV, 12.

Sarah Perkins is given no baptism date in the Manchester Branch Records. She later emigrated to Nauvoo, returned to Manchester, and was excommunicated. Manchester Branch, "Records," 74.

Elizabeth Poole was baptized November 25, 1838. She lived on Edward Street and later emigrated. *Ibid.*, 72.

Mary Powell was baptized December 23, 1838 at Manchester. By 1852 she had died, apparently without marrying the John named in the January 3, 1840 entry of Clayton's diary. *Ibid.*

Orson Pratt was born September 19, 1811, in Hartford, New York, and was a younger brother of Parley P. Pratt. One of the Church's most active missionaries, he was ordained an apostle in 1835. During his mission to England of 1840 and 1841, he labored for nine months in Edinburgh, Scotland, where he founded a branch of over 200 people. IIe was one of the Church's most learned leaders, and became one of its most prolific writers. He died in 1881 in Salt Lake City.

Parley P. Pratt was born April 12, 1807 at Burlington, New York. He joined the Baptist Church and the Disciples of Christ before his conversion to Mormonism. His mission to Ohio resulted in the conversion of Sidney Rigdon. After coming to England in 1840, he became editor of the *Millennial Star*. After moving to Utah, he went to the Southern States on a mission where he was murdered in 1857. Reva Stanley, *A Biography of Parley P. Pratt: The Archer of Paradise* (Caldwell, Idaho: Caxton Printers, 1937); Parley P. Pratt, *The Autobiography of Parley P. Pratt*, ed. Parley P. Pratt, Jr. (7th ed.; Salt Lake City: Deseret News Press, 1968).

Eliza Prince was baptized on February 20, 1839, and lived on Loom Street in Manchester. She later emigrated to the United States. Manchester Branch, "Records," 72.

Willard Richards, first counselor to Joseph Fielding, was apparently living in Preston, having married Jenetta Richards, the daughter of a clergyman. He was born in 1804 at Hopkinton, Massachusetts, and was ordained an apostle on April 14, 1840 at Preston. He became Second Counselor to President Brigham Young in April 1854 and died in Salt Lake City in December of the same year. Claire Noall, *Intimate*

Disciple: A Portrait of Willard Richards: Apostle to Joseph Smith—Cousin of Brigham Young (Salt Lake City: University of Utah Press, 1957); Smith, *History of the Church*, II, 492; Evans, *A Century of Mormonism*, 71; Whitney, *Life of Heber C. Kimball*, 144.

Jane Rigby was baptized April 2, 1839. She later emigrated to the United States. Manchester Branch, "Records," 80.

Sidney Rigdon was consecutively a Baptist and Campbellite minister before joining the Church in 1831 in Ohio. He then became a close associate of Joseph Smith and a counselor in the Church's first presidency. He was away from Nauvoo on a journey to Pennsylvania at the time of Joseph Smith's murder and he returned in an attempt to lead the Church as Guardian. After his excommunication by the Twelve Apostles, he moved to Pittsburgh and organized the Church of Christ. He died at Friendship, New York, in 1876. F. Mark McKiernan, *The Voice of One Crying in the Wilderness; Sidney Rigdon, Religious Reformer, 1793-1876* (Lawrence, Kansas: Coronado Press, 1971).

Alanson Ripley was a bishop in Ohio and was active in Missouri. He was an agent in land purchases in Iowa and Illinois and served as surveyor of Nauvoo. Smith, *History of the Church*, IV, 12; III, 209, 252; V, 270; Robert Bruce Flanders, *Nauvoo, Kingdom on the Mississippi* (Urbana: University of Illinois Press, 1965), 35.

Henry Royle was baptized on March 17, 1839. He later emigrated to the United States. Manchester Branch, "Records," 80.

Anby Sands lived on Hart Street and emigrated on March 1, 1844. *Ibid.*, 86.

No **Arthur Smith** is listed in the Manchester Branch Records for this period, but this may have been **A. Sidney**

Smith who was baptized on March 16, 1839. He eventually became an elder and was later cut off. He lived on Oxford Street. In the early days of the Church, it was common for mature men to hold the office of deacon, teacher, or priest, in contrast to the current practice of giving these offices to all "worthy" young men beginning at age twelve. It is clear from the context that Church members considered this an important calling. In this branch, the deacons undoubtedly performed a number of important tasks in connection with keeping the temporal affairs of the branch in order. *Ibid.*

Either **Emma Hale Smith,** wife of Joseph Smith, or **Mary Fielding Smith,** sister of Joseph Fielding and wife of Hyrum Smith is referred to in the diary. Since Clayton had purchased land from Hyrum Smith, the unclear reference on March 19 and 20, 1841, is probably to the latter.

George A. Smith was born in Pottsdam, New York, June 26, 1817. A cousin of Joseph Smith, he joined the LDS Church in 1832, moved to Kirtland, to Missouri, and to Nauvoo. Ordained a member of the Twelve Apostles in 1839, he was one of the missionaries to England in 1840. After moving to Utah, he served as first counselor to Brigham Young from 1863 to 1875 when he died. Jenson, *LDS Biographical Encyclopedia,* I, 37-42.

Hyrum Smith, Joseph Smith's oldest brother, was born February 9, 1800, in Tunbridge, Vermont. He was perhaps the prophet's closest friend and advisor, serving as a counselor to Joseph and also as Patriarch to the Church. He was murdered with Joseph in 1844. Smith, *History of the Church,* I, 45; III, 313; IV, 229; VI, 617.

John Smith of Manchester was baptized on March 18, 1839. He became a high priest before he emigrated. He lived on Dalton Street. Manchester Branch, "Records," 86.

John Smith, uncle of Joseph Smith, was the father of

George A. Smith. He was president of the Iowa Stake in 1841. Smith, *History of the Church*, I, 348; III, 338; IV, 12.

William Smith of Manchester is shown as having been baptized on February 14th rather than 16th as Clayton says. Smith lived on Hart Street. He emigrated on March 1, 1844. Manchester Branch, "Records," 86.

William Smith, the fifth son of Joseph Smith, Sr. and Lucy Mack Smith, was born in Royalton, Vermont, on March 13, 1811. He was baptized soon after the Church was organized. He served for a time as an apostle in the Church, but was excommunicated after Joseph Smith's death. Smith, *History of the Church*, I, 86, 322; III, 345, 364; VII, 483.

Ralph Stafford and **Edwin Stafford** were both baptized March 31, 1840, and both emigrated. It is not clear to which the entry of February 2, 1840 refers. It is interesting that Clayton refers to "brother" Stafford, even though he was apparently not yet baptized. Manchester Branch, "Records," 86.

Sarah Stirrup was baptized March 1, 1840. *Ibid.*

Nancy Street was baptized on May 5, 1839. She lived in Pendleton. *Ibid.*

Elizabeth Summers is listed in the branch records, but no baptism date is given. *Ibid.,* 89.

John Taylor was a native of Milnthorpe, Westmoreland County, England, where he was born in 1808. He emigrated to Canada and settled near Toronto where he was converted by Parley P. Pratt in 1836. He was ordained an apostle on December 19, 1838, and succeeded to the Presidency of the Church on October 19, 1880. He died on July 25, 1887 at Kaysville, Utah. B. H. Roberts, *The Life of John Taylor* (Salt Lake City: George Q. Cannon & Sons, 1892).

Robert Blashel Tompson was born October 1, 1811 in Great Driffield, Yorkshire, England. He emigrated to Canada and was converted by Parley P. Pratt. He moved to Kirtland where he married Mercy Rachel Fielding in 1837. He subsequently moved to Far West where he engaged in the battle of Crooked River. He moved to Illinois in 1839 and moved to Commerce with the Saints. He served as scribe to Joseph Smith and became an officer in the Nauvoo Legion. He died in 1841. Smith, *History of the Church*, IV, 411.

Margaret Townshend was baptized May 14, 1839, lived in the suburbs of Newton, and was later excommunicated. Manchester Branch, "Records," 95.

Theodore Turley was born in April, 1801, at Birmingham, England. He emigrated to Toronto, Canada, where he was converted to Mormonism. He returned to England on a mission with members of the Quorum of Twelve Apostles. Turley first went to Birmingham where he preached to his relatives. He then went to Staffordshire where he was imprisoned for a debt but released without coming to trial through the efforts of his brother John. Theodore Turley, "Journal of Theodore Turley," MSS Special Collections, Brigham Young University Library, January 30, 31, April 17, May 8, 1840; George A. Smith, "My Journal," *The Instructor*, LXXXII, 323; Evans, *A Century of Mormonism*, 93, 136.

Charlotte Walker was baptized on April 2, 1839, and lived on Cookson Street. Hannah Walker was baptized on November 28, 1838, and lived at 2 Maria Street. It is not clear which of these is the Sister Walker mentioned on January 3, 1840. Charlotte emigrated to the United States in 1844. Hannah was eventually excommunicated. Manchester Branch, "Records," 103.

Robert Walker was baptized on June 19, 1839. He lived on Cookson Street and later emigrated. *Ibid.*

Mary Webb is listed in the Manchester Branch Records, but no baptism date is given for her. She later moved to Bristol. *Ibid.*, 106.

Joseph West was baptized on June 16, 1839, and later emigrated to the United States. He lived on Cookson Street. *Ibid.*, 103.

William Whitehead was baptized March 3, 1839. He lived in the suburb of Moston and later emigrated. *Ibid.*

Jemima Whitaker was baptized April 12, 1840, and lived on St. Georges Road. She later became Jemima Jones. *Ibid.*

No **Rob Williams** or Robert Williams is listed in the branch record. However, this is probably the same **Robert Williams** who was ordained a priest at the July, 1840, conference, and who volunteered to devote full time to the Church at the October, 1840, conference after Clayton left England. He emigrated in 1842 and was met in Nauvoo along with many other old acquaintances by Clayton. Smith, *History of the Church*, IV, 148, 217; Clayton to William Hardman, *Millennial Star*, III (August 1, 1842), 75.

David Wilding represented the branches in Bolton, Bury, and Elton in the July, 1840, conference. Wilding was also one of those who volunteered to devote his time as a missionary for the Church in the July, 1840, conference. Smith, *History of the Church*, IV, 149.

Ann Williamson was baptized July 21, 1839. Manchester Branch, "Records," 103.

Mary Wood was baptized March 29, 1839; she lived on Tibb Street and emigrated March 1, 1844. *Ibid.*

Wilford Woodruff was born in 1807 at Avon, Connecticut. He moved to New York where he was converted in 1833. He was ordained an apostle on April 26, 1839, by Brigham Young, became President of the Church on April 7, 1889, and served in that capacity until his death at San Francisco, California, on September 2, 1898. Matthias F. Cowley, ed., *Wilford Woodruff: Fourth President of the Church of Jesus Christ of Latter-day Saints: History of His*

Life and Labors as Recorded in His Daily Journals (Salt Lake City: Bookcraft, 1964).

Brigham Young was born June 1, 1801, at Whitingham, Vermont. His family moved to New York state where he joined the LDS Church. He became an original member of the Quorum of Twelve Apostles and was called to England on a mission in 1840 in spite of ill health. He succeeded Joseph Smith as President of the Church in 1847, served as Governor of Utah Territory, and died in 1877.

INDEX

A

Ague, Clayton sick with, 214
Albany, New York, 187
Alston, England, 9, 86
Altrincham, England, 151
America, John Moon's first impression of, 42
Angels, visitation of, 161
Anti-Corn-Law League, 19
Apostasy, 163n
Apostles: views on working classes, 2; writings on England, 3; conversion of James Fielding congregation, 6; success in Preston, 7; advice on helping poor, 9; impressions of Manchester, 20, 72, 74; sympathy with working class, 22; comments on English social conditions, 23; comments on English working conditions, 23; missionary work, 80; mission to England, 137; meeting with Clayton, 140
Ashley, England, 110

Athens, New York, 187

B

Baptism. See Mormonism, religious ordinances
Battersby, Ellen, 25
Bedford, England, 63
Bennett, John C., 206, 213n
Beurdwood, Elizabeth, (Aunt), Clayton baptized for, 212
Bewshaw family, 26, 67, 74, 88, 100, 102, 103, 120, 136, 144, 147
Bewsher. See Bewshaw family
Birmingham, England, 39, 167, 168
Blackburn, England, 129
Bolton, England, 147, 164; unemployment in, 11
Bolton Railroad, 69
Book of Covenants, 94
Book of Mormon, copyright for, 141n

241

put out fire on new house, 202-203; land dealings of, in Iowa, 203; land summons served on, 204; organized with high priests, 205; attends conference, 205-206; appointed to high council and as clerk, 212; rebaptized, 212; illness of, 213, 214; moves to Nauvoo, 217; tithing for temple entered by, 218.

Coal wharf, 187

Cobden, Richard, and Manchester School, 19

Cock Pit (Preston, England), 128, 140

Coles, Austin, 207

Collegiate Church (Manchester England), 20

Colonel Young's village, New York, 187

Commerce, Illinois. *See* Nauvoo, Illinois

Condor of Halifax (ship), 182

Congress (ship), 185

Constable, notice to W. Clayton to appear to answer to William Miller, 204

Contributions to William Clayton, 93

Cook, William, 35

Cordon, Alfred, 94, 101, 108, 116, 118, 127, 132, 135, 138, 166

Corn laws, England, 12

Crooks, Sarah, 26, 32-35, 69, 76, 78, 83, 86, 88, 91, 93, 94, 97, 101, 103, 104, 105, 110, 111, 113, 114, 115, 116, 117, 118, 121, 124, 125, 127, 128, 130, 131, 132, 134, 135, 136, 138, 139, 142, 143, 144, 145, 146, 147, 148, 149, 150, 151, 154, 155, 157, 158, 159, 160, 161, 163, 164, 165, 167, 169, 171, 172; dreams concerning William Clayton's wife, 73; dream about marriage, 133

Cruden Concordance, 134

Cuerden Factory, 129

Cutler, Alpheus, 206

D

Detroit, Michigan, 194

Detroit River, 194n

Dixon, Illinois, 196

Doctrine and Covenants, 132; copyright for, 141n

Dreams, 92, 117, 118, 121n, 133

Drugs, 216n

Duckworth, Sarah, 27, 70, 77, 79, 83, 84

Dunkinfield, England, 70, 87, 131, 132, 148

E

Eccles, England, 120, 126, 132, 136, 147, 149, 155, 160

Eccleston, England, Alice Moon's sale, 129

Ellis Island, New York, 184n

Emigration, 39-40, 43-46, 86, 92, 98, 167, 168, 170, 173; of British companies, 12-13, 50; Brigham Young's advice on, 141; problems of, 175, 182; mortality rate of Mormon groups during, 177; confusion aboard ship during, 181

England: increased industrialism in, 11; conflict between agriculture and industry in, 12; manufacturing in, 15; educational institutions in, 150

Erie Canal, 188; locks described by Clayton, 190

F

Fairport, Ohio, 194

Farrington, England, 95, 170

Faucher, Leon, 16

Fielding, Hannah, 10

Fielding, James, 6, 24

Fielding, Joseph, 4, 7, 8, 39, 50, 67, 68, 70, 75, 87, 90, 93, 94, 95, 96, 104, 116, 119, 120, 121, 125, 127, 130, 132, 135, 136, 137, 139, 141, 156; comments of, on conditions of the world, 10; advice of, concerning emigration of Saints, 40

Folk medicine, 115, 117

Foster, Robert, 35

209, 212; church doctrines of, 31, 91, 92n, 113, 114, 121, 132, 135, 139, 207, 209; church practices of, 36, 38-39, 85n, 88, 205; theology of, 36, 41, 158; customs of, 38, 39, 106-107; concept of gathering of, 42; discipline of members of, 153

Mormons: conditions among, in England, 8; problems of, with apostasy, 9; emigration of, from England, 11, 12, 169, 171; class origin of English, 15, 21; profile of English, 20-22; relation to reform movement of, 21; difficulties of, in England, 24; English, in 1840, 166n; mortality among emigrant, 177

N

Nauvoo, Illinois, 46, 192, 200; upon completion of trip to, William Clayton praises the Lord, 200; public building in, 210n; William Clayton moves to, 217

Nauvoo Legion, 208

Nauvoo Steamboat, William Clayton to work on, 201

Nauvoo Temple, 49, 208

New York City: first impression of, by William Clayton, 184, 187; view of, 186

Newton, England, 121, 148

North America (ship), 43, 185; captain's desire to bring more Mormons across, 185

O

Owenites, 21, 103
Oxford, England, 148

P

Page, John E., 206

Palmyra, New York, 190

Parkinson, Reverend R., 20

Partington, Rebecca, 33, 83, 91, 94, 101, 103, 105, 111, 113, 114-115, 116, 117, 118, 124, 125, 126, 127, 128, 130, 131, 132, 133, 134, 135, 136, 138, 139, 142, 143, 144, 146, 147, 148, 151, 154, 155, 157, 158, 159, 160, 163, 171

Patriarchal Blessing, Peter Melling to Thomas Moon and William Clayton, 156

Patricroft, England, 133, 144, 150

Patten, D. W., 206

Pendlebury, England, 119, 135, 161

Pendleton, England, 103, 130

Penwortham, England, 7, 42, 128, 167

Peover, England, 79, 116, 127

Perkins, Sarah, 26, 69, 80, 86, 90-91, 94, 100, 101, 104, 108, 111, 114, 116, 122, 125, 127, 165

Plural marriage, 110, 145

Plymouth Brethren, 126

Potteries (Staffordshire, England), 139

Pratt, Orson, 137n, 139, 141, 158n, 206

Pratt, Parley P., 3, 20, 92n, 137, 139, 141, 143, 144, 146, 147, 150, 153, 154, 156, 157, 159, 161, 164, 165, 166, 167, 206; literature by, 140; spoke of visitation of angels, 161

Presque Isle, Michigan, 195

Preston, England, 6, 41, 86, 95-96, 104, 116, 137, 139, 141, 142, 147, 157, 165, 170

Prestwich, England, 93, 101, 125, 132, 146, 159

Princess Dock (Liverpool, England), 170

Q

Queen Victoria, 11, 92n
Quinine, 214